Writing
Chicago

The Social

Foundations of

Aesthetic Forms

Jonathan Arac,

Editor

The Social Foundations of Aesthetic Forms

A SERIES OF

COLUMBIA UNIVERSITY PRESS
Jonathan Arac, Editor

Writing Chicago

Modernism,
Ethnography,
and
the Novel

Chicago

Carla Cappetti

Columbia
University
Press
New York

Columbia University Press

New York   Chichester, West Sussex

Library of Congress Cataloging-in Publication Data

Cappetti, Carla.

    Writing Chicago : Modernism, Ethnography, and the Novel / Carla
Cappetti.

       p.   cm. — (The social foundations of aesthetic forms)

    Includes bibliographical references and index.

    ISBN 0-231-08128-6; 0-231-08129-4 (pbk.)

    1. American fiction—Illinois—Chicago—History and criticism.
2. Modernism   (literature)—Illinois—Chicago.   3. Literature and
society—Illinois—Chicago.   4. City and town life in literature.
5. Chicago (Ill.)—Intellectual life.   6. Chicago (Ill.) in
literature.   7. Ethnic groups in literature.   8. Ethnology —
Illinois—Chicago.   I. Title.   II. Series: Social foundations of
aesthetic forms.

    PS285.C47C36   1993

    813'.5209977311—dc20   92-41092

                                                 CIP

∞

Printed in the United States of America

c 10 9 8 7 6 5 4 3 2 1

To Tom,
Corinna,
and Monica

Contents

Contents

Acknowledgments

To Steven Marcus and Werner Sollors I owe my greatest debt and warmest thanks. In their seminars, at my oral examination, as dissertation advisers first, as friends and colleagues later, they made it possible for me to thrive intellectually and to pursue my research interests.

The English department at the City College of New York, the American Council of Learned Societies, the American Philosophical Society, the Newberry Library, the CUNY Research Foundation, and the CCNY Rifkind-Eisner Center all generously contributed fellowship and research money, and release time to this study.

Many are the individuals—teachers, colleagues, editors, friends, and relatives—who have contributed in one form or another to this work. I especially wish to thank Jonathan Arac, Tom Bender, Bettina Berch, Mary Campbell, Ida Cappetti, James Clifford, Lizabeth Cohen, Jennifer Crewe, Mary Jo Deegan, Andy Delbanco, Michael Denning,

Acknowledgments

Herbert Gans, Eileen Gillooly, Diana Haskell, Karen Hornick, Miriam Klein, Karl Malkoff, Susan Pensak, Silvana Patriarca, Richard Popp, Walter Rideout, Paul Sherwin, Nancy Stepan, Fred Stern, James Stronks, Alan Wald, and Joshua Wilner. In the form of comments and critiques, confidence and encouragement, distraction and sanity, they too have made this work possible.

Tom, Corinna, and Monica Klein have contributed the largest share to this project.

Writing
Chicago

Introduction

James T. Farrell, Nelson Algren, and Richard Wright, the authors to whom this study devotes closest attention, are at once the most emblematic products and the best known representatives of a currently neglected tradition. Their names bring into sharp focus the sociological imagination of Chicago literature, of the American urban novel, and, more broadly, of American literature.

Richard Wright explicitly acknowledged the special role that the Chicago sociologists Robert Park, Robert Redfield, Horace Cayton, and Louis Wirth played in his career when he stated: "But I did not know what my story was, and it was not until I stumbled upon science that I discovered some of the meanings of the environment that battered and taunted me."[1] These words hold true for a generation of writers who in the 1930s, sometimes consciously and openly, sometimes indirectly or inadvertently, responded to the new discipline of sociology.

Farrell's, Algren's, and Wright's appropriations from Chicago urban sociology and the ways such an intellectual exchange shaped their literary work provide the main focus for the present study. The trilogy of *Studs Lonigan* by James T. Farrell,[2] *Never Come Morning* by Nelson Algren,[3] *Black Boy-American Hunger* by Richard Wright,[4] I argue, cannot be understood within a restrictively literary context— proletarian, ethnic, naturalist, or otherwise—but must as well be framed within a larger tradition of urban writing. Central to this tradition are the sociological writings, theoretical and empirical, on the city, produced by Chicago urban sociologists just before or at the same time as these novels and autobiographical narratives. Characters in books by Farrell, Algren, and Wright walk along the streets that the sociologists charted, join gangs that they studied, encounter problems that they explained, and come to the sorry ends they foretold.

At the crossroad where Chicago literature and Chicago sociology meet are two groups of texts written between 1915 and 1945—texts that exemplify the connections between these two schools of urban writing. James T. Farrell's Irish street youths, Nelson Algren's Polish thieves and prostitutes, Richard Wright's Black boys, and the neighborhoods in which these characters live find their sociological counterparts in W. I. Thomas and Florian Znaniecki's Polish peasants and unadjusted girls, in Robert Park's marginal men, in Robert Redfield's urban "folks," in Frederic Thrasher's youth gangs, and in Louis Wirth's metropolitan types. The aesthetic and thematic analogies, exchanges, similarities, and even identities that inform the sociologists' and the novelists' respective readings of the city provide the primary material in the present study.

Writing Chicago directs attention to an important chapter of the American literary tradition. This tradition has frequently been identified through worn-out labels such as *naturalism, proletarian literature, ethnic literature,* or through limiting definitions such as *Chicago literature* and *midwestern literature.* These terms foreclose the need for critical analysis and abandon the authors to float alone in a literary firmament inhabited by other unhelpful, if more famous constellations such as the *transcendentalists,* the *modernists,* and the *Lost Generation.* Naturalism— whose critical fortunes typify those of the others—has become a catch-all term. It reveals little about so-called naturalist authors and

2

texts but a great deal about an institution—post-WWII American literary criticism—which has been, to put it mildly, unsympathetic to social literature and sociological criticism.[5]

One cannot simply argue that these labels have become obsolete, or that "naturalism," "proletarian literature," and the like do not exist in the real world of literature. They exist as much or as little as "modernism" or the "Harlem Renaissance." However, in the United States the lack of critical insight, sympathy, and interest toward the literary products and practices encompassed by those labels has created a de facto situation where to use the label naturalism is either to be patronizing or dismissive: "naturalism" has second-rate status in literary studies. The solution is not to discard the labels or the literatures—this has covertly been done all along—but to develop new frameworks that will allow us to judge them with new critical standards. New assumptions, categories, and methods must be invented to free critics of the aesthetic biases and ideological burdens that naturalism and the many literatures associated with that label—ethnic, proletarian, African-American, urban, realist—carry with them at present and have carried with them for the last fifty years in the United States.

Attempts are made periodically to show that this or that naturalist author is indeed deserving of attention, is indeed a Great American Novelist, does indeed belong to American literature on the basis of some newly discovered irony, gothicism, ambiguity, self-reflexivity, or general anti-realism. Several of these recent attempts have focused on Richard Wright, whose critical fortunes can be seen as paradigmatic.

Exemplifying the best of these revisionist critics, Robert Lee rightly challenges the limiting view of Wright as simply a naturalist or realist novelist, to argue, less fruitfully, that those two aesthetic levels constitute a superficial outer shell for the more complex nonrealistic "inside narratives."[6] The intent of this type of revision is praiseworthy: to attack the simplemindedness of reducing Wright and others to aesthetic forms that have been judged lacking in complexity and originality. More specific goals are even more commendable: to recover the symbolism, the mythical and Biblical allusions, the surreal, hyperreal, and metaphysical elements that form such an important core in Richard Wright's work. The final results, however, are less promising: the interior landscape rather than the external ghetto of Native Son becomes the focus of the critic's attention; no connection is established between the two poles of realism and "unrealism," which are therefore once again reified—fully subservient to the predominant paradigms of American literary criticism—as essentially distinct and antithetical rather than generally historical, sometimes contingent, often heuristic concepts. Finally, the premises of a critical practice that routinely associates naturalism with artistic failure are not challenged but reproduced.[7]

Houston Baker has recently evoked the immediate context for these well-meaning but ultimately misdirected revisions. Retracing the steps that from the mid-seventies have brought African-American studies within the Yale compass and occasioned the rewriting of the "Black tradition" around "influence" and "tropes," Baker notes that, as a result, all contacts between this literature and the social world of the street were erased.[8] Indeed, the inner landscape, not the outside ghetto, language as consciousness, not the empirical object or the historically inseparable tension between these spheres, became the critic's concern. Few comments spell out more clearly the premises that have made Richard Wright persona non grata within the African-American literary tradition and have produced a stubborn dilemma for the American literary canon.[9] Wright is in fact one of the most important representatives, within modern American literature, of the irreducible ties that have historically bound the novel—specifically the American novel—and the street.[10]

While it is true that the debate on realism and naturalism has languished far from the centers of critical debate of the literary institution, it would be inaccurate to imply that no scholars have taken steps toward reconceptualizing American naturalism and realism. I am not referring here to the occasional studies that periodically devote attention to some aspect of American literary realism and naturalism without engaging the epistemological status of those genres within American literature, and to that of mimesis and referentiality in contemporary American intellectual thought.[11] Although few in number and heterogenous in their methodological, ideological, and theoretical orientation, a number of scholars in the last few years have contributed important starting points toward this most essential task awaiting critics of American literature.

June Howard has brought to the fore the "literary form" that naturalism has traditionally been faulted for lacking, and has conceptualized this form as an "immanent ideology" that "shares its imaginative horizons" with such contemporaneous formations as "criminal anthropology and political progressivism."[12] Lee Clark Mitchell critiques the predominant view of naturalism as "pessimistic realism" or "a low-rent version" of realism. Like Howard he asks that we "relax the stranglehold of literary 'standards,'" and instead turn attention to the "philosophical terms" underlying what has been labeled "bad writing" and what Mitchell refers to as "problematic style."[13] Within an even broader conceptual canvas Barbara Foley has proposed that we view the "documentary novel" as a genre that exists on the border between "factual" and "fictional" modes, and more broadly all "major modes of fictional narrative . . . as simply variations on the basic form of the mimetic contract." A pluridimensional continuum rather than an antithetical polarity, Foley implies, is a more fruitful way to address referentiality and self-referentiality.[14] More recently Amy Kaplan has denounced "the history of realism in American literature" as a futile "history of failure." Arguing that "realism cannot be understood only in relation to the world it represents," and that it is also, and more importantly, "a debate within the novel form, with competing modes of representation," Kaplan like Foley proposes that we "move beyond that dichotomous judgment [success and failure] to explore the dynamic relationship between changing fictional and social forms in realistic representation."[15]

Inspiring much of this debate has been the effort to recontextualize realism and naturalism both historically and aesthetically, intellectually, and comparatively, and the belief that a reexamination of American naturalism and realism must at the same time engage the fundamental paradigms of American literature and literary criticism. Through such reformulations scholars are beginning to bring mimesis and referentiality back within the relative axes of history, and to rediscover individual texts and literary traditions as they actively and dynamically negotiate the terms and forms of mimesis.

To draw attention to Farrell, Algren, and Wright and to the sociological tradition they represent is on one basic level to address an appeal to American literature—to rediscover three major novelists of Chicago, of modern American literature, and of the twentieth century, and through them to rediscover itself. Should the sociological and the larger urban tradition of the American novel that the present study reclaims be acknowledged as yet another dot in that landscape of rapidly proliferating traditions which American literature has become? At present the term tradition is so loosely used within and without scholarly discourse—somewhat as ideology was ten years ago— that its power has become seriously diluted. In today's pluralistic landscape any group of authors and texts with something in common—form, race, ethnicity, gender, sexual orientation tend to prevail at present over history, class, and ideology—can turn into a tradition and claim a seat at that parliament of literary criticism which is the MLA.[16] One uses the term *tradition* with caution, aware that literary pluralism is turning too frequently into peaceful and contented coexistence with and within the very literary theories, practices, and ideologies that have kept many of the "new" literatures out to begin with.

To focus on Farrell, Algren, and Wright, it would be naive to ignore, is also and more importantly to scrutinize the premises and challenge the biases of their neglect. The reader must ask what it means in the present contexts of American literary criticism and literary history to write a book about three authors who were not part of *the* Chicago renaissance; who were from Chicago and not New York or Boston; who wrote about a northern industrial immigrant city and not a pre-industrial North, a rural South, a precapitalist West, or a pastoral America; who belong to the literary thirties and not the generally more appreciated literary twenties. What does it mean, at present, to claim that the Chicago urban novelists of the 1930s were directly influenced by an indigenous, even local intellectual school—the Chicago school of sociology—and to suggest that the urban sociological tradition is a predominant and characteristic tradition in American literature? What are the consequences of arguing that the urban sociological novel represents one of the most original contributions of American letters to the novel in a comparative perspective?

The literary history of Chicago—much like the literary history of the United States—has not spared attention to "modernism" and to the Chicago renaissance, constituted as its epitome and climax. To write about the Chicago literature of the 1930s is thus to be confronted with a long and illustrious list of literary predecessors known as *the* Chicago renaissance of the 1910s–1920s, the local equivalent and, in many respects a precursor, of what is generally known as American modernism. Some critics have recently argued that the period 1890–1910 does not merely precede but is also an essential part of this renaissance. In so doing they have made room for an important group of early realist novelists, journalists, humorists, and poets who paved the way for the aesthetic and social experimentation of the Chicago modernist twenties. The period 1890–1920 is as a result the most studied period of Chicago literary history, and critics and

6

historians have been right to research and proud to celebrate its products. It is a story that has been told and retold as it represents the golden age of the Chicago historiographical tradition.

To reassess the literary thirties does not mean to downplay or discard the many literary and artistic monuments of the Chicago renaissance but simply to rethink the outlines of that history. The mecca of modern journalism and newspaper humor, the home of a great deal of early American literary realism, and arguably the birthplace of American urban literature, Chicago brought together around the turn of the century such well-known humorists as Field, Ade and Dunne, and such pioneer realist novelists as Henry B. Fuller, Hamlin Garland, Robert Herrick, and Theodore Dreiser. Through these pioneers the living speech and the stories of the city, of migrants and immigrants and of modern industrial America were first given literary form. Better known are the names and institutions that make up the second and arguably greatest phase of the Chicago literary renaissance. With Harriet Monroe's *Poetry: A Magazine of Verse*, Stone and Kimball's *Chap-Book*, Margaret Anderson's *Little Review*, Floyd Dell's *Friday Literary Times*, and Francis Fisher Brown's *The Dial* on the literary front, with such avant-garde and radical editors as Stone and Kimball, Covici, Kerr, and such visionaries of mass circulation as Walsh and McClurg on the publishing front, and with The Little Theatre, the Players' Workshop, and the Hull House Theatre on the theatrical front, Chicago for the decades between 1890 and 1920 was in touch with the most avant-garde artistic and intellectual expressions of Europe and the most original experiments of the United States "west of the Hudson." This network of magazines, journals, presses, and theaters, brought European modernists like Joyce, Pound, Yeats, D. H. Lawrence, Ibsen, and Shaw, and American vernacular modernists like Edgar Lee Masters, Sherwood Anderson, Carl Sandburg, Vachel Lindsay, Floyd Dell, Ben Hecht, Ring Lardner together, and it brought both to an audience of great sensibility. In short, it brought the world to Chicago and Chicago to the world. Combining the aesthetic genius and sensibility of local intellectuals deeply in touch with vernacular America and just as hungry for the larger world, and of New England and European emigré intellectuals in touch with the most modern continental aesthetic and philosophical developments, the Chicago renaissance stands 7 for a time of acute artistic, social, and political experimentation and intensely cosmopolitan awareness.[17]

The Chicago literature of the 1930s has not yet been properly framed within this context even though, in the estimation of the present study, it represents the true climax of a half century of aesthetic experimentation and intellectual research for the creation of vernacular forms of expression and thought, vernacular to the Midwest as well as to the United States.[18]

To write about Farrell, Algren, and Wright is to suggest that Chicago literary history—and by implication American literary history—reconsider its limiting emphasis on the Chicago "modernist" renaissance of the 1910s and 1920s.[19] This emphasis passively reiterates the embattled paradigms of American literary history, but is a disservice to the interests and nature of that very literature and of what it represents nationally and internationally.

If the notion of the Chicago renaissance poses difficulties for the present study because of its neglect of the authors under discussion and the unprestigious status of the Chicago literary thirties as the "aftermath" of a renaissance, the concept of literary *renaissance* poses even larger problems.[20] The idea of *renaissance* carries with it the notion of a flowering or rebirth, often from mysterious sources, in the midst of an equally mysterious creative sterility, and complements the vulgar Romantic notion of the artist as irrational genius, representing its closest correlative at the level of literary groups and currents. Why, we need to ask, are some literary periods and traditions called "renaissances"—New England, Chicago, Harlem come to mind—while others are called "literatures"—modernism, Western literature? Why is it that some regions, nations, groups remain indefinitely identified by and restricted to their "renaissances"—Chicago, Ireland, African-Americans—while others—the New England renaissance, the Italian renaissance—progress to become full-fledged national and international literatures—*the* American Renaissance, *the* Renaissance?

The notion of the "regional" novel, Raymond Williams indicates, poses analogous critical problems. Implicit in the concept of "regional" literature is not principally the assumption that it is about Chicago as opposed to New York, or that it is by a Chicago author as opposed to a Boston author. Rather the concept implies and stresses that some places are "regions"—Chicago, the Midwest—while others are not—New York, New England. It implies that some novels are about a specific geographic space, while others are about life; that some are about a specific society while others are about human experience; that some are about a specific class—the working class—while others are about people in general.[21] Eric Sundquist has noticed the biased use of similar categories within American literature. "Those in power" he states "have more often been judged 'realists' while those removed from the seats of power . . . have been categorized as regionalists."[22] In addition, within American literary realism some authors have been acknowledged within broader national and international canons—Henry James, who in any case qualifies as an early modern, and a few select others, W. D. Howells, Stephen Crane, William Faulkner—and most others have been patronized within the more restricted, discrete, and localized literary traditions of gender, race, ethnicity, region, and class, approximately in that order of importance.

Hazel Carby confronts an analogous dilemma in attempting to contextualize the African-American intellectual movements of Boston at the turn of the century, a period that preceded and overlapped with the Harlem Renaissance.[23] The "elusive" yet constraining centrality of the Harlem Renaissance in the literary historiography, Carby notes, obfuscates rather than explains its relationship to what came before and to what came after. More useful than the iconography of the Harlem Renaissance as a "unique, intellectually cohesive and homogeneous historical movement," a mythology, Carby claims, "invent[ed by] the literary and cultural historian," would be to understand "the shift in concerns of the intellectuals of the twenties as opposed to the previous two decades . . . [and] the discontinuities surrounding issues of representation."[24] The same can be said of the Chicago renaissance and of its "elusive" relationship to the Chicago literary thirties.

The case of New York is equally revealing of the double-edged quality of the "renaissance" construct. Why is New York so lacking in renaissances, with the exception of the Harlem Renaissance, which, as the very name implies, is in New York but not of New York? Precisely because one does not need to resort to such concepts when discussing New York, a place that no one assumes ever to have been culturally barren and that indeed is synonymous with culture. On the other hand, certain cities, regions, classes, and certain gender, race, and ethnic groups often, and sometimes exclusively, produce renaissances, and sociologically, historically, and geographically localized literatures. These renaissances and localized literatures represent conventional entry points for previously disregarded groups of authors and texts. They are the first door to be unlocked by literary critics of emerging literatures. However, those very notions too often

9

bring the literatures in question out of invisibility only to relegate them into "regional," "provincial," "renaissance" marginality, thus reinforcing even more the hegemonic literatures as "national," "international" literatures, or simply "humanities."

While the debate over the "canon" has turned into a field without visible boundaries, little of this critical reexamination has been directed toward "literary history." True, literary historiography has not competed with textual analysis—canonical or anticanonical—in the United States for at least fifty years, much less now.[25] While many new literatures have emerged in the course of the last two decades, these literatures continue to formulate their own literary histories on the basis of paradigms that were the infrastructure of that very same old canon. Whether national or international, bourgeois or proletarian, "literary history"—no less than the canon—is in serious need of reconceptualization, precisely on the basis of the critical work of the last decades.

Much as to study the literature of the South is to evoke slavery and the plantation economy, and much as to study the literature of New England is to confront early merchant and industrial capitalism, to study the literature of the Midwest is to encounter the forces that made the United States the world's greatest economic power in less than a century. To call attention to this literature is to emphasize the forces of advanced capitalism, of modern corporate industrialism in the city where such events took place in most dramatic, sudden, and exaggerated form.

To tell the story of Chicago is to tell the story of a modern miracle. Frontier and Metropolis, Great Fire and World Fair, Babel and Babylon, Pork and Plato, heroic labor leaders and ruthless industry magnates, oxymora and hyperboles abound wherever observers have tried to capture this phenomenon of modern capitalism.[26] From newly created frontier in 1803 to world metropolis in 1890, Chicago traveled the route of other American cities at twice the speed, ending up ahead of all but one. In between it burned down and raised itself up anew, like the proverbial phoenix, adding more fuel to the rhetorical fires of later historians and providing them with a handy date, 1871, on the two sides of which the city history seems to hang.

10   Before the Great Fire Chicago's history boasts more of gore than of glories. Explorers, trappers, and adventurers traded with and stole from the Potawatomie Indians, exchanging fish hooks and diseases for furs. The symbolic date of birth of Chicago, its incorporation date,

followed by only a few years the bloody Black Hawk war of 1832, when an attempt by the Sauk and Fox Indians to regain control over their Illinois lands was defeated, and a large number of men, women, and children were killed during their retreat westward. This was the last important attempt to resist white invasion and repudiate earlier land settlements. From this point on the region became "free" of Indians.

Between 1825, when the Erie Canal opened connecting through the Great Lakes Chicago and the Atlantic, and 1869, when Chicago became the hub of American railways, the city nursed its dreams of economic grandeur while also accommodating as best it could the newcomers—laborers and speculators alike. Cosmopolitan in accent if not yet in refinement, by 1890 Chicago had a population of over a million people—a figure that would triple by 1930. As the century came to a close the wheels were turning at full speed. Cattle, hogs, sheep, iron ore, coke, lumber, farm produce went in; meat, machinery, paper, and commodity futures came out. Through the waterways first and the railways later everything was carried everywhere, and this mass of people that had sprouted in the middle of the prairie found itself in touch with the raw materials as well as the raw ideas, the main markets as well as the main philosophies, of the American continent and indeed the world.

The exceptional 2 percent annual growth rate of the Midwest between 1860 and 1880, double that of the United States at a time of rapid expansion, was from an economic point of view "the nineteenth-century equivalent of the near double-digit growth rates recorded in some rapidly developing nations in Asia today."[27] Although a disparity between industrial and financial capital kept Chicago dependent upon New York, by 1900 the region became "a capital exporting region," a major shift from its previous condition as a "capital poor" and "resource rich" area. "This is" remarked the 1900 census writer, "the most notable and rapid advance in position which has occurred in industrial history."[28] Some Chicagoans, however, were less than enthusiastic. Henry B. Fuller would disconsolately admit that Chicago was "the only great city in the world to which all its citizens have come for the avowed purpose of making money. There you have its genesis, its growth, its object; and there are but few of us who are not attending to that object very strictly."[29] With some qualifications the same 11 might have been said of the United States, whose history Chicago seems to have telescoped and grandly reproduced, making it both more awsome and more surreal.

Starting with the 1890s, and for a long half-century, Chicago came to embody the most advanced sectors of the U.S. economy, the most radical sectors of the U.S. reform movement, and the most avant-garde expressions of American art.[30] The periphery had turned into the center, the frontier into the metropolis. The literary thirties are an integral part of this long historical period. While the literature of Chicago traditionally emanates the magic dreams of wealth and the allure of American capitalism, Chicago's literary thirties highlight the bankruptcy of those same dreams at a time—the Depression—and in the place—Chicago—where such bankruptcy is most tangible.

Why is it important to emphasize the vernacular intellectual sources of the Chicago urban novels of the 1930s, a literature that has been generally understood as the ideological by-product of the Popular Front and of the Communist Party's aesthetic policies, and of Farrell, Algren, and Wright, authors whose political allegiance to the international left and to European realism has gained them little standing as American authors?

To emphasize the vernacular intellectual debts of this literature is to challenge two clichés that have defined it: first, that it was dictated by the cultural policies of the Comintern and that it was un-American and unoriginal; second, that it flourished—badly, according to prevailing aesthetic criteria—despite, against, and outside the essential nature of the American novel and of American literature. This literature, so the received story goes, is not centrally concerned with social issues, society, and classes, since the only reality available is that of a "self" in pursuit of transcendence, precisely from reality. And, in any case, there are no classes in America to speak of, at least not in the European sense, nor is there a thick enough social fabric to sustain that kind of literature. Therefore, the writer who deals with such subjects produces inferior literature lacking in the ambiguities, paradoxes, and ironies that define Great American Books.[31] The writers of the 1930s were retrospectively rebuked for doing precisely that.

My claim that Chicago sociology was an important source for the work of Farrell, Algren, and Wright is not intended to depoliticize these authors, downplay their activities within the Communist Party and around the literary left during the 1930s, nor minimize their life-long if variegated Marxist humanist orientation. This is particularly a risk in the case of Richard Wright, whose prolonged membership in the Communist Party has made the need to politically "purify" him more pressing and whose eventual contribution to *The God That Failed* anthology has been taken out of context and used precisely for that purpose. "Wright was an avowed Communist, and even after repudiating the CP, he remained a Marxist-humanist for the remainder of his life" Margaret Walker wrote in her memoir-biography of Wright, *Daemonic Genius*.[32] The same, mutatis mutandi, can be said of Farrell and Algren.[33]

This study does not address the view that the Communist Party and Marxism influenced or shaped Wright's writing—or Farrell's or Algren's for that matter—in general and his writings of the 1930s in particular. I am arguing something that is at once narrower and broader. First, the theories and methodologies developed by the Chicago urban sociologists played a central role in the overall shape and specific content of Wright's autobiography; they exercised a life-long influence on his work, and played as important a role on Wright's writing as Marx, Freud, Dostoyevsky, and Sartre, his more frequently acknowledged intellectual sources. Second, much as the anthropological imagination can be said to be a predominant undercurrent of Zora Neale Hurston's work, of the Harlem Renaissance and, more generally, of American modernism, so the sociological imagination—in a larger sense than simply that of the Chicago school—was the overarching source and inspiration of Wright's creativity, of the African-American Chicago renaissance of the 1930s, and of American realism.[34]

Writing Chicago directly assumes that, at the present time, the task of evaluating the literature of the 1930s, given the biases of American literary criticism, must originate in and proceed from its vernacular sources. Most certainly, this task cannot be deductively accomplished on the basis of a priori assessments of the aesthetic policies of the Soviet Union or the American Communist Party. The influence on such novels and on the larger urban sociological tradition in American letters was by far much broader than the Comintern and its aesthetic policies, reaching back to at least two centuries of novels dealing with urban growth, migration, and change, and reaching across several European national traditions.

To write this kind of book, clearly, is to ask for more than simply that a new tradition be instituted or three authors reinstated. To write this kind of book in the present context is to find oneself going 13 against the grain of much that passes and has passed for Chicago literature, African-American literature, and American literature, and to be forced to challenge many cherished notions of American literary history: that Chicago, African-American, and American literature consist essentially of all the works that lead into and grow out of their respective renaissances restrictively defined as the modernist precursors and ancestors; that the literature of the 1930s was the crude version of a foreign dogma; that American realism is derivative of a European tradition, a foreign genre, imported, un-American, and uncongenial to American society; that the urban tradition is a secondary genre and pastoralism the predominant mode; that American novelists have cared little for social representation and those who have cared must perforce be alien to the tradition.

Exceptional as they were, Farrell, Algren, and Wright were not alone in Chicago. The same sociological imagination, orientation, and emphasis characterized a contemporaneous group of African-American authors—Margaret Walker, Arna Bontemps, Water Turpin, Alden Bland, Willard Motley, and Gwendolyn Brooks. With Richard Wright, Robert Bone has argued, they formed a Chicago renaissance as impressive as, and generally overlooked in favor of, the Harlem Renaissance of African-American writing.[35]

Original as they were, Farrell, Algren, and Wright were not formed in a literary vacuum. They were preceded by a long lineage of authors—poets, novelists, journalists, social reformers—who had been equally committed to and inspired by social and sociological themes, theories, and methods. Among these proto- and neosociologists figure such familiar names as Hamlin Garland, Henry B. Fuller, Theodore Dreiser, Clarence S. Darrow, Hutchins Hapgood, Robert Herrick, Carl Sandburg, Vachel Lindsay, Edgar Lee Masters, Jane Addams, Ben Hecht, W. R. Burnett, Floyd Dell, Meyer Levin, William Attaway—all of them midwesterners and, by birth or adoption, Chicagoans.

Finally, Farrell, Algren, and Wright were far from alone within the larger American and European novelistic traditions. Clustered about Chicago during the 1930s but in fact reaching east, south, and west in the United States and across the Atlantic to Europe, was a well-established novelistic tradition among whose members one finds Jack London, Upton Sinclair, John Steinbeck, William Faulkner, John Dos Passos on the one hand, and Defoe, Balzac, Flaubert, Maupassant, Hugo, Thackeray, Dickens, Zola, Gorky, Chekhov, Dostoyevsky, Kuprin, Joyce on the other, names that evoke the most original elements of the realist novel across three centuries. Much as the aesthetic experiments of modern art foreshadowed, for Walter Benjamin, the birth of cinema, and the pairing family adumbrated, for Friedrich Engels, the birth of the monogamous family and of modern society, this literature presaged the birth of sociology, took active part in the new developments of the social sciences, and contributed to the development of the sociological novel.[36]

James T. Farrell, Nelson Algren, and Richard Wright are representative of a literary tradition that has characterized the novel from its inception. This tradition was born of the curiosity, passion, and commitment that have driven American and European novelists across class and race boundaries, into invisible or willfully neglected corners of society: the slum, the ghetto, the consciousness of the delinquent, the mind of the prostitute.

To write this kind of study is to suggest that the theory of the novel and the history of the American novel should take into account the role played by sociological and anthropological writings and, reciprocally, that Wright, Farrell, and Algren must be reexamined as representatives of an important novelistic tradition that significantly links the Chicago novel, the American novel, and the European novel. The sociological novels of Chicago and of the 1930s, it is time to discover, are one of the most significant and characteristic traditions both in American literature and in the history of the novel.

What F. H. Matthews has perceptively noted of anthropology— "[a]nthropology in the 1920's was for some of its recruits a fruitful method of *internal expatriation*"[37]—applies equally well to sociology and to the 1930s. Such is the larger framework of the present study and of its dual focus on sociologists and novelists as ethnographers at home. On the one hand we encounter the sociologists who traveled from their middle-class, generally "nonethnic" families and communities to the peasant, ethnic, and lumpenproletarian neighborhoods in order to penetrate the mysteries of Chicago's "urban jungles"; on the other hand there are the writers who belonged to those ethnic and newly urbanized communities, and who in sociology found the inspiration to become sociological informants and observers of their own neighborhoods.

Much as the initial representation of the colonized that one finds in novels, films, and plays is often indebted to the scientific research and discourse that had preceded it—ethnosociology, medicine, geology, botany in Africa, Alain Calmes argues, can be read as monologues of the colonizer over the colonized[38]—the Chicago urban literature of the 1930s is indebted to the urban sociology of the 1910s and 1920s.

15

Somewhat like missionaries, explorers, and ethnographers, who for centuries had traveled across continents and oceans, these modern-day urban travelers crossed the intangible boundaries that separate neighborhoods, classes, ethnic, and racial groups. Sociologists and novelists contributed to and worked both within and against a well-established tradition: the representation of "others" within the West. Chicago sociologists often represented people from peasant backgrounds—immigrants from southern and eastern Europe, migrants from the South and from rural America—as "primitives," "exotics," and ultimately "others" to be civilized, modernized, and urbanized. Chicago novelists, on the other hand, sometimes uncritically reproduced, but more often creatively undermined these stereotypes. The ideological, cultural, and class presuppositions of Chicago sociology notwithstanding, writers found in sociology important conceptual tools—not unlike what Zora Neale Hurston had called the "spyglass of Anthropology"—with which to write about immigrants, juvenile delinquents, and the slum, so as to go beyond the post-Darwinian biological and social determinism of their naturalist precursors. James T. Farrell, Nelson Algren, and Richard Wright not only explored but kept alive the radical possibilities embedded in the discipline of sociology.[39]

While belonging to different "disciplines" and expressing themselves through different forms and genres of writing, sociologists and novelists worked in close intellectual proximity. Before "disciplinary" divisions separated them, personal, artistic and political ties joined the sociologist and the novelist and influenced their work. The product of such creativity was an impressive number of studies and novels about the city, immigration, and deviance, which shaped the representation of urban America and indeed the perception of American society altogether between the two world wars.[40]

The study consists of two parts. I analyze, first, selected theories, ethnographies, and case studies of the Chicago sociologists W. I. Thomas, Robert Park, Ernest Burgess, Frederic Thrasher, Robert Redfield, and Louis Wirth on immigrants and deviants, the city and the slum. Second, I explore selected works of James T. Farrell, Nelson Algren, and Richard Wright on migrants, immigrants, and their children.

Chapter 1 examines the use of literary materials and methods in the courses, studies, and methodologies of Chicago sociologists to argue that they openly competed with and even imitated the creative writer and the literary critic in their study of society, and were themselves heirs of the literary urban tradition and the social novel.

Chapter 2 and 3 focus on a number of well-known studies on the city, migration, and urbanization by Chicago sociologists, which shaped the fictionalization of the slum, of immigrants, and juvenile delinquents. Chapter 2 focuses on Robert Park's essay "The City: Suggestions for the Investigation of Human Behavior in the Urban Environment" (1915),[41] Ernest Burgess's essay "The Growth of the City: An Introduction to a Research Project" (1924),[42] and Frederic Thrasher's volume *The Gang: A Study of 1,313 Gangs in Chicago* (1927).[43] This section also provides important background material for the novels of Farrell and Algren, both of them stories of a Chicago gang youth in an ethnic neighborhood.

Chapter 3 focuses on the distinction between country and city and on the "transition" model that underlies "modernization theories" as originally formulated by Chicago sociologists, at the same time providing important conceptual material against which to read *Black Boy-American Hunger* as a sociological story of "transition."[44] The discussion examines how Robert Park—in "Human Migration and the Marginal Man" (1928)[45]—and Robert Redfield—in *Tepoztlán: A Mexican Village* (1930)[46]—elaborated the distinctions rural and urban, ethnic and cosmopolitan, traditional and modern to explore the borderline where racial, cultural, and social differences meet. The discussion then moves on to Louis Wirth's "Urbanism as a Way of Life" (1938)[47] and Robert Redfield's later study *The Folk Culture of Yucatan* (1941)[48] and to the way they polarized those same distinctions.

Wright's autobiography also finds close sociological contexts in W. I. Thomas and Florian Znaniecki's *The Polish Peasant in Europe and America* (1918–19)[49] and in W. I. Thomas's *The Unadjusted Girl* (1923).[50] Chapter 4 is devoted to the analysis of this second and lesser known monograph. Thomas found the girl-who-goes-to-the-city both a well-established literary type and a powerful means for representing the social, cultural, and moral conflicts sparked by migration. His study of juvenile female delinquents reads as a bildungsroman of modern society in which migration and deviance induce either to growth and liberation—not unlike that experienced by the autobiographical narrator of *Black Boy-American Hunger*—or to crime and degeneration—of the type experienced by the protagonists of *Studs Lonigan* and *Never Come Morning*.

17

The trilogy of *Studs Lonigan* (1932–35)[51] by James T. Farrell and the novel *Never Come Morning* (1942)[52] by Nelson Algren—the focus of chapters 5, and 6, and 7 respectively—are versions of a similar story, parallel attempts to narrate the life of a juvenile delinquent.

Chapter 5 examines Farrell's radical use of Chicago sociology in the trilogy of *Studs Lonigan*. Farrell found in Thrasher's study of urban gangs a means through which he could represent the world of youth and specifically the gang as a microcosm of an Irish middle-class neighborhood. He appropriated a sociological model originally developed for the study of the slum and the urban poor and used it to represent a middle-class neighborhood undergoing change. These changes had been conceptualized by Ernest Burgess in "The Growth of the City." Burgess's essay, which is paraphrased at the very center of the trilogy, provided Farrell with the epistemological position from which to observe and therefore write about urban change.

Chapters 6 and 7 focus on the city and the gang in *Never Come Morning*. Algren's representation of the slum and the immigrant community, the youth gang and the delinquent boy, the brothel and the prostitute is heavily indebted to sociology. At the same time the sociological representation complements a poetic one that, borrowing from symbolism, expressionism, and surrealism, counteracts the sociologists' vision of the slum and the deviant as sources of degeneration and pathology, and substitutes instead a view of the slum as a microcosm of the city and of the delinquent as a true representative of American society.

Chapters 8 and 9 are devoted to Richard Wright and to the ways a rereading of *Black Boy-American Hunger* (1944)[53] within a sociological framework allows one to rethink the outlines of the African-American literary tradition and of the American literary tradition as well. Chapter 8 addresses a number of recent tendencies within African-American literary criticism that have accused Wright of being "un-Africanamerican" and sexist, and that have led to the marginalization of this author and to recentering the tradition around Zora Neale Hurston. Within such shifts are to be found the causes of some serious misreadings of *Black Boy-American Hunger*. The ways sociological concepts and methods directly traceable to the Chicago sociologists shape this work is the subject of chapter 9. The conflict between individual and group, a characteristic theme of Chicago sociology, structures Wright's autobiography into a case history of migration from country to city, from community to society, from juvenile delinquent

18

to prominent writer. This framework allows one to reevaluate Wright's position in relation to the African-American tradition in light of larger cultural and epistemological frameworks rather than private and individual ambivalences.

One might rightly wonder why the sociologists appear *before* and *apart from* the novelists in a study that questions the validity of such epistemological and disciplinary distinctions and argues that such distinctions were actually blurred in the writing practice of Chicago sociologists and novelists. The decision to present the sociologists before the novelists and to separate the sociological theories and monographs from the novels should be understood as a way of highlighting chronology and as a choice of practice rather than faith. While organizing the discussion along thematic and nonchronological lines would have been more congruent with the argument of the study, it also would likely disorient readers unfamiliar with the periodization of Chicago sociology and literature. If this study had focused on a better known group of American authors, it would have enjoyed greater latitude in organizing its material. Like freedom of speech, the freedom of formal experimentation is a right of all but a privilege of few.

Between Literature and Science: Chicago Sociology and the Urban Literary Tradition

1

If one cannot properly understand the urban novels of James T. Farrell, Nelson Algren, and Richard Wright apart from the urban sociological studies that preceded and accompanied them, it would be equally a mistake to ignore the literary and, specifically, the novelistic influences that the Chicago sociologists themselves derive from the early European and American urban literary tradition.[1] While the long term and complex dynamic between the novel and sociology of which they are part is beyond the scope of the present study, a brief examination of these earlier exchanges will both contribute to such a future project and provide a context for the novelists under study.

The importance of the Chicago school of urban sociology in the context of both American and European intellectual history has been variously assessed.[2] William Sharpe and Leonard Wallock have identified the Chicago school as one of the three main traditions of analysis of the modern city and have placed it side by side with the English school of Charles Booth and (perhaps oddly) Friedrich Engels and the German school of Max Weber, George Simmel, and Oswald Spengler.[3] Even more emphatically, Alessandro Pizzorno writes:

> Chicago sociologists were certainly not the first ones to take on the systematic study of the city. From the monumental work of C. Booth on London at the turn of the century, to the long series of studies successively collected as the "Grossstadt Dokumente," by H. Ostwald (1905), to the collection of essays compiled by Peter-mann which includes Simmel's *Die Grossstadt und das Geistesleben*, a masterpiece of psychological and sociological intuitions, the Chicago school had illustrious predecessors.[4]

The literary predecessors of the Chicago school were no less illustrious. Traditionally of interest neither to the literary critic nor to the intellectual historian, the conceptual and methodological intuitions of the literary urban tradition did not escape the attention of the Chicago sociologists, who methodically relied on these protosociologists as pathbreakers of social observation. The influences at play between the urban novel and urban sociology historically had moved in two directions, resembling a system of interconnected channels more than a one-way street.

William Isaac Thomas, arguably the founding figure of Chicago sociology, came late to this new discipline, after several years of research and teaching in classical and modern languages. To that earlier period Thomas refers in the following recollection:

> The character of my visits to the Cumberland and Smoky Mountains changed. Formerly they had been hunting and shooting expeditions, but now I collected a list of about 300 "Chaucerian" and "Shakespearean" words surviving in the speech of the mountaineers, which I gave later, in Berlin, to the American dialectologist George Hempel.[5]

At the time, Thomas, who was originally from rural Virginia, was completing his Ph.D. at the University of Tennessee, where he remained as a teacher of Greek, French, German, and English for a few years until he went to Germany for further study. How inadequate he had been as a teacher of modern languages, he discovered, "may be judged by the fact that when I reached Berlin I could understand hardly the simplest German sentence. I had been taught German and French without conversation, precisely as Latin and Greek were taught at that time."[6] In Berlin and Göttingen Thomas concentrated on the study of "old English, old French, and old German," in other words on philology, the discipline that at the turn of the century was preeminent in literature departments; here he was first exposed to such new disciplines as ethnology and folk psychology. Though only thirty years of age, Thomas was a respected and experienced language and literature professor when he decided to leave his professorship at Oberlin College and enroll as one of the first graduate students in the newly organized department of sociology of the University of Chicago.[7]

While it is hard to gauge what precisely Thomas brought from philology and comparative literature to sociology, the methodologies that remain associated with his name afford generous clues. According to Thomas, "personal life-records, as complete as possible, constitute the *perfect* type of sociological material."[8] This often quoted statement is the synthesis of a methodology that Thomas originated, that the Chicago school of sociology contributed to, and came to inform the studies of at least three generations of sociologists. The literary import of this methodology can be assessed in an outline prepared for the Carnegie Corporation–Americanization Studies.[9] Noting that while sociologists have studied "formal organization[s]," they have neglected "the field of behavior," which has been "undertaken seriously only by literary men [sic]—Zola, Ibsen, Shaw, Meredith, etc.—and psychiatrists," the document explicitly views the sociologist as a first cousin of the novelist and dramatist. It then goes on to classify the "important classes of 'human documents'" for sociological use:

1. Letters; diaries; communications to newspapers; records of the juvenile courts, criminal courts, legal aid societies, charity organizations, etc. . . . [that] contain data of personal life. . . .

2. Life-records prepared by arrangement with the individual . . . a relatively large number . . . prepared by average or proletarian persons, and a smaller number by selected idealists and intellectuals. . . .

3. Extant autobiographies, especially those printed in the native language of the writer . . . and also unprinted manuscripts of this kind.[10]

In emphasizing literary records as essential materials for the study of society, the document spelled out what may be Thomas's most original contribution to the discipline of sociology. As important, the document articulated a pioneer position for the retrieval of literary forms and expressions produced by groups who were hardly considered human let alone capable of producing literature. These notes were thus also forerunners of the proletarian literature theories of the 1930s.

Thomas's emphasis on literary records, and unsolicited ones especially, and on "subjective" experience informed his pedagogy as well. Commenting on the use of such material by one of his students, he wrote: "[I]t seems to me that these cases and the others you mention as in preparation could be brought together in a volume which would have something of the quality of the stories of Chekov"; such a volume, he added, "would be of sociological as well as literary value." The superiority of these case histories in relation to fictional stories, Thomas suggested, derived from their being free of the "imagination" and "characteristics" that the "dramatist" and "story writer" bring to similar material. Exhorting the student to "leave out the moralizing," Thomas revealed that the case histories were more valuable for being less encumbered by the standards of a given time or class.[11] Through these documents the sociologist no less than the literary artist was taking part in the aesthetic movement to modernize and broaden the social range of American literature.

Robert Park's recollection of Thomas is also suggestive of the literary personality and background of this philologist turned sociologist: "Thomas' interest was always, it seems, that of a poet . . . and of a literary man in the reportorial sense. . . . He wanted to see, to know, and to report, disinterestedly and without respect to anyone's policies or programs, the world of men and things as he experienced it."[12]

Similar views characterized Park as well, the scholar whom Thomas brought to the University of Chicago and who became his collaborator and successor. As Park's life has received the benefit of two full-length biographies the importance of literature for this soci-

23

ologist has been noted.[13] Grey, Goldsmith, Tennyson, Whitman, Goethe, Turgenev, Tolstoy, Gorky, Dickens, Twain, Zola, Ibsen, Dreiser, Anderson are names that recur in the biographers' accounts and in Park's own writings. They are names that evoke the confrontation of country and city and the attendant phenomena of migration, industrialization, urbanization, and modernization in British, French, German, Russian, and American literature. While the unfamiliar reader would be justified in taking these references as mere signs of a well-read intellectual such as Park no doubt was, some familiarity with Park's work and life leaves no doubt as to the importance, epistemologically and even emotionally, of these authors and literatures.

Park's path to sociology, like Thomas's, was neither a straight nor an orthodox one. He received graduate training in philosophy both in the United States and Germany, studying with William James, John Dewey, George Simmel, and Wilhelm Windelband, among others. He repeatedly interrupted his academic career and spent years, first as court reporter, police reporter, and city newspaper reporter—as an "intellectual vagabond," he recalls, "exploring and writing about the life of the city"[14]—then as in-house journalist for the Congo Reform Association and, later yet, as personal assistant to and ghost writer for Booker T. Washington. These experiences he eventually came to consider as integral to and even his only sociological training. His graduate training in sociology—he was fond of explaining—took place in the newsroom of a large metropolitan newspaper, and he claimed that journalism was analogous to sociology. "Sociology, after all, is concerned with problems in regard to which newspaper men inevitably get a good deal of first hand knowledge. . . . One might fairly say that a sociologist is merely a more accurate, responsible, and scientific reporter."[15] And Park insistently recommended to his students: "[w]rite down only what you see, hear, and know, like a newspaper reporter."[16]

If journalism represented an important aspect in Park's definition of sociology, literature opened for him a window into the world of cities. When asked about the late start of his career in sociology, Park explained: "I can trace my interest in sociology to the reading of Goethe's *Faust*. You remember that Faust was tired of books and wanted to see the world—the world of men."[17] A few years later, he added: "I made up my mind to go in for experience for its own sake, to gather into my soul, as Faust somewhere says, all the joys and sorrows of the world."[18]

In a lecture entitled "Walt Whitman" Park recalled having been in youth a devout follower of Whitman and having encountered the poet when still "an ardent rebel," in other words, a typical member of the bohemian generation that had grown so numerous in the Midwest and that fully emerged in the 1910s. "In *Leaves of Grass*," Park explained, "I encountered a new type of man; a man who had broken with tradition but had found, nevertheless, a new vocation and a new faith."[19] Park was at the time a "newspaper man . . . as Whitman had been:"

> A newspaperman, more than most people, I suspect, knows, and feels, and is thrilled by the vast, anonymous and impersonal life of the city. . . . I began to read with a certain amount of enthusiasm Whitman's musings on the city's surging life. . . . I felt, as he did, that there was something inspiring, majestic—in the spectacle of the manifold and multitudinous life of the city. . . . something at once moving and mystical. [20]

Likewise it was through the eyes of poets and novelists that Park, the journalist turned sociologist, taught his students to look at the city. Asked to recall what he had learned from Park, the anthropologist Leslie A. White stated:

> Park's genuine interests were in particulars, not generalizations. He was . . . concerned with individuals, pictures of the life of groups—immigrants, denizens of skid row, hoodlums, etc., much as Dreiser, Gorky, et al., were. . . . I remember well his showing me a doctoral thesis written under his direction. . . . It was an intimate account of a small town in the west. He had everything in it about the characters, both respectable and otherwise. It was exactly the sort of things that Sherwood Anderson and Dreiser wrote. Park was fascinated by it.[21]

Park's interest in "particulars" and "individuals" and his impatience with abstract theoretics could be rudely evident in his relations with other academics. "We give a damn for logic around here! What we want to know is what people do!" Park shouted at a European scholar who was empahsizing the need to analyze something "logically."[22] The same predilection was evident on the shelves of his library where "[t]he majority of the books were travelogues, journalistic reports, novels and the like. . . . He explained his preference for books of this kind, saying, 'Of course, these books are not sociology, but those

25

who wrote them have one advantage over sociologists—they know people!'"[23] In the words of his biographer, "Park brought to the study of urban life not only the compulsive curiosity of the city beat report- er but the romantic sensibility developed among poets and novelists by a century of observing with fascinated horror the growth of indus- trial cities."[24]

If Park was a poet of the city in spirit, Robert Redfield, his student and eventually his son-in-law, was a poet in fact. In the estimation of some the most important successors of Franz Boas, Redfield was un- equivocally and unabashedly a poet with ambitions and some skill, judging from his submissions and occasional disappointments. " 'We are Poets,' you say, 'Of course the others can't understand us.' / Why, we are all poets! / Only half of us don't know it," Redfield scornfully wrote once in response to a rejection. Entitled "Addressed to Certain Writers of Verses," this verse reply challenges unappreciative critics:

I know this isn't poetry I'm writing
But neither is half of the stuff you write,
And I wish you realized that fact.
I don't care so much about your verse form
Or lack of form ——
Though you are insufferably conceited about
The immense importance of the way
You space the little black marks supposed to represent ideas ——[25]

The poem warns the new poets that though modern aesthetics repre- sents a change for the better, emptiness of genuine ideas and lack of true emotions are once again a threat. If Redfield's poem does not qualify as great literature, it does reveal an understanding of the for- mal disputes that were being fought in the first decades of the century. Like Thomas, who searched for the literature of the people, Redfield was anticipating some of the themes of the populist poetics that would inspire much of the 1930s modernism and much of that peri- od's reaction against the more rarefied and elitist modernism of the 1920s. The notion that "we are all poets" hinges on the same view that perceives sociological documents to have literary value and that sees sociology, like literature, to be concerned with people.

26

In his lecture "Social Science as Humanity"[26] Redfield explicitly claimed that the social sciences are centrally concerned with human beings, and that the sources for that study are "the records of human living [that] . . . exist in ethnography and history . . . in biography and in psychiatric case records; and . . . in creative literature." He added:

> No one is more deeply engaged in the examination and understanding of human nature than are the dramatist and the novelist. . . . I doubt that the results so far achieved by the social scientists are more communicative of the truth about human nature than are the results achieved by the more personal and imaginative records of the artist. . . . The man [sic] of literature and art has been longest interested in the subject.[27]

Chicago sociologists identified not just with writers and artists but with literary critics as well, seeing, for example, in Freud's reading of case histories not a physician at work but a literary critic to be emulated.[28] Placing the sociologist in a position analogous to that of the artist and the literary critic, Redfield acknowledged the relationship between "literary" and "sociological documents," between "novelist" and "proletarian author," between literary "character" and sociological "informant," between literary "critic" and "sociologist":

> The humanistic scholar studies culture chiefly as it appears in literature and art . . . a culture from the top, so to speak. The anthropologist begins at the bottom where the ordinary people work out their ways of life without benefit of books or Socrates. The student of art or literature is concerned with the finest flowers on a tree whose roots are investigated by anthropologists. But it is the same tree.[29]

The difference, Redfield implies, between "high" and "low" is one of degree, not kind, of class, not essence. Chicago sociologists and anthropologists saw themselves, in part, as scholars and critics of "popular culture" before such a field had been invented.

Because of just such views Redfield belongs to the second generation of Chicago sociologists, one that while trained within more sharply defined disciplinary boundaries continued to look upon fiction, poetry, and drama as important sociological referents. As a result of training and sometimes personal inclination, this generation maintained its humanistic emphasis, and systematically brought into their courses a variety of "literatures"—of the city, of the family, of immigrants, of the Negro, of the muckrakers, of labor—some of which have but very recently become acceptable fields within literature departments.[30] Park, for example, used a great deal of "Negro poetry."[31]

Burgess routinely referred students to authors like Theodore Dreiser, Upton Sinclair, and Sherwood Anderson, and to "literature that depicted family life or communities or crime delinquency."[32] Other authors whose work was used in sociology courses at Chicago include Ole E. Rolvaag, Edith Wharton, James Branch Cabell, Joseph Hergesheimer, H. L. Mencken, and James T. Farrell. And professors widely drew from autobiographical materials written by both students and sociological informants.[33]

"Study of the City Through Literature and Art" is an example of the pedagogical use of literature by Chicago sociologists.[34] This course outline, by Ernest Burgess, breaks down into such subheadings as "a new literary form for the City," "rural to urban transition," "City working men [sic]," "skyscrapers, crowds, subways"; among Louis Wirth's papers are also a number of index cards about urban literature that complement Burgess's outline.[35] Some of the titles are "The city in Literature," "American Writers and the city," "The small town in fiction," "The Deserted Village," and "The novel and the city."[36] A few of these notes condense material from such works as the Old Testament, Charles Dickens's "Travels in America," Oliver Goldsmith's "The Deserted Village," and Thomas Gray's "Elegy," and one makes a pointed comment about Dickens:

> Nor is even Dickens fully aware of that silent throng on whom rested the whole social fabric: the productive class. His people, workers though they be, live by selling, not by making. His knowledge, though not his sympathy, fails when he approaches industrial conditions, and the slight, pathetic figures of Rachael and Stephen Blackpool in "Hard Times," are almost his only examples of manual laborers. The time of the proletariat in art has not yet come.[37]

That time did come; it came with special force in the United States, in the 1930s, and in Chicago, and is most centrally represented by Farrell, Algren, and Wright.

A typed page in the same folder contains excerpts from Jules Romains's *Men of Good Will*, excerpts that describe a large city when its dwellers and working guests are between work and home and through a narrator acutely aware of class relations in the streets: "It was the hour when the proportion of wealthy people in the streets is the highest . . . and when the children of the poorer quarters chase one another shouting along the sidewalks." And aware of power relations embodied in the city: "Four, seven, eleven express trains were on their way to Paris. The four which were creeping along far away had barely emerged from the provinces. They had just left the big cities which Paris allows to grow at a certain distance away from her."[38]

Much like Park's celebration of Whitman, Wirth's feeling for such passages typifies the special sensitivity that attracted the Chicago sociologists to the realist novels of the nineteenth and early twentieth century—a literature that grandly staged the human drama of the city, of its pilgrims, immigrants, merchants, workers, and flâneurs—and to the humanistic brand of sociology that was its direct descendant.

The literature "of the city" that Burgess taught and Wirth annotated was complemented by a number of related literatures. One of these was the literature "of the Negro" before it became African-American literature, works Park used in his courses and regularly reviewed between 1918 and 1935 for the *American Journal of Sociology*.[39] One typescript in his files includes pages of comments about African-American authors and genres and discusses how sociologists should view this literary material.[40] Another poses the following question:

> What is Negro Literature as the term is used in this course? What are the characteristics of Negro Literature?
> 1. During the period of slavery?
> 2. During the period of Reconstruction?
> 3. During the last two decades?
> What is the relation of Negro Literature to race consciousness?[41]

"The Muck-rake or the Literature of Exposure," another of the genres Chicago sociologists studied, was the title of a paper presented at the 1924 Summer Institute of the Society for Social Research.[42] It was part of a panel that included talks on the "Sociological Use of Literary Materials," "The Use of Poetry and Folklore in Social Science," and "Literature in Relation to the Problems of the Social Worker."[43] Park's files also contain a detailed discussion of muckraking literature:[44]

> Fifty years from now, when the historian of American literature writes of the opening years of the century, he [sic] will give [one] of his most interesting chapters to the literature of exposure, and he [sic] will pronounce it a true intellectual force, a vital element in the creative activity of later years.[45]

The literary winds have not blown as the author of these remarks predicted.

Labor poetry was also of interest to Chicago sociologists and an essay by Nels Anderson identifies two main phases of its development: first, when poets "sang of the open road, of the wild and wooly . . . cowboy songs, lumberjack songs, railroad songs, mining songs and rollicking narrative poems. . . . But they were not radical"; second, when "the poet was taken over . . . [by] the rebel press" and "became the intellectual in a movement."[46] Neither sentimental nor patronizing, Anderson celebrates the "rebel poet" as a true "cosmopolitan" who, like a true modernist poet, openly opposes his enemies, "the boss," "the judge," "the policeman," and cares little for the "uncompromising loyalties of the provincials" or of the "reformer whom he regards as a juggler of platitudes."[47]

Students of sociology at Chicago made extensive and novel use of literature in their readings and writings. One of Park's assignments was: "write the history of a marginal man selecting from the materials of autobiography those which you think are characteristic of the type."[48] Using excerpts from Ludwig Lewisohn's *Up Stream, An American Chronicle,* and *Israel,* a student created, out of these different literary texts and in the form of a literary montage, a familiar paradigm of Parkian sociology: marginal man as a split figure between cultures.

Ernest Burgess's course, Family Study II, also required students to utilize autobiographical and biographical texts. The list of forty-nine texts for this interesting hybrid of sociological analysis and literary criticism ranges from Margaret Fuller to Carlo Goldoni, from Edward Bok to Charles Darwin, from St. Augustine to Benjamin Franklin, with a preponderance of Romantic and Victorian figures.[49] And a handwritten list by Burgess of essay topics for one of his courses further indicates the pedagogical use Chicago sociologists made of literary material:

An Event in the City
A Vivid City Experience
A Thrilling Adventure
This Could Only Have Happened in the City
An Incident of City Life
A Personal Experience in Urban Life
Narratives of City Life
Poems of City Life
City Life in Art (typical representations)
Legends and Myths of the City[50]

As for the effect of such instruction on students, not untypical is a dissertation written by Hugh D. Duncan in 1948, and supervised by Wirth, which examines the roots of Chicago literature and assesses its contribution to the literature of the United States when this was still "a young nation" and far from having "a national literature."[51]

At a time when literature courses taught in English departments ended with the seventeenth century, and American literature, African-American literature, ethnic literature, although they were read, were not considered worthy of critical attention, Chicago sociologists acted to constitute, preserve, and promote them. They were teaching courses and using materials of the type one now finds in most English and American literature departments deserving of the name, but that until ten, fifteen years ago were still quite rare. These literatures were not merely used out of context for the purpose of providing colorful illustrations to the sociology but rather existed within the Chicago sociology department as self-contained and self-defined fields. Although the sociologists' view of literature was not, strictly speaking, informed by aesthetic criteria, or concerned with the conceptualization of form, it contributed to some of the earliest classifications and commentaries of the texts. Like missionaries, natural scientists, and ethnographers who, in the colonial context, preserved many cultural artifacts while engaged in the political and economic destruction of those cultures, Chicago sociologists were ahead of the literary critics in conceptualizing and constituting the literatures of immigrants, African-Americans, the city, and workers, even while their theories of urbanization and modernization created powerful ideologies against some of those same cultures. Chicago sociologists represent important if problematic precursors of ethnic studies and literary multiculturalism with whom we cannot avoid confronting ourselves critically. Whether we like it or not, social scientists, whose main goal was knowledge of the group for the purpose of social control, have been historically important agents in the process that turns cultures into literatures. At once disinterestedly curious and politically compromised, these social scientists were among the first systematizers of the literatures of the United States.

Beneath their scholarly practice lay the perception that sociological life history and literary autobiography, sociology and literature, belong on the same continuum rather than separate spheres. "If we knew the full life-history of a single individual in his social setting," Wirth claimed, "we would probably know most of what is worth 31 knowing about social life and human nature."[52] These words sum up the Chicago sociology department's inclination toward empirical research and firsthand contact with the subjects of study, and toward personal documents and life histories as primary repositories of social experience. Commenting on the new generations of sociologists who look down on the rough and archaic methods used by these pioneers of the social sciences, Alessandro Pizzorno has noted that their success and strength were derived precisely from the "wealth of intuitions and uninterrupted exchange between theory and research, in other words from opening up theory to the innovations and surprises that the unrigorous methodology of participant observation favored."[53] Combining the empirical tradition that had characterized American philosophy and social reformers' activities and writings as well as the theoretical orientation of the European sociological tradition, Chicago sociologists brought social theory physically into the city; they also brought autobiographies, life histories, case studies, and personal letters into the sociologists' monographs, and in general they brought sociology closer to literature than to hard science.

Referring to the "abstract" representation of Chicago by the novelists who preceded the Chicago urban sociologists, Fred H. Matthews has noted: "[I]n one sense the school of urban sociology which developed under the guidance of Park and Ernest Burgess sought to remove the blindfold of the artist, and capture the particular texture and color of the neighborhood subcultures—the Gold Coast, the Ghetto, the slums and hobohemias of Chicago."[54] James T. Farrell, Nelson Algren, and Richard Wright represent the generation of novelists that inherited and built upon such a view of the city.

If sociology and literature have come to be seen routinely as antithetical, that has not always been the case. Chicago urban sociologists and novelists intellectually rubbed elbows, and conceptually and methodologically, aesthetically and thematically stood as primary reference points for one another. They felt no qualms about acknowledging this kinship. While the critical practice of the last few decades has been fairly consistent in decreeing that when a literary text is "sociological" it is not "art," the practice of Chicago sociologists and novelists points to a time when good sociology and good literature held hands.

That forms, conventions, and language have become the main preoccupation of literary critics as the only apprehensible reality, and that quantifiable forms of behavior have become the main preoc-

cupation of social scientists as the only observable reality reveal, paradoxically, that the increasing polarization of these two disciplines
might hinge on a basic complementarity: the disregard for the subjective experience and consciousness of historically, socially, and existentially specific people, be they Authors or authors, Characters or sociological subjects.

Maps, Models, and Metaphors: Theories of the City

2

This chaos of alleys, courts, hovels, filth—and human beings—is not a chaos at all. Every fragment of disarray, every inconvenience, every scrap of human suffering has a meaning. Each of these is inversely and ineradicably related to the life led by the middle classes, to the work performed in the factories, and to the structure of the city as a whole.

—Steven Marcus, "Reading the Illegible"

Thus has Steven Marcus explained Friedrich Engels' discovery that the urban space, specifically the slum, encompasses the political economy of the whole society. As Marcus puts it, it was precisely the "invisibility" of the "dark, dense belt formed by Manchester's working class and their dwelling," that made the overall structure of Manchester "unintelligible" and "illegible."[1] Through his reading of the working-class slum, Marcus points out, Engels uncovered much more than just the structure of a physical space called Manchester: Engels read the structure of industrial capitalism itself, for the nineteenth century the true mysterious center of things.

If the modern city, as Marcus notes, continues to be perceived as "unintelligible and illegible," and is experienced as "the structure of a chaos," the content of this estrangement has varied not only with different individuals but at different times and in different places, finding its historical focus in different parts of the city. For Engels and for many of his middle-class contemporaries, the heart of the illegible city was in its working-class slums. In the United States during the first decades of the twentieth century, the illegible city was sought less and less in the working-class sections. Urban illegibility found its focus in the slums of the American industrial city, which, at the height of migration—Chicago urban sociologists argued—consisted of many distinct neighborhoods and were inhabited by several classes of the "poor": the immigrant colonies, "gangland," "Hobohemia," the "Black Belt," the "red-light region," the "vice district." Sociologists like Robert Park, Ernest Burgess, and Louis Wirth set out to do for the modern American city what Engels had done for the early industrial city: they would proclaim the city and all its parts readable, the processes of its growth and change intelligible.

While the Romantic and Victorian travelers have recently become familiar presences within literary studies, and, more generally, nineteenth-century travel writing a respectable field for literary critics, the twentieth-century heirs of those urban investigators and proto-ethnographers and of those literary traditions have yet to become meaningful objects of examination. To be sure, sociologists and intellectual historians have not neglected the Chicago school of urban sociology. Yet their studies have been less concerned with the language, the prose, and the modes of signification of Chicago sociology than with evaluating the methodological and theoretical legacies of this school. They have asked what is left of this science rather than what was remarkable in this literature. Generally found to be lacking in methodological and theoretical rigor, Chicago sociology survives mostly as antiquated vintage or the monument of another intellectual era. The questions that Steven Marcus asked of Engels' study of Manchester, on the other hand, have not been asked of the Chicago school. How did Chicago sociologists negotiate the relation between the "visible" and the "invisible," the "legible" and the "illegible," the larger city and the specific and numerous slums? What is the structure of modern American society that Chicago sociologists read into and out of the city? What role did language play in mediating between or 35 interfering with the conceptual and empirical study of the city by the Chicago sociologists?

"The City: Suggestions for the Investigation of Human Behavior in the Urban Environment" by Robert Park, "The Growth of the City: An Introduction to a Research Project" by Ernest Burgess, and *The Gang: A Study of 1,313 Gangs in Chicago* by Frederic Thrasher are significant documents of the Chicago sociological tradition and are emblematic of the conceptual efforts and tensions at the heart of that tradition.[2] Pioneering works of modern sociological discourse, they are representative of the Chicago sociologists' main intellectual thrust: to counter the traditional view of the modern American city as chaos, invisibility, "unnatural nature," and outside history—in essence as temporal and spatial otherness—through the production of some of the earliest and most original frameworks for the analysis of the city as both culture and change. As Morris Janowitz has noted, these works are expressions of the desire "to view the city as an object of detached sociological analysis" and to discover "patterns of regularity in its apparent confusion."[3] Central to Chicago sociologists' enterprise was the effort to define the city conceptually and to make urban change and migration worthy objects of scientific investigation. Arguing for a specific science of the city and seeking out its system of signification—its *langue* and *parole*—Chicago sociologists, these three exemplary texts show, did for the city what Saussure had but recently done for language: they brought order where there had been chaos, established a semiological relationship among the parts—the neighborhoods—and between the part and the whole—the neighborhood and the city, where there had been an undistinguishable amalgam, articulating, overall, both synchronic and diachronic models for the anlysis of the city. Paradoxically, when they turned attention to the slums, the Chicago sociologists reproduced and reaffirmed the very same views that had made the city—and language—inaccessible for study: nature, rather than culture, natural disorder, rather than conventional order, reemerged as explanatory paradigms. It is these different and incongruous aspects of Chicago urban theory and ethnography that the present and following chapters examine.

At the center of the Chicago sociologists' theories and studies of the city are two interrelated conceptual frameworks: Park, Burgess, and Thrasher conceptualized the city as harmonious space and intelligible time but envisioned the slum as contagious, degenerative, and unintelligible fragment. This is a central discrepancy of Chicago urban theory, which should not be simply dismissed as yet another proof that Chicago sociologists were pseudoscientists. Rather, it is argued here, these discordances are meaningful in and of themselves, much as poetic dissonance—self-conscious or otherwise—is understood by literary critics as meaningful within a given context of signification. Moreover, they are especially meaningful in relation to the sociological novels and autobiographies of James T. Farrell, Nelson Algren, and Richard Wright, authors who by writing about migration to and deviance within the city could not avoid a headmost confrontation with this powerful conceptual apparatus.

I

"The City: Suggestions for the Investigation of Human Behavior in the Urban Environment," by Robert Park, represents the first programmatic and theoretical call for the scientific study of the city, a task which, Park complains, has been left largely to the pens of writers.

> We are mainly indebted to writers of fiction for our more intimate knowledge of contemporary urban life. But the life of our cities demands a more searching and disinterested study than even Emile Zola has given us in his "experimental" novels and the annals of the Rougon-Macquart family.[4]

Park begins by denouncing as false the image of the city as artificial and unnatural. Beneath this stereotype, Park claims, lies the perception of the city as "mere artifact":

> The city, particularly the modern American city, strikes one at first blush as so little a product of the artless processes of nature and growth, that it is difficult to recognize it as a living entity. The ground plan of most American cities, for example is a checkerboard. The unit of distance is the block. This geometrical form suggests that the city is a purely artificial contruction which might conceivably be taken apart and put together again, like a house of blocks.[5]

Not only is the city more than "merely a physical mechanism and an artificial construction," it is also something more than just "a congeries of individual men and social conveniences" or "a mere constellation of institutions and administrative devices." The city, Park suggests, is "a product of nature, and particularly of human nature." The "human" nature of the city is visible in its overall structure, which "first impresses us by its visible vastness and complexity. But . . . has its basis, nevertheless, in human nature, of which it is an expression."[6] And

37

the human nature of the city is especially visible in its culture when one begins to see that "[t]he city is . . . a state of mind, a body of customs and traditions, and of the organized attitudes and sentiments that inhere in these customs and are transmitted with this traditon."[7] Thus the modern city no less than "primitive" society takes the form of its culture. Making the analogy more explicit by quoting Oswald Spengler, Park closes these prefatory remarks by stating that "'What his house is to the peasant, the city is to civilized man.'"[8]

Living on two different continents yet drawing from the same intellectual tradition—the German sociological and philosophical tradition—and formulating these particular insights probably within a few months of each other, both Georg Lukács and Robert Park addressed modern consciousness and modern society in terms of exile, marginality, and homelessness. Lukács defined the existential condition of the modern individual as one of "transcendental homelessness." Park, on the other hand, gave the modern individual a new "home."[9]

Having defined the city as "natural" but "human," "primitive" but "civilized," as the "culture" of human "nature," in other words, having blurred some of the basic dichotomies of his age and culture, Park proceeds to the important tasks of defining a method and identifying the morphological units for the study of the city:

> Anthropology, the science of man, has been mainly concerned up to the present with the study of primitive peoples. But civilized man is quite as interesting an object of investigation. . . . The same patient methods of observation which anthropologists like Boas and Lowie have expended on the study of the life and manners of the North American Indian might be even more fruitfully employed in the investigation of the customs, beliefs, social practices, and general conceptions of life prevalent in Little Italy on the lower North Side in Chicago, or in recording the more sophisticated folkways of the inhabitants of Greeenwich Village and the neighborhood of Washington Square, New York.[10]

If anthropology is the "science of man," Park proposes sociology as the anthropology of "civilized man." The claim that Italian immigrants—or any group of new immigrants for that matter—have a culture no less than the North American Indians reproduced on one level a predominant view of immigrants as exotics and foreigners while at the same time modestly advancing their neighborhoods from un-

38

intelligible chaos to intelligible primitive space. More original, especially in light of Farrell, Algren, and Wright's narratives, was Park's suggestion that one might study the wealthier urban dwellers—and by extension the whole culture—ethnographically, and that the sociologist should become a foreigner at home.

Park's discussion of the way human nature shapes the physical structure of the city is especially significant. Within the general limits imposed by the "city plan," Park explains, neighborhoods are freely constituted by "personal tastes and convenience, vocational and economic interests" as well as by "sympathy, rivalry, and economic necessity."[11] The results of this spatial laissez-faire are on one hand the ecological macrostructure of the modern city, in which different areas are occupied by "business and industry," "fashionable residence quarters," the "slums"; and on the other hand the cultural microstructure, wherein each section is transformed into a "neighborhood . . . that is to say, a locality with sentiments, traditions, and a history of its own."[12] The nature of the city, Park was claiming, is to be many separate cities at once, each inhabited by distinct groups, and each following semiindependent historical and social trajectories. Whether inspired by Park's formulation, which he knew well, or by his own experience, or most likely by both, James T. Farrell articulated the same view of the urban neighborhood when he recalled:

> The critics and reviewers . . . have committed themselves in print to the assertion that Theodore Dreiser was the biggest influence in my literary career . . . [but] I felt closer to Anderson's intimate world than I did to that depicted in Dreiser's massive novels. The neighborhoods of Chicago in which I grew up possessed something of the character of a small town. They were little worlds of their own. Many of the people living in them knew one another. There was a certain amount of gossip of the character that one finds in small towns. . . . To [Dreiser] Chicago was new, exciting, wonderful. . . . Chicago sang for him, and he sang with it. To me Chicago was different. I never felt the wonder of Chicago until I had left it and returned to it many times.[13]

Closer to Dreiser than to Farrell in their own perception of the city, Chicago sociologists, one might say, translated their "wonder" into sociological concepts that, in turn, later allowed Farrell intellectually to leave the "little neighborhood."

The neighborhood, according to Park, represents both the mor-

39

phological unit of study and the most visible product of the interaction between physical space and human nature, macro- and microstructure, encompassing the characteristic form of the modern city:

> Every great city has its racial colonies, like the Chinatowns of San Francisco and New York, the Little Sicily of Chicago, and various other less pronounced types. In addition to these, most cities have their segregated vice districts, like that which until recently existed in Chicago, their rendezvous for criminals of various sorts. Every large city has its occupational suburbs, like the Stockyards in Chicago, and its residential enclaves, like Brookline in Boston, the so-called "Gold Coast" in Chicago, Greenwich Village in New York, each of which has the size and the character of a complete separate town, village, or city, except that its population is a selected one. Undoubtedly the most remarkable of these *cities within cities* . . . is East London, with a population of 2,000,000 laborers.[14]

Cultural difference—for Park the real essence of human nature—incorporates itself, so to speak, as a neighborhood. The illegibility of the modern city is, accordingly, not an intrinsic but a contingent trait due to the isolation and segregation that are its dominant features. Where Engels discovered that the illegibility of the city was premised on the invisibility of the working-class slums and that the invisibility of class relations resulted in unintelligible spatial and social relations, Park claimed that the illegibility of the city was premised on the "natural" self-segregation of individuals into different neighborhoods, and that the invisibility of "cultural" relations—"ethnicity," "vice," "occupations," and "wealth"—resulted in unintelligible human nature.

"Temperament and the Urban Environment," the fourth and last section of Park's essay, is less frequently discussed and yet the most significant in this reading. More than just a conclusion for what remains an original essay on the culture of the city, this section shifts attention from the city to the slum, producing a radically different reading of the urban space that is as inconsistent with Park's analysis up to this point as it is revealing of its ideological scope.

Park here redefines the city as a biological rather than cultural expression. "Great cities," he writes, "have always been the melting-pots of races and of cultures. Out of the vivid interactions of which they have been the centers, there have come the newer breeds and the newer social types." In this formulation the city appears less as a cultural crossroad than as a biological one. Anticipating both his later es-

40

say on the marginal man and Louis Wirth's theory of urbanization, Park notes that

> the great cities of the United States, for example, have drawn from the isolation of their native villages great masses of the rural popula-tions of Europe and America. Under the shock of the new contacts the latent energies of these primitive peoples have been released, and the subtler processes of interaction have brought into exist-ence not merely vocational, but temperamental, types.[15]

Earlier in the essay Park had argued that the city—with its wealth of vocational opportunities—liberates individuals by allowing them "to choose [their] own vocation and develop [their] peculiar individual talents."[16] In the last section, however, Park transposes the same mod-el in biological terms, arguing that as immigrants are transformed from "primitive people" into urban people, their "latent energies"—that is, biological energies—are also freed: "The lure of great cities is perhaps a consequence of stimulations which act directly upon the reflexes. As a type of human behavior it may be explained, like the attraction of the flame for the moth, as a sort of tropism."[17] In a lan-guage that becomes more and more conceptually unstable, Park tries awkwardly to modify this metaphor of self-destruction, which threat-ens his broader theory of the city as liberating modernity, by falling into yet more biological language, exchanging a metaphor of self-destruction for other biological and innate traits:

> The attraction of the metropolis is due in part, however, to the fact that in the long run every individual finds somewhere among the varied manifestations of city life . . . the *moral climate* in which his *peculiar nature* obtains the *stimulations* that bring his *innate dispositions* to full and free expression. It is, I suspect, motives of this kind which have their basis, not in interest nor even in sentiment, but in some-thing more *fundamental* and *primitive* which draw many, if not most, of the young men and young women from the security of their homes in the country into the big, booming confusion and excite-ment of city life.[18]

Rather than "unnatural," in this formulation the city is home to the most "natural" parts of human nature, those intangible entities vaguely labeled "peculiar nature," "innate disposition," or something "fundamental" and "primitive." With minute but drastic shifts Park has gone from reading the city as an expression of human nature to read-

41

ing it as nature tout-court, and, paradoxically, to viewing migration to the modern city as a return to a hypothetical primitive aspect of human nature.

Much as the impulse to migrate to the city is now identified as a biological one, and as equally biological is the effect of the city on new immigrants, so biological are the effects of the city on people who freely "move" within it.

> The processes of segregation establish *moral distances* which make the city a *mosaic of little worlds* which touch but do not interpenetrate. This makes it possible for individuals to pass quickly and easily from one *moral milieu* to another, and encourages the fascinating but dangerous experiment of living at the same time in several different contiguous, but otherwise widely separated, worlds. All this tends to . . . produce *new and divergent individual types.*[19]

Following the familiar discourse of "morality-cum-biology" that historically has been the cornerstone of deviance studies and theories, Park also captures the cultural schizophrenia of the immigrant—Park's later marginal man—who, living within distinct and sometimes incompatible cultures, becomes by default an ethnographer and relativist, culturally as well as "morally." Richard Wright, one might fairly say, chose to write his autobiographical narrative through the eyes of this "deviant" personality, and it is this self-conscious pattern of deviance—deviance of action as well as of point of view—that provides a fundamental motif for *Black Boy-American Hunger.*

The "newer breeds," the "temperamental," and "divergent" types generated by the city are especially visible to Park in the contrast between the city on the one hand and the small community, the town, and the village on the other. "If they had the making of criminals, the restraints and inhibitions of the small community rendered them harmless. If they had the stuff of genius in them, they remained sterile for lack of appreciation or opportunity."[20] What the village barely tolerates, the city, and the slum especially, rewards, and vice versa. The criminal and the genius share in this fate: unable fully to develop in the village, both types find in the city their congenial environment. Two distant literary texts illustrate Park's theory of wasted geniuses:

42

> Mark Twain's story of *Pudd'n Head Wilson* [sic] is a description of one such obscure and unappreciated genius. It is not so true as it was that

Full many a flower is born to blush unseen
And waste its fragrance on the desert air.
Gray wrote the "Elegy in a Country Churchyard" before the rise of
the modern metropolis.[21]

Through its divergent types, Park suggests, human nature shapes
the physical environment no less than through its conventional types.
The success of the criminal in the urban environment, more than that
of the genius, concerns Park. "In the city," he writes, in a language
more and more laden with biological metaphors, "many of these divergent types now find a milieu in which, for good or for ill, their dis-
positions and talents parturiate and bear fruit."[22] If the larger structure
of the city is shaped by the "occupational interests" and the "economic conditions" of the people who concentrate in distinct neighborhoods, the structure of the slum bears the imprint of the "tastes" and
"temperaments" of those who concentrate in the slum, or in the
"moral regions" as Park labels the neighborhoods that most conspicu-
ously embody the "immoral" sides of human nature. These areas are
"detached milieus in which vagrant and oppressed impulses, passions and ideals emancipate themselves from the dominant moral order."[23] Park here significantly moves in the direction of both psychoanalysis and aesthetics to reflect on the origins of the slum and the
city:

> Men are brought into the world with all the passions, instincts, and
> appetites, uncontrolled and undisciplined. Civilization, in the in-
> terests of the common welfare, demands the suppression some-
> times, and the control always, of these wild, natural dispositions. In
> the process of imposing its discipline upon the individual, in mak-
> ing over the individual in accordance with the accepted commu-
> nity model, much is suppressed altogether, and much more finds
> vicarious expression in forms that are socially valuable, or at least
> innocuous. It is at this point that sport, play, and art function. They
> permit the individual to purge himself by means of symbolic ex-
> pression of these wild and suppressed impulses. This is the cathar-
> sis of which Aristotle wrote in his Poetic [sic], and which has been
> given new and more positive significance by the investigations of
> Sigmund Freud and the psychoanalysts.[24]

43

Pushing this analogy to its logical conclusion, one notes that Park's
"moral zones"—"Bohemia," the "half-world," the "red-light district,"
the "vice districts"—turn out to function as the id of a hypothetical ur-

ban psyche, as an unconscious which expresses itself spatially in the slum and behaviorally in the deviant.

This view of the slum is much simpler than that of the city as a mosaic of cultural tiles, and indeed provides, in the language of the natural sciences, the real conclusion for Park's essay:

> In this great city the poor, the vicious, and the delinquent, crushed together in an unhealthful and contagious intimacy, breed in and in, soul and body, so that it has often occurred to me that those long genealogies of the Jukes and the tribes of Ishmael would not show such a persistent and distressing uniformity of vice, crime, and poverty unless they were peculiarly fit for the environment in which they are condemned to exist.[25]

The congregation of the "poor," "vicious," "criminal," and "exceptional" types produces more of the same. Indeed, their congregation and reproduction in the slum tautologically confirms the slum to be their natural environment and the slum dwellers to be naturally deviant. From seeing the city as a study of cultural difference, Park arrives here at postulating the city as a study of behavioral and moral difference.

In bringing the discussion to a close, Park returns briefly to his ethnographic and culturalist premises to remark that "these moral regions" must be accepted "as part of the natural, if not normal, life of a city"; they should not be seen, therefore, as "necessarily criminal or abnormal" but rather as "regions in which a divergent moral code prevails," and "in which the people who inhabit it are dominated, as people are ordinarily not dominated, by a taste or by a passion or by some interest which has its roots directly in the original nature of the individual."[26] The hidden center of the city, it turns out, is identical with the hidden center of human nature. Historically the port of entry of immigrants and migrants, the slum is the region from which the modern city draws demographic sustenance, as well as the region of the chronically unemployed, who are just as essential for the economic well-being of both the city and the larger economy; it was therefore more appropriate than Park had intended that both the city and its "vice areas" should originate in the same source: the "original nature of the individual."

44   On one hand Park posited the city as a world of cultural and social difference embodied in neighborhoods. On the other he distinguished between "natural" and "moral" areas, creating what is in fact a definition of difference within difference. With this shift from the lan-

guage of art and anthropology to the language of science and medicine, Park's essay closes with two views of the city. The "mosaic" city projects a world of fragments and cultural differences, where neighborhoods are to each other in the same relation as the tiles of a mosaic, and where the sociologist observes as an art critic these fragments' role in the overall harmony of the design. The "laboratory" city projects the image of a physical rather than cultural space, the image of a secluded space where observation is subordinated to intervention, where difference is biological rather than cultural, and where the sociologist's function is that of a social physician.

Behind Park's shift was a conceptual shift from human nature as culture to human nature as nature. Biological impulses turn out to be the original motivation for immigration, and therefore for the modern city, and biological the effect that the city has on human nature. With this new focus Park put aside the larger city for some specific neighborhoods—the "vice districts"—and abandoned the dialectic of culture and space for a determination of biology over space. Whereas Engels came to understand the city as the spatial embodiment of industrial capitalism and to claim that the slum was the key that made sense of that urban hieroglyph, Park came to understand the city as the spatial embodiment of human nature and to claim that the slum embodied the most "innate" and "primitive" traits of that nature.

II

Published almost ten years after Park's "The City," Ernest Burgess's "The Growth of the City: An Introduction to a Research Project" added to Park's synchronic model a diachronic model that conceptualized the city in terms of linear and temporal developments, specifically in terms of evolution, progress, and upward mobility.

Against the dominant view of cities as large amorphous aggregates of services and people, Burgess claims that urban growth results from processes of expansion rather than of mere agglomeration: "The typical processes of the expansion of the city can best be illustrated, perhaps, by a series of concentric circles, which may be numbered to designate both the successive zones of urban extension and the types of areas differentiated in the process of expansion."[27] Aiming to show that meaningful rather than accidental processes underlie urban

45

growth, Burgess proposes that the physical changes of the city should be imagined as consecutive stages and visualized as a series of concentric circles. In "the Loop," the first circle, is located "the central business district"; this is surrounded by "the zone of transition," the second circle, "which is being invaded by business and light manufacture"; encircling this area is the "zone of workingmen's homes," the third circle, which is "inhabited by the workers in industries who have escaped from the area of deterioration but who desire to live within easy access of their work." On the outer edge is the "residential area," composed of "high-class apartment buildings" and "exclusive 'restricted' districts of single family dwellings," and the "commuter zone," located "beyond the city limits" and composed of "suburban areas" and "satellite cities." Burgess here captures not only the abstract circularity of the city but, more important, the laws that shape each circle, "namely, the tendency of each inner zone to extend by invading the next outer zone."[28] Urban growth thus is envisioned as a ripple phenomenon that starts at the center and spreads outward, affecting every part.

Having outlined the general model of urban growth as a dynamic structure that expands outward along imaginary radii, Burgess proceeds to examine what triggers that movement, and the changes that this in turn produces at the individual and collective levels. Launching into a daring analogy, Burgess here abandons the ecological metaphor for a physiological analogy: "Urban growth [is] a resultant of organization and disorganization analogous to the anabolic and katabolic processes of metabolism in the body."[29] The arrival of immigrants, the primary cause of change, functions in two stages. First, the city goes through the "katabolic" stage, physiologically the destructive part of metabolism when food is broken down into simpler compounds. "Disorganization . . . is almost invariably the lot of the newcomer to the city, and the discarding of the habitual, and often of what has been to him the moral, is not infrequently accompanied by sharp mental conflict and sense of personal loss."[30] Subsequently the city goes through the "anabolic" stage, the constructive part of metabolism when food is built up and assimilated: "Oftener, perhaps, the change gives sooner or later a feeling of emancipation and an urge toward new goals."[31] Burgess thus reads the city as a physical body, as an organism endowed with complex digestive functions. Extending the analogy, he goes on to analyze the "incorporation" and "assimilation" of individuals and the "rate of increase of population" as meta-

bolic processes. Social disorganization, for example, is seen as analogous to the anabolic and katabolic phases of digestion; disorganization *and* organization—both in the physiological and in the urban
metabolisms—exist in "reciprocal relationship," "co-operating in a
moving equilibrium"; social disorganization is not a "pathological"
but a "normal" stage "preliminary to reorganization."[32]

On the basis of this extended analogy, and of the details it adds to
the initial image of concentric circles, Burgess introduces now a new
and less abstract image of the concentric city:

> Within the central business district or on an adjoining street is the
> "main stem" of "hobohemia," the teeming Rialto of the homeless
> migratory man of the Middle West. In the zone of deterioration en-
> circling the central business section are always to be found the so-
> called "slums" and "bad lands," with their submerged regions of
> poverty, degradation, and disease, and their underworlds of crime
> and vice. Within a deteriorating area are rooming-house districts,
> the purgatory of "lost souls." Near by is the Latin Quarter, where
> creative and rebellious spirits resort. The slums are also crowded to
> overflowing with immigrant colonies—the Ghetto, Little Sicily,
> Greektown, Chinatown—fascinatingly combining old world heri-
> tages and American adaptations. Wedging out from here is the
> Black Belt, with its free and disorderly life. The area of deteriora-
> tion, while essentially one of decay, of stationary or declining pop-
> ulation, is also one of regeneration, as witness the mission, the set-
> tlement, the artist's colony, radical centers—all obsessed with the
> vision of a new and better world.
>
> The next zone is also inhabited predominantly by factory and
> shop workers, but skilled and thrifty. This is an area of second im-
> migrant settlement, generally of the second generation. It is the re-
> gion of escape from the slum, the *Deutschland* of the aspiring Ghetto
> family. For *Deutschland* (literally "Germany") is the name given, half
> in envy, half in derision, to that region beyond the Ghetto where
> successful neighbors appear to be imitating German Jewish stan-
> dards of living. But the inhabitant of this area in turn looks to the
> "promised Land" beyond, to its residential hotels, its apartment-
> house region, its "satellite loops," and its "bright light" areas.[33]

In this new picture the initial model of urban growth merges and indeed clashes with a more empirical map of the city. The circles in the
first picture projected the possibility for the city of endless expansion,
for the immigrant of endless upward mobility. They embodied the

47

ideal of a *normal* metabolism where disorganization and organization, immigration and assimilation "co-operate" and exist in "equilibrium," allowing the city to easily "digest" the people who arrive; where newcomers distribute themselves without tension in the different areas of the city on the basis of preference, division of labor, social class, in other words on the basis of relatively free choice.

Quite different is the second picture that Burgess proposes. Having imagined the city as an organism, Burgess inevitably begins to see "social problems" as "disturbances of metabolism" or as "symptomatic of abnormalities."[34] Among the causes of these disturbances, Burgess lists any "marked variations" in the population, in the proportion between males and females, young and adult; likewise, he includes "any excessive increase [in population] as those which followed the great influx of southern Negroes into northern cities since the war."[35] The second version of the concentric city contains the ideologically problematic—and empirically more accurate—image of an "abnormal" metabolism where disorganization never disappears but rather becomes a permanent attribute of the city. "[Immigrants'] invasion of the city has the effect of a tidal wave inundating first the immigrant colonies, the ports of first entry, dislodging thousands of inhabitants who overflow into the next zone, and so on and on until the momentum of the wave has spent its force on the last urban zone."[36] In this second version the arrival of immigrants from Europe or migrants from the South is more analogous to an uncontrolled sexual process than to a discrete digestive phase. Indicating the effects of this excessive human "flood" as "increases in disease, crime, disorder, vice, insanity, and suicide," Burgess has reconceptualized migration from a source of fertility to one of pathology.[37]

Like Park, Burgess was drawn to the slum in his search for hypotheses and explanations concerning the modern city and modern society, and, like Park, Burgess struggled to theorize difference and change, culture and history, as processes rather than essences. He succeeded in theorizing the city as a constellation of dynamic, interacting, and changing parts. Yet ultimately, like Park, he reproduced the very same paradigms of degeneration that had traditionally been associated with the larger city, when he directed attention to the slum. The result, once again, were two incompatible conceptual frameworks, one for modern society, the modern city and the modern immigrant, the other for the slum and the deviant. Both James T. Farrell, in the *Studs Lonigan* trilogy, and Nelson Algren, in *Never Come*

Morning, appropriated this model and turned it inside out. Farrell did so by framing Studs Lonigan's narrative firmly within and against the patterns of urban change and upward mobility articulated by Burgess, and by showing his audience that degeneration and deviance are to be found in the stable, upwardly mobile middle-class community represented by the Lonigans and are indeed endemic to that class and to its view of the world. Algren did so by reconnecting the ties between slum and city that Chicago sociologists had severed, showing his audience that, rather than an aberration, the slum is an intrinsic and indeed a most emblematic part of the city. The young delinquent, the young prostitute, and their "green-horn" families, Algren points out, are most successful in overcoming the poverty and surviving the brutality of the slum when they most closely follow the jungle ethics of modern American society.

III

A student of W. I. Thomas, Robert Park, and Ernest Burgess, Frederic Thrasher is one of many graduate students at Chicago who, in the 1920s and 1930s, chose as a dissertation project the ethnographic exploration of a small region of the city. Like other graduate students at Chicago,[38] Thrasher chose, not one of the stable working-class, middle-class, or wealthy neighborhoods central to Park's and Burgess's theories of the modern city, but rather Gangland, a subregion of Chicago's large slums, and Gangs, its inhabitants—in other words, an apparently peripheral aspect of those theories.

Thrasher set out on his investigation with the research tools for which Chicago sociology remains famous: maps, taxonomies, interviews, life histories, and direct observation. The result of his research was *The Gang: A Study of 1,313 Gangs in Chicago*, a work that sociologist James Short recently described as a "modern classic" and "the most comprehensive study of the phenomenon of adolescent gangs ever undertaken."[39] *The Gang* is of particular relevance for the three narratives under discussion. Both Farrell's *Studs Lonigan* trilogy and Algren's *Never Come Morning* are centrally concerned with the life of a gang youth and his gang. And while Richard Wright's *Black Boy-American Hunger* deals directly with a gang in only a couple of episodes, the nature of the conflict between the autobiographical narrator and the social groups he systematically challenges and the success of his physical escape and spiritual emancipation are predicated on Richard's inability

49

to be part of a "gang," however that might be represented, and to follow a gang "code," whatever form that might happen to take.

From a methodological point of view, Thrasher's study is a classic of urban ethnography, a literary tradition that, characteristically, represents small-scale societies and strives for total description—the tradition of Franz Boas and Ruth Benedict in anthropology and of the Chicago school in sociology. Ethnography is the written text that the anthropologist produces upon returning from the field. One might speak of ethnography, as opposed to historiography, as a narrative that moves spatially rather than temporally; that recounts in the present rather than in the past tense; that organizes its material synchronically rather than diachronically. Within this literary genre and form Thrasher's *The Gang* occupies an important position as well.[40]

From the very beginning gangland is defined as an ecological region emblematic of the larger slum. *The Gang*, Park explains in the introduction, is "a study of the gang and its habitat, and in this case the habitat is a city slum." This area, in turn, is characteristic of the "modern American city," and shared by gangs with different social groups such as "hoboes," "new immigrants," "Negroes," "Chinese," and, at one time, "Jews." Further drawing from the language of plant ecology, Park goes on to characterize the Gang as "a specific type or variety," "elementary" in form, "spontaneous" in origin, that "grow[s] like weeds," and prospers in particular climates and latitudes. And in like language Park formulates one of the premises of Thrasher's study: "It is not only true that the habitat makes gangs, but what is of more practical importance, it is the habitat which determines whether or not their activities shall assume those perverse forms in which they become a menace to the community."[41] That premise has interesting ramifications in the case of Studs Lonigan and his gang, whose degeneration Farrell traces directly to the bigoted and narrow-minded views of the Irish-American middle class, and in the case of Bruno Bicek and his gang, whose ethos of violence and exploitation reproduces in glaring form the perversions of a society much larger than just the slum.

The primary motivation for Thrasher's study lies precisely in the potential "menace" to the community that gangs pose. As Thrasher unequivocally acknowledges in his own introductory remarks,

> [T]he gang touches in a vital way almost every problem in the life of the community. Delinquencies among its members all the way from truancy to serious crimes, disturbances of the peace from

street brawls to race riots, and close alliance with beer running, labor slugging, and corrupt politics—all are attributed to the gang, whose *treatment* presents a puzzle to almost every public or private agency in the city, which deals with boys and young men.[42]

Thus, as these remarks indicate, *The Gang* is not just a study of "gangs" and their "habitat." Rather it is a study of gangland as a cross section of the slum, the urban region where the "criminal," "the Hobo," the "immigrant," the "Black," and the "Jew" meet, where class and culture, race and morality become incorporated as an "urban wilderness," menacing an unnamed but ever present urban "civilization."

In keeping with the conventions of ethnographic and travel writing, Thrasher begins with a physical survey of the lanscape:

> The characteristic habitat of Chicago's numerous gangs is that broad twilight zone of railroads and factories, of deteriorating neighborhoods and shifting populations, which borders the city's central business district on the north, on the west, and on the south. The gangs dwell among the shadows of the slum. Yet, dreary and repellent as their external environment must seem to the casual observer, their life is to the initiated at once vivid and fascinating.[43]

This is the opening paragraph of the study and a meaningful initial representation if not of the slum certainly of the subjectivity invoked by the account. Stirring in this opening invocation are the blurred picture of "deteriorating neighborhoods" and "shifting populations," the impression of an impending descent into Hades, a "dreary" and "repellent" netherworld of "shadows" and "twilight," and the image of a mysterious world which only to the "initiated" reveals its true essence.

Then the slum suddenly lights up—as a stage—"vivid" and "fascinating." "It is in such regions as the gang inhabits that we find much of the romance and mystery of a great city. Here are comedy and tragedy. Here is melodrama which excels the recurrent 'thrillers' at the downtown theaters. Here are unvarnished emotions."[44] Thus, Thrasher brings the invisible, menacing, and unreal slum close to the reader by imaginatively enclosing it within the curtains of a stage and by discovering in it the familiar genres of fiction. The "real" menacing slum is familiarized and tamed, paradoxically, as just another form of representation, as "fiction."

51

The Gang is, overall, the travel record of Thrasher's solitary expedition into gangland, a region located at the center, and yet beyond the frontier of urban civilization. Thrasher himself acknowledges the study as "an exploratory survey of life in an area little understood by the average citizen," and warns his reader that "the type of life described here may not even be apparent to the average citizen of the district, who is chiefly occupied in his own pursuits."[45] To the description of the landscape, of its boundaries, composition, and characteristics Thrasher devotes the first and most significant chapter of the study, appropriately entitled "Gangland."

> The broad expanse of gangland with its intricate tribal and intertribal relationships is medieval and feudal in its organization rather than modern and urban. . . . In some respects these regions of conflict are like a frontier; in others, like a 'no man's land,' lawless, godless, wild.

Conceptualized as a spatial phenomenon, Gangland and gangs are also located in time, although not the time of the present. In gangland one finds a "primitive democracy." Life is "rough and untamed." And finally,

> The hang-out of the gang is its castle and the center of a feudal estate which it guards most jealously. Gang leaders hold sway like barons of old, watchful of invaders and ready to swoop down upon the lands of rivals and carry off booty or prisoners or to inflict punishment upon their enemies.[46]

Frontier, empires, kingdoms, and domains all bespeak a time neither urban nor modern. Through the historical dislocation of gangs Thrasher promises to take us on a time voyage that extends to the middle ages, to primordial times, and as far back as the geologic past, exorcising a menacing present reality with a familiarized ahistorical unreality.

Thrasher goes on to provide a minute description of the terrain. "In Chicago," he explains, "the empire of the gang divides into three great domains, each of which in turn breaks up into smaller kingdoms. . . . The first of these we may call the 'North Side jungles'; the second, the 'West Side wilderness'; and the third, the 'South Side badlands.'"[47] Shaped as a semicircle, these three regions surround "the central business district (the Loop)," thus functioning as "a sort of *interstitial* barrier between the Loop and the better residential areas"—in

52

other words, between the productive and reproductive parts of the city.[48]

Thrasher proceeds to describe the geographic, social, and ethnic composition of each region by starting on the northern edge of the hemicycle. The North Side jungles, he explains, are the first main division of gangland, with physical boundaries in Lake Michigan to the east and the Chicago River to the west. They are located in the "unique area known as the 'Grand Canyon of Chicago' because of the great diversity of its 'social scenery.'" Its physical and social boundaries are the wealthy and fashionable Gold Coast to the north, and the "artists' colony" or Bohemia to the south. To the west they border on "a cosmopolitan and rooming-house district which includes the haunts of a gang of dope-peddlers," and is the base for some "notorious bootlegging groups," as well as on "the north stem of 'Hobohemia'" and "'Bughouse Square,' a center for hobo intellectuals."[49] Gangland itself concentrates along the river in "Little Sicily," also known as "Little Hell," and in the Polish colony "called by the gang boy 'Pojay Town,' in contradistinction to 'Dago Town.'" Internal animosities among gangs notwithstanding, Thrasher explains, "[A]ll the gangs of this region together are known as the 'North Siders,' and they wage continual warfare across the river bridges with their enemies the 'West Siders.'"[50]

The West Siders occupy the "West Side Wilderness," the second and "most extensive of gangland domains." This region finds its natural boundaries in the Chicago River on the northeast side—a natural barrier that separates it from the "North Side jungles"—in the Loop on the east, and in the lower branch of the river on the south and southeast.[51] Thrasher's description of this area relies on exuberant metaphors reminiscent of Victorian prose about the slums:

> Across these turbid, sewage-laden waters lie the crowded river wards. In the drab hideousness of the slum, despite a continuous exodus to more desirable districts, people are swarming more than 50,000 to the square mile. Life is enmeshed in a network of tracks, canals, and docks, factories and breweries, warehouses, and lumber-yards. There is nothing fresh or clean to greet the eye; everywhere are unpainted, ramshackle buildings, blackened and besmirched with the smoke of industry. In this sort of habitat the gang seems to flourish best.[52]

The largest of the domains, the West Side Wilderness is also ethnically and racially the most "cosmopolitan," and economically the most de-

53

pressed: Polish, Italians, migratory workers, Blacks, Irish, Jews, Russians, Greeks, Gypsies, Mexicans, Lithuanians, Bohemians, Croatians. And in this area are located as well "the main stem of 'Hobohemia,'" and its main institutions: "Bum Park" and the "slave market." Here one also finds that "greatly congested immigrant community" known as "Moonshine Valley" and the "Bloody Nineteenth" where Jane Addams "established Hull-House."[53]

Moving further to the south, Thrasher takes his reader through "the third major division of gangland—the South Side badlands." This region is defined by the Loop to the north, the Chicago river to the northwest, and the lake to the east. Here are Italians, Irish, Polish, Germans, Lithuanians as well as the Black Belt, "Chicago's most extensive negro area." Here is also the "odorous expanse of pens and packing-houses of the Union Stock Yards," and next to it "is an immigrant colony, dominantly Polish, known as 'Back-of-the-Yards,' . . . one of the grimiest, most congested slums of the city."[54]

The "empire of gangland" includes also the "boundary lines and borderlands between the non-gang areas of the city" (19). These "[t]hreads of social disintegration tend to follow alongside rivers, canals, railroad tracks, and business streets . . . and permit gangs to thrive in the interstices between very good residence areas."[55] Finally, gangland includes a number of "appended ganglands" located in the "satellite communities near Chicago." These outer territories develop in the "residential" and "well-organized suburbs" of Chicago because "even in these regions . . . . gangs develop in interstitital zones."[56]

Thrasher's topography of gangland reveals a characteristic way to know the city through spatial visualization. First it imposes order on chaos, fixity on flux. Thrasher's prose is a poetic reenactment of his physical voyage through the urban "heart-of-darkness." There is a major effort behind Thrasher's topographical precision. The greater the confusion on the part of the observer, the greater the effort to visualize and chart. The observer describes as if he were suspended in mid-air and did not have to move physically along an accidented terrain. The language transforms an impenetrable into a penetrable space, an invisible into a visible structure. The urban cartographer, at least at the level of language, moves unimpeded from north to south. In his verbal and graphic map is inscribed the precondition of his movement—the immobility of the landscape—and the result—victory over a socially impenetrable territory.

If maps are a main vehicle for imposing order on what appears to

54

the outsider as chaos, words are another of at least equal importance. The slum is at once the territory to be mapped out and a region in constant, dangerous flux. The gang habitat is a region of "deteriorating neighborhoods, and shifting populations." The gang is "a protean manifestation." The slum is crossed by "turbid, sewage-laden waters," and by "a continuous exodus to more desirable districts." Its inhabitants are "swarming more than 50,000 to the square mile." Their "[l]ife is enmeshed in a network of tracks, canals, and docks, factories and breweries, warehouses, and lumber-yards."[57] There is a tangible contradiction between Thrasher's cartographic image and his verbal description. While the first bespeaks an observer who has the landscape under control, immobilized, so to speak, the second conveys restlessness and movement, not the regular and paced movement of the observer, but rather the nervous and menacing movement of waters and insects.

Most revealing in this respect is the language through which Thrasher tries to "capture" the slum in relation to the surrounding city. Two contradictory metaphors—the frontier and the empire—alternate as Thrasher attempts to convey the nature of gangland, not simply as an isolated territory but as a world that exists within a larger space with which it interacts and intersects.

Thrasher conceptualizes gangland as an "interstitial" region, and a number of significant images cluster around this concept. Park introduces the "frontier" image in his preface: "Gangs flourish on the frontier, and the predatory bands that infest the fringes of civilization exhibit, on the whole, the same characteristic traits displayed by the groups studied in this volume."[58] Gangland is also a "twilight zone of railroads and factories," in other words, an area suspended between day and night. And it is a zone suspended between frontiers: "In some respects these regions of conflict are like a frontier; in others, like a 'no man's land,' lawless, godless, wild."[59] Gangland thus at once constitutes a frontier and exists between frontiers. This is especially the case with the gangs that develop on the borders between "non-gang areas of the city . . . alongside rivers, canals, railroad tracks, and business streets." These are the areas that "permit gangs to thrive in the interstices between very good residence areas."[60]

Thrasher explains at the end of this chapter: "The most important conclusion suggested by a study of the location and distribution of the 1,313 gangs investigated in Chicago is that gangland represents a geographically and socially interstitial area in the city." Here he also provides a

55

definition of "interstice," the concept he uses most self-consciously throughout the study:

> Interstitial—that is pertaining to spaces that intervene between one thing and another. In nature foreign matter tends to collect and cake in every crack, crevice, and cranny-interstices. There are also fissures and breaks in the structure of social organization. The gang may be regarded as an interstitital element in the framework of society, and gangland as an interstitital region in the layout of the city. . . . This zone is a distinctly interstitial phase of the city's growth.[61]

In this metaphoric carousel "interstice" is the central pivot around which a number of images follow one another in a none too coherent fashion: the geologic city—with cracks and crevices; the woodframe city—with fissures and crannies; the temporal city—where space reads like time. Whether interstitial "element," "region," or "phase," the conceptualization of gangland as "foreign," "in between," and essentially unreal space accomplishes the overall task of exiling social and cultural "otherness" by physically and spatially locating it outside Chicago, the city, civilization.

Related to and equally important as the "interstice" concept is another set of images clustered around the metaphor of empire. Gangland, Thrasher explains, is an "empire" that divides into "domains" and "smaller kingdoms." Just as an empire consists of a center and a periphery—the provinces and far territories—so the empire of gangland extends outward. Its provinces are as "tentacle[s] of gangland extending [their] baleful influence into an orderly residential area"; sometimes they are as "threads of social disintegration [that] tend to follow alongside rivers, canals, railroad tracks, and business streets."[62] Conversely, Thrasher goes on, "[T]his process is seen, too, in the way in which a business street, stream, canal, or railroad track running through a residential area tends to become a 'finger' of the slum and an extension of gangland." Indeed, much as Chicago stretches out into "satellite communities," so the "central empire of gangland" stretches out into "appended ganglands."[63]

Gangland as interstice-frontier and gangland as empire-octopus produce related but distinct and perhaps not fully compatible representations of the urban landscape. The analogy with empire constitutes gangland as a menacing enemy, threatening to expand into and conquer border regions. The analogy with frontier, on the other

56

hand, constitutes gangland as something hopelessly foreign but also as something from which "civilization" can defend itself. Sometimes the metaphors just slip out of control and metamorphize into surreal images of a frontier thrusting its fingers or tentacles outward, or they verge uneasily toward a Dantesque netherworld—"the shadows of the slum"; a "region of life [that] is in a real sense an *underworld*."[64] The paragraphs where the two metaphors mix so awkwardly speak not of stylistic but of conceptual difficulties, particularly the difficulty of sustaining a frontier image for something that lies physically and economically at the center of the "civilized" and "industrial" city.

In representing gangland and by extention the slum, Thrasher resorted to two distinct systems of representation. On one hand he consciously relied on the map, a teleological and progressive form that allowed him to read the illegible and visualize the invisible city. On the other he relied, more unconsciouly, on figurative language, on metaphors, similes, analogies that, in the form of conceptual fragments and oxymora, accommodated all that did not fit in the linearity of the map. Through maps, icons of topographic control, Thrasher tried to impose order on chaos, to bring light into darkness. In the metaphors, however, Thrasher more truly recorded the historical experience of a class besieged as it experiences and tries to come to terms with the estrangement, chaos, and social disorder of mass migration and urban poverty. The final product of Thrasher's study was the image of a wilderness in the midst of the city—a jungle in the garden—inhabited by warring gangs and tribes made up of the children of the immigrants, historically the primitives of the modern city. The country and the city, we have been told, represent an underlying dichotomy of American culture. It may very well be so. But either we can reconceptualize that dichotomy so as to accommodate the type of historical and social conflicts within modern cities illustrated by Thrasher's study of gangland or that paradigm might as well be declared useless for modern American culture.

Robert Park and Ernest Burgess's theoretical essays and Thrasher's ethnographic study represent important, if exemplary, reference points for the urban novelists of the 1930s. They constituted a powerful universe of discourse for authors who, like James T. Farrell, Nelson Algren, and Richard Wright, chose to write about immigrant and racial ghettos or about immigration and migration to the modern city. The Chicago sociologists articulated for the urban novelists of the 1930s sophisticated and culturally radical views of the city, in the absence of which the very fabric of *Studs Lonigan, Never Come Morning, Black Boy-American Hunger* are inconceivable and against which those narratives moved: Farrell contrapuntally framed the degeneration of Studs Lonigan against Burgess's paradigms of urban mobility and urban degeneration; Algren's viewed the relationship between the Polish ghetto and the larger city through Park's view of the city as a mosaic even as he appropriated that language against Park's own theory; Wright's pathbraking transformation of the ex-slave narrative into an immigrant narrative of emancipation both appropriated and exposed the paradigm of the individual's emancipation and rebirth into modernity underlying Park and Burgess's theories of the city as well as W. I. Thomas's study of juvenile female delinquents, Robert Redfield's study of modernization in the Yucatan, and Louis Wirth's theory of urbanization.

Thrasher's ethnographic study, Robert Park's and Ernest Burgess's theories of the city exemplify a sociology for which urban diversity was a fine line separating cultural difference and moral deviance, and urban mobility an equally fine line separating social change and moral degeneration. They illustrate how much the Chicago sociologists' theories of the city were in fact theories of the slum, and their theories of urban progress were in fact theories of urban pathology. Their sociology systematically tried to conceptualize the urban slums as "margin" and "periphery." The urban spaces and the social processes they represented resisted, however, and even defeated those attempts. In the language of the sociologists themselves at first and in the narratives of their literary heirs later, the urban slum ultimately emerges as the true center of the modern city, just as Engels had discovered the working-class slum to be the center of the early industrial city.

3

"The Folk in a City World": Narratives of Transition, Theories of Modernization

"Ethnic and cosmopolitan," "rural and urban," "traditional and modern": these have become deeply rooted distinctions in the thought and speech of our time. Equally entrenched is the idea of a "transition" that supposedly leads people from one pole of these dichotomies to the other. Cruises and travel packages advertised in travel sections would lure us to places that have yet to start on this transition, while magazine sections of the same Sunday papers measure the success of recent immigrants by how fast they move through this hypothetical transition. So ingrained have these categories become that their metaphoric content is no longer visible to us: born as abstractions to make sense of the world, they have become "natural" phenomena; they have become the world itself. First developed in order to understand and represent complex social changes, these sociological concepts have become a "reality" that hides what they were meant to explain. From these original categories, social scientists have derived a collection of terms that represent social change as a unified linear phenomenon. They speak of "assimilation," "Americanization," "urbanization," "acculturation." When social scientists apply these terms to immigrants it is immediately clear in what direction the arrow of progress is pointing. And yet, beneath processes conceptualized as unilinear and unidirectional is a complex reality of uncertain outcome.

"Transition" is a figure of speech. It reproduces a sociological model that has its own beginnings and history not far removed from us. Urban historian Thomas Bender paved the way for a reexamination of the two concepts—"community" and "society"—that for several decades have formed the infrastructure of modernization theories in the United States. In his study *Community and Social Change in America* Bender has traced the origin of that distinction back to the concepts *Gemeinschaft* and *Gesellschaft* originally coined by German sociologist Ferdinand Tönnies in the 1880s.[1] Bender follows these concepts through their adoption into American sociology and through their hegemony, for almost fifty years, in American sociological and historical studies dealing with migration and urbanization. American sociologists and historians, according to Bender, have for several decades, followed a model of urbanization and modernization that has been proven inaccurate not only for the United States but for other countries as well. Such a model, he also claims, revolves around a distinction between community and society that actually distorts Tönnies's original formulation.[2] The way Chicago urban sociologists borrowed the original distinction from German sociology and developed a "transition" model that still permeates our culture represents the primary focus of this chapter. James T. Farrell, Nelson Algren, and Richard Wright, subsequent chapters will show, sometimes critically and sometimes unproblematically participated with their narratives in the discourse of modernization and urbanization originally formulated by the Chicago sociologists.

Robert Park's essay "Human Migration and the Marginal Man," Robert Redfield's model of a "folk-urban" continuum as formulated in his monographs *Tepoztlán: A Mexican Village. A Study of Folk Life* and *The Folk Culture of Yucatan*, and Louis Wirth's essay "Urbanism as a Way of Life" are both important early formulations, in the United States, of modernization and urbanization theories and illustrative of the way Chicago sociologists adapted Tönnies's concepts to modern American society.[3] In general, they exemplify Bender's claim that Tönnies's typological distinction, in the United States and at the University of Chicago most of all, came to be translated into empirically verifiable and distinct realities. At the same time these theoretical and ethnographic studies show in greater detail than Bender has done how these concepts and paradigms actually evolved in the course of approximately a decade of active theoretical and empirical research in Chicago. Finally and more importantly in light of the present study, a close examination of Park's and Wirth's urbanization and modernization theories and of Redfield's modernization ethnographies allows one to discover and properly weigh how deeply the trilogy of Studs Lonigan, Never Come Morning, and Black Boy-American Hunger reproduced even as they challenged the discourse of modernization of Chicago sociology. Park's marginal man is the prototype for both Danny O'Neill, James T. Farrell's well-known autobiographical character, and for Richard Wright's autobiographical persona in Black Boy-American Hunger. With varying degrees of optimism, each is represented, like Park's marginal man, as a lone and alienated consciousness and as an individual who actively and consciously chooses homelessness, exile, and society over intimacy, harmony, and community. Both the Polish immigrants of Never Come Morning and the Black migrants that Wright encounters in the South and in Chicago are modeled after Redfield's notion of the "folk in a city world." Collective representations of marginal man, they are no longer at home in the peasant universe they have left, and just as spiritually and culturally homeless in modern and urban America. Wirth's and the later Redfield's view of the city and urbanization as a universal telos may not represent the ideological intent of these narratives, and yet it is much closer to them than the nostalgia for a lost pastoral America that critics periodically tease out of Farrell's, Algren's, or Wright's work.

I

Robert Park's famous essay "Human Migration and the Marginal Man" revolves around two main themes: catastrophism as a model of social change and marginal man as agent and emblem of modern urban civilization. Park set himself the ambitious task of reformulating the notion of "civilization" so that multiethnic urban American could become part of it. As long as civilization continued to be imagined through evolutionary metaphors and premised on notions of racial homogeneity, America would continue to exist outside of civilization.

Park takes a first step by juxtaposing evolutionary and catastrophic models of social change. Contrary to commonsense and clichés, progress and civilization have always been induced by catastrophic changes. Under the label of catastrophic change, Park includes human migrations as well as wars, revolutions, religious movements, commerce. By contrast, racial and cultural isolation have produced social stagnation. The "catastrophic theory of progress" allows Park to claim that "the most important . . . influences have been . . . migration and the incidental collisions, conflicts, and fusion of people and cultures which they have occasioned."[4] Behind Park's far-reaching argument was the social upheaval of migration and rapid industrialization out of which the main twentieth-century American cities had emerged—Chicago foremost among them. The need to accommodate these specific aspects of American history made catastrophism appealing to Park. Through this theory Park can argue that "immigrants," "Blacks," "Jews" are now to be recognized as instigators of civilization and no longer as threats or symptoms of its decay:

> In fact, races and cultures, so far from being in any sense identical . . . are perhaps to be set over against one another as contrast effects, the results of antagonistic tendencies, so that civilization may be said to flourish at the expense of racial differences. . . . If it is true that races are the products of isolation and inbreeding, it is just as certain that civilization . . . is a consequence of contact and communication.[5]

Having resolved that catastrophic and not evolutionary changes are the basis of progress, Park was here confronting the thorny issue of race, so central to evolutionary theories of progress and one no American sociologist could ignore. In the United States the science of race had articulated degrees of difference, so that certain European immigrants were labeled more "different" than others. If in Europe, as Nancy Stepan notes, "the laboring poor were represented as the 'savages' of Europe, and the criminal as a 'negro,'" in the United States, by the early twentieth century, it was the southern and eastern European immigrants and the southern Black migrants who were increasingly represented in that way: the shift from "peasant savages" to "urban savages" must not have appeared all that significant.[6]

62

Park proceeds by openly challenging the xenophobic idea that only race purity can guarantee civilization. Race purity, actually, causes a "peace disease" whose symptoms are social stagnation and inertia. Once the prerequisite of progress, Park turns race closure into the antithesis of change and civilization.

The personification of Park's theory is a new sociological character altogether. Between the tearing down of the medieval ghetto walls and the growth of metropolitan cities there emerges, out of Park's essay, marginal man, a poetic product of the American sociological imagination. Culturally and racially a mixed blood, he is "a man on the margin of two cultures." A symbol of newly achieved freedom and of metropolitan enlightenment, marginal man is the individual who breaks loose from "local bonds . . . from the culture of tribe and folk . . . from the sacred order of tribal custom." He is the individual who steadily moves toward the "metropolitan cities . . . the freedom of cities . . . the rational organization which we call civilization." He is the spiritual brother of Simmel's "stranger." Exceptional and isolated as he may seem, marginal man is truly a type, for the moral dichotomy and conflict that define his existential condition are, according to Park, "probably characteristic of every immigrant during the period of transition."[7]

If in general Park views marginality and conflict as temporary phenomena, his essay closes with a haunting image of marginal man in permanent conflict:

> But in the case of the marginal man the period of crisis is relatively permanent. . . . Ordinarily the marginal man is a mixed blood . . . one who lives in two worlds, in both of which he is more or less of a stranger. . . . It is in the mind of the marginal man that the moral turmoil which new cultural contacts occasion, manifests itself in the most obvious forms. It is in the mind of the marginal man—where the changes and fusion of culture are going on—that we can best study the processes of civilization and progress.[8]

Park failed in the attempt to lead marginal man through a smooth transition from one side of his split self to the other and created yet another version of the tragic mulatto stereotype: the tragic migrant. The nineteenth-century science of race—Nancy Stepan explains— had proclaimed mulattoes to be products of "un-natural" unions, hybrids sterile crossings of different races; it had declared both "mulattoes" and "hybrids" emblems of degeneration and threats to civilization.[9]

Park succeeded in altering the traditional associations between race and civilization on the one hand, and between hybrids and degeneration on the other. Marginal man measures the distance separating the old science of race and its eugenist descendents from the new social sciences. In giving life to marginal man, Park created an American icon of historic and social change, of progress and civilization. He made marginal man not just an an emblem of civilization but, to use J. M. Berthelot's suggestive image, a geological metaphor, a body whose scars and layers tell us the history of civilization.[10]

II

Equipped with Park's ideas on migration, marginality, and social change, but more interested in "urbanization" and "modernization," Robert Redfield went to Mexico in order to study migration as the origin of new social and cultural formations. A student of Park, Redfield studied at the University of Chicago when anthropology and sociology still comprised the same department. His theories and studies of the interaction between urban, folk, and primitive cultures as well as his model of a "folk-urban continuum" came to enjoy great popularity in anthropology and sociology and remain a major asset of urbanization-modernization theories. The choice for his fieldwork fell on Tepoztlán, at the time a small, predominantly Indian rural community located south of Mexico City, along what Chicago sociologists conceptualized as a sociological border between urban and peasant Mexico. Park's theory of migration and marginality allowed Redfield to approach Tepoztlán as a phenomenon analogous to marginal man, a "mixed blood" community alien to both peasant and modern Mexico.

Tepoztlán: A Mexican Village is the ethnography of a village that, in Redfield's words, exists on a "frontier of contact" between modern urban civilization and traditional rural culture. Rejecting ethnology's antiquarian interest in the rescue of aboriginal survivals, Redfield defines his study as part of "social anthropology," that is, the discipline that studies "current" and "contemporary" change. The primary intent of the fieldwork was a "description of changes occurring in . . . folk culture due to the spread of city ways," and of Tepoztlán as "an example . . . of the general type of change whereby primitive man becomes civilized man, the rustic becomes the urbanite."[11]

Already moving beyond Park, Redfield was groping for what he

64

would later formulate as a continuum theory, the idea that "primitive," "folk," and "urban" constitute an uninterrupted line leading in the direction of the latter, and that a process called "transition" linked the hypothetical infinite number of points along the continuum. This is the conceptual infrastructure of Redfield's monograph and of its close examination of cultural and social change. Thus, the "state of holydays" in Tepoztlán suggests something "intermediate between the condition in a primitive tribe and that in a modern city." The rituals of life and death "provide another opportunity to study the process of transformation from folk to urban culture." The same process is taking place in the division of labor, in the practice of magic and medicine, and even in the field of music, now that "several phonographs are . . . making city songs popular." "As the urbanization of Tepoztlán slowly progresses," Redfield prophesizes, "the city songs will become more usual; there will be a shift of emphasis from folk songs to popular songs."[12]

The above formulations show Redfield already engaged in what Bender has rightly identified as a false polarization between community and society, rural and urban, traditional and modern. On the other hand the method that Redfield followed, a single community as case study, and his use at the end of the study of a long life history, the story of a marginal man from Tepoztlán, indicate that such reification was not yet a foregone conclusion.

One of the two concluding chapters is entitled "The Folk in a City World," an oxymoronic title that self-consciously suggests a relationship of tension between two poles postulated as essentially different. Here Redfield introduces a man who, like many others, migrated to Mexico City during the revolution, but who, unlike most, returned to Tepoztlán.[13] Furnished with the familiar themes of mobility, dislocation, hope, disillusionment, and conflict between two cultures, this life history represents a variation on the general type of immigrant autobiographies with which we have become familiar. Redfield's Mexican marginal man experiences the conflict between city and country as well as the racial and ethnic conflicts that Park had presented as causes of "mental turmoil." Redfield's marginal man exemplifies "the experience . . . of the individual who springs from the folk, is no longer entirely at home in it and yet can never quite leave it, and who lives . . . with one foot in one world and the other foot in another."[14] Recounted in the third person in a manner not devoid of literary merit, the life history tells the story of a "pure-blooded Indian" native of

65

Tepoztlán from a poor family who is sent away to school, first to Cuernavaca and later to Mexico City. In the metropolis he develops a profound interest in his native Indian language through the agency of a "North-American priest and amateur archeologist." From this cultural mentor he receives a grammar of his native language and is introduced to its literary heritage, with the result of becoming more "race conscious" and proud of his "pure Indian blood." The man eventually marries, perhaps strangely, a *mestiza* woman who is part Indian and part Spanish, and after a number of years as a white-collar worker in Mexico City, decides to move himself, his reluctant wife, and his children back to his native village. In Tepoztlán he unsuccessfully engages in the preservation of the local cultural heritage and in civic reform, the only visible result being that he becomes more and more "isolated" and "disillusioned." By the end of the story, approximately coinciding with Redfield's fieldwork, the man has departed for Mexico City and "talks now of learning English and coming to the United States. There one can make money, and there scientists are interested in his language."[15]

For Redfield the transformation of this immigrant into a marginal man is produced by the conflict between folk and urban cultures. Ironically, a North American priest, a representative of modern, urban culture, triggers the spiral of marginality; toward North America, a country most populated at the time with marginal men, and like the priest an embodiment of modern urban culture, this Mexican marginal man is looking for escape. Redfield's comments on this typical Chicago sociology life history are that as marginal man "sees Tepoztlán partly through the eyes of a man of the wider city-world, so are the folk of Mexico coming to see themselves."[16] This new way of seeing, according to Redfield, was transforming the people of Mexico from a "folk" into an "urban" people. It requires no great leap of the imagination to estimate how important this prediction was to Chicago sociologists, living as they did in a city that had been invaded by the "folk" of southern and eastern Europe and by the Black "folk" of the South, neither group in a great hurry or with the resources to divest itself of its "peasant" heritage.[17]

As Bender has claimed, Redfield's study polarizes folk and urban, community and society where the terms are understood as geographically and socially separate, and where one moves, almost physically, from one to the other. On the other hand, the choice of Tep oztlán, of the case study, and the image of the town emerging from Redfield's study reveal, like the story of marginal man, uncomfortable proximities more often than simple dualities. Park's marginal man and Redfield's Tepoztlán articulate the dialectical version of this duality, where the conflict is *internal* to both individuals and communities. In this version, the two poles of community and society are still seen as coterminal and inseparable. They coexist within the same physical and social space.

It was in part the case study method that prevented the type of reification that later would become predominant. In the Tepoztlán monograph Redfield explored the folk-urban dichotomy *inside* one community, much as Park had explored it *inside* one individual. Not surprisingly, the topographic image of Tepoztlán drawn by Redfield was charged with imagery of center and periphery that borders on paradox. When Redfield attempted to spatialize the frontier of change between city and country, he referred to the *plaza*, the village central square, as the site where contact with the city takes place and change originates. Redfield characterizes the plaza as a central zone where two culture "areas" overlap: a "culture of the folk" and "a culture of the city." This central zone is built not on the assumption of clear-cut separations but rather on the observation of profound interpenetrations whose conflictual nature is actually embodied in the oxymoron Redfield, inadvertently perhaps, created: "the periphery of change is at the center."[18]

Redfield's study of Tepoztlán complemented Park's theory of migration and marginality. Tepoztlán represents the social world that surrounds marginal man. In both Park's marginal man and Redfield's Tepoztlán two opposites meet, the old and the new, the ethnic community and the cosmopolitan city, tradition and modernity.

III

The analysis of the social changes caused by the migration of people toward urban centers and of the spreading influence of these centers over larger areas took a different direction in the late thirties. Louis Wirth's famous essay on the city lies precisely at this juncture. Published in 1938, "Urbanism as a Way of Life" remains, after almost fifty years, a pivotal sociological statement on the city.[19] In Thomas Bender's words, "As yet, no alternative theory has seriously challenged its ascendancy among students of community and urban life."[20] Attracted, like his colleagues, to the social processes of migration into the city, Wirth's work took an openly theoretical direction.

Taking the substance of Park's argument for granted—that urbanism and civilization are synonymous terms—Wirth went on to grapple with a different problem. Foremost on his agenda appears the need for a conceptual framework that could once and for all provide the sociological definition of the city. Wirth begins by sketching out two separate worlds: the urban world and the rural world. The inflow of immigrants from rural areas, drawn to the city by "the attraction and suggestions . . . it exerts" bridges these two otherwise separate worlds. Without these immigrants, Wirth confidently writes, "the difference between the rural and the urban modes of life would be even greater than they are."[21] Euphemisms for the foreclosure of farms, regions, and even countries in the context of a world economy where rural and urban were far from separate, Wirth's comments exemplify the culturally acute but economically shallow premises of Chicago urban theory.

Wirth's characterization of the two worlds is so familiar that it requires little description. The rural world is the world of kinship, solidarity, sentimental, and emotional ties. The urban world, to which Wirth's attention is devoted, is the world of sophistication, rationality, freedom, tolerance; it is also the world of indifference, loneliness, insecurity, impotence.

Two metaphors convey Wirth's conception of the urban world. He writes: "[T]he distinctive feature of man's mode of living in the modern age is his concentration into gigantic aggregations around which cluster lesser centers and from which radiate the ideas and practices which we call civilization." In conceptualizing the position that the city occupies in the larger world, Wirth imagines the city as a sun, the civilizing center of the universe; from this center of civilization and urbanism "ideas" radiate outward toward the peripheries of the orbit. Appropriately, the image of the orbit reemerges in the subsequent paragraph. "For the city . . . is the initiating and controlling center of economic, political, and cultural life that has drawn the most remote communities of the world into its orbit and woven diverse areas, peoples, and activities into a cosmos."[22] Wirth makes the city into a god-like power that can "weave" distant and fragmented things into a "cosmos" and turn chaos into order.

Thomas Bender has explained the prolonged favor enjoyed by

68

Wirth's theory in these terms: "Wirth's theory of community break-down . . . offered a vision of unilinear and inevitable progress toward a rationalized and homogenized world which might have been encouraging even if it was tinged with nostalgia for the vanishing community."[23] And yet it is the profound urbo-centricity of Wirth's theory that resonates throughout his essay, from beginning, "[T]he growth of cities and the urbanization of the world comprise one of the most impressive facts of modern times," to end, "[T]he direction of the ongoing changes in urbanism will for good or ill transform not only the city but the world."[24] Wirth assigned to the city absolute cultural hegemony over the social universe. This is the framework that became the dominant one in community and urban studies.

It is a curious paradox that Wirth has been accused repeatedly, with other Chicago sociologists, of nourishing a nostalgic bias for the rural world and yet was described by his own daughter in the opposite way in his attitude toward his native village in Germany.

> For Wirth, Gemunden, a settlement of only nine hundred persons, was always an exemplification of the narrowness and monotony of village life. In "Urbanism as a Way of Life" (1938) and other writings, he was later to pay tribute to urban civilizations, which he contrasted implicitly with the deficiencies of the rural setting. . . . Certainly Wirth was never tempted to romanticize rural life or to bemoan the rural-urban migration.[25]

One is left with the difficult task of mediating between Wirth the romantic, nostalgically yearning for the rural community, and Wirth the apologist of modernization, preaching a gospel of triumphant world urbanization. It may be that the two views of Wirth actually complement each other. As Bender indirectly suggests, what was most influential in Wirth's theory was the simplified version of a cultural paradox. Having split country and city in order to foretell the urbanization of the world, the part that was suppressed, the rural world of community, intimacy, and being-at-home, continues to come back to haunt our culture under the guise of nostalgia.

IV

Robert Redfield's study The Folk Culture of Yucatan, published shortly after Wirth's famous essay, illustrates a similar conceptual rethinking within Chicago sociology.[26] In this later monograph Redfield developed the idea of a folk-urban continuum, incipient in *Tepoztlán*, into a fully articulated theory. This time he chose to study the peninsula of Yucatan for its relative isolation, when the opposite motivation had led to the choice of Tepoztlán, and within the Yucatan region he selected four points, a city (Merida), a town (Dzitas), a peasant village (ChanKom), and a tribal village (Tusik), each community distributed at increasing distance from Merida itself, the state capital. Around these four communities Redfield constructed a telos leading toward the city and, like Wirth, created the master sociological narrative of modern urban civilization.

While in many respects the Yucatan study reelaborates the insights first developed in the study of Tepoztlán, a significant change underlies the methodological choice of focusing on these four communities in an isolated region. This shift in the mode of representation parallels a shift in the conceptualization of the city and of modernization. The uncomfortable tensions present in the previous study were somehow erased here. In *Tepoztlán* Redfield had chosen to represent one community experiencing the process of transition from "primitive" to "urban" culture, a sort of migrant community moving toward the city culturally if not physically. In the Yucatan study Redfield translates a sociological typology, primitive, folk, and urban, into an empirical progression. Redfield lines up his four communities, and chooses them so that their geographical distribution will bear this out as so many examples of urban penetration. In the process he collapses geographical space into historical time, a well-known practice in the natural sciences. Out of different social formations, the four communities in question, he elicits the sequence tribe-village-town-city, a sequence that reads as the autobiography of the metropolis and by extension of Western civilization. The immigrant moving from one country-region-community to another could now be imagined as moving in time from past to future.

From the original ideal types of *Gemeinschaft* and *Gesellschaft* formulated by Tönnies with the intent of conceptualizing differences in degree and not in kind, we now reach the point where such distinctions were turned into extended sociological metaphors. In Redfield's later study the metaphor bridges the distance that separates Tusik, the primeval tribe in the heart of the tropical forest, and the metropolis Merida, but it might as well be Chicago. The metaphor erases, however, that very distance as it existed and could be observed daily by Chicago

70

sociologists in the center of "civilization," in the immigrant and Black ghettos of Chicago.

In Redfield's study of the Yucatan peninsula one can also observe the conceptual transformation whereby the original polarity rural-urban was transposed into the polarity primitive-civilization. This was a remarkable realignment when one remembers the "heart of darkness" iconography of the city popular in the nineteenth century. This iconography allowed little doubt regarding the place occupied by the city in the scale of progress; the city stood for regression and degeneration.

V

The purported antiurban bias of the Chicago school and more generally of American culture might yet turn out to be, upon closer scrutiny, one of the most powerful apologetic ideologies of the city and of modernity. Park, Redfield, and Wirth were all concerned with migration—between races, cultures, regions, and communities. However, Park and the early Redfield represented this "transition" as innumerable points where opposites meet. Marginal man and Tepoztlán were but two instances containing and reproducing the tensions, ruptures, and conflicts that constitute social change. Conversely, Redfield's later study of the Yucatan and Wirth's theory of urbanism externalized and reified the "transition." Redfield reified a continuum between village and city, while Wirth created a discontinuous duality, the urban and the rural, two apparently opposite but actually complementary views of the city and modernity.

Park and the early Redfield show in what direction one could take the distinctions between traditional and modern, ethnic and cosmopolitan. They used them to explore the points of tensions where opposites meet. Park represented these innumerable points through the figure of marginal man, the racial and cultural hybrid type of a society undergoing rapid change. Redfield did the same with Tepoztlán, a hybrid community that is at once primitive and modern, where the world of Indian tribal culture and modern Mexico City culture merge in uneasy and unstable combinations. Marginal man and Tepoztlán, as a result, argue for dialectical tensions internal to the individual and the group rather than for polarized dichotomies separating them into either modern or traditional, urban or rural, cosmopolitan or ethnic.

71

Louis Wirth and the later Redfield, on the contrary, moved toward increasingly clear-cut distinctions. No longer treated as abstractions but as tangible realities, these distinctions were finally used to constitute the progressive stages in a teleology of modernity that culminates in the twentieth-century metropolis. It is this second version that was consistently used in later decades, and that made Wirth's essay the official pronouncement on the city.

Richard Wright chose to tell his own story, in *Black Boy-American Hunger*, as the story of a Parkian marginal man:

> From far beyond the horizons that bound this bleak plantation there had come to me through my living the knowledge that my father was a black peasant who had gone to the city seeking life, but who had failed in the city; a black peasant whose life had been hopelessly snarled in the city, and who had at last fled the city—that same city which had lifted me in its burning arms and borne me toward alien and undreamed-of shores of knowing.[27]

It is in part the modernity of that construct that preserves the power of his narrative half a century later. When he turned his recollection to his father, his family, the rural south, and the past, Wright relied on the conceptual apparatus exemplified here by Wirth and the later Redfield. Too optimistically perhaps by contemporary standards, Wright in this badly misunderstood and most important passage of *Black Boy* envisioned his escape from the rural South to the urban North as an accelerated escape into the future and a miraculous escape to a faraway planet. One need only compare this passage with Walter Benjamin's view of the angel of history to sense how much the discourse of modernity in the early twentieth century, whether in sociological discourse, narrative, or philosophy, within Marxist or simply liberal frameworks, hinged on visions of utopia and apocalypse.[28]

Deviant Girls and Dissatisfied Women: A Sociologist's Tale

4

[M]y past . . . seems very remote to me. The changes in ways of life have recently been so great as to separate all of us from our early years profoundly, and in my case this separation seems to be more profound because I was born in an isolated region of Old Virginia, 20 miles from the railroad in a social environment resembling that of the 18th century, and I consequently feel that I have lived in three centuries, migrating gradually toward the higher cultural areas. The fact that I reached civilization at all is evidently due to some obscure decision on the part of my father to attend an institution of learning. . . . In this decision he provoked a certain amount of resentment from his own father, a Pennsylvania Dutchman, rich in land but with peasant attitudes.
—William Isaac Thomas, "My Life," 1928

From far beyond the horizons that bound this bleak plantation there had come to me through my living the knowledge that my father was a black peasant who had gone to the city seeking life, but who had failed in the city; a black peasant whose life had been hopelessly snarled in the city, and who had at last fled the city—that same city which had lifted me in its burning arms and borne me toward alien and undreamed-of shores of knowing.   —Richard Wright, Black Boy, 1945

Had he been a European immigrant or a Black migrant from the South with such literary talent, Thomas might have contributed to the immigrant narratives which form such an important genre in American literature. Both W. I. Thomas and Richard Wright came from the South, both described their lives as voyages, both recounted a story of migration from country to city and, finally, both indicated knowledge as their final destination. The parallel experiences of a white middle-class academic and a Black proletarian novelist, both of whom migrated to Chicago, explain perhaps the echoes that the two above excerpts produce. William Isaac Thomas was more self-consciously an intellectual migrant whose voyage north overlapped with his decision to become a sociologist. When, at the turn of the century, he joined the still infant discipline at the University of Chicago, Thomas brought two crucial assets to it: his identity as a migrant from rural Virginia to urban Chicago and a special sensibility for words, for storytelling, for personal narratives.[1] By 1918 Thomas had become, with his coauthorship of *The Polish Peasant in Europe and America* (1918–20), the founding figure of American sociology.[2] Making extensive use of immigrant letters and life histories, Thomas had combined science, migration, and storytelling, and produced what, in 1937, was voted the single most important contribution to American sociology.[3] He had successfully staked out sociology's claim to immigrant narratives, a privilege that had remained largely the territory of autobiographical writing.

When in the early twenties he decided to study juvenile female delinquents Thomas implicitly decided to retell his favorite story—the story of the immigrant voyage across centuries and to "civilization"—with a set of new characters and in a new setting. The result was a female story of migration and change from premodern, rural, traditional, ethnic community to modern, urban, freer, often deviant society. W. I. Thomas's *The Unadjusted Girl: With Cases and Standpoint for Behavior Analysis* was the final version of the narrative.[4]

At the center of *The Unadjusted Girl* stand a number of social phenomena—female deviance, corruption, prostitution—that had become dramatically visible during the first two decades of the century. The rapid urban growth of the period, nourished not only by foreign immigrants but by internal migrants from the rural regions of America as well, was the most obvious cause of such social problems. The sociologist's earlier effort to explain the maladjustment that occurred when Polish immigrants moved from the "old" to the "new" world, from the rural villages of Poland to the industrial cities of America, became, in this later study, an attempt to understand the maladjustment that *all* people experience, not just immigrants from rural Europe when they migrate to "modernity," that abstraction which is so often synonymous with "city." In *The Unadjusted Girl* the deviant girl and women in general replaced the Polish immigrant as emblems of all the hopes and threats implicit in the transition.

74

I

The female deviant in the modern world exists, in Thomas's study, in the space defined by two main axes: on one side is a theory of human behavior that relies on psychological, anthropological, and physiological concepts; on the other is a theory of social change that narrates the decline of the old world and the rise of modern society.

Thomas's theory of human behavior and personality relies on two basic concepts for his portrait of deviant modernity: the "wishes" and the "definition of the situation."[5] Thomas identifies four basic wishes as universal and innate behavioral components: the wish for new experience, the wish for security, the wish for response, and the wish for recognition. Without delving into the details of this taxonomy one notices that these wishes form two sets of complementary opposites. The wish for "new experience" originates in what Thomas considers the best traits of our primitive ancestors: courage, anger, disregard for death, impulses of attack and pursuit. The wish for "security," on the other hand, points to the negative attributes of our forebears: fear, avoidance of death, timidity, flight, caution.[6] Transferred to the modern universe the first two wishes divide people into two main groups: those who want change, disregard standards, and have no fear of instability, and those afraid of change, especially of economic insecurity. The second set of wishes locates the individual among other human subjects. The wish for "response" triggers, in fact, desires for love and appreciation, and finds expression in activities relating to love.[7] The wish for "recognition," on the other hand, animates the pursuit of political, artistic, or scientific careers, and the desire for fashion and elegance.

In this mirror of behavioral dualities not only do the four wishes form two sets of opposites, Pasteur vs. the philistine, Florence Nightingale or Jane Addams vs. Napoleon, but each wish contains complementary and morally opposite types as well: the inventor and the vagabond; the philistine and the miser; the self-sacrificing woman and the promiscuous one; the leader and the exhibitionist:

> The moral good or evil of a wish depends on the social meaning or value of the activity which results from it. Thus the vagabond, the adventurer, the spendthrift, the bohemian are dominated by the desire for new experience, but so are the inventor and the scientist; adventures with women and the tendency to domesticity are both

75

expressions of the desire for response; vain ostentation and creative artistic work both are designed to provoke recognition; avarice and business enterprise are actuated by the desire for security. (38)

By showing that moral judgments are socially and culturally defined and by uncovering their arbitrary nature, Thomas sets the stage for the human material he examines in the subsequent chapters: a procession of cases illustrating precisely the complementarity of morally and socially dichotomous behaviors.

After he dismisses the question of whether certain forms of behavior are "good" or "evil" Thomas raises two new questions: first, what causes one or the other wish to become predominant? Second, what causes two individuals who are equally directed by the same wish, for example, the wish for new experience, to become an artist, a scientist, a hobo, or a criminal? In order to account for the highly individual nature of behavior, Thomas introduces, at this point, two new variables: temperament, a physiological variable, and social experience, a cultural variable. While the first is "a chemical matter dependent on the secretions of the glandular systems" (39), the second is a record of all the external influences acting upon the individual.

Little interested in the "chemical" component of his scheme, Thomas turns his attention to the interaction between wishes and social experience. Such interaction distinguishes "man" from the "lower animals" and allows the former the privilege of choosing whether to obey stimulations, a choice that is exercised on the basis of memory and "past experiences" (41). "Preliminary to any self-determined act of behavior there is always a stage of examination and deliberation which we may call the *definition of the situation*. And actually not only concrete acts are dependent on the definition of the situation, but gradually a whole life-policy and the personality of the individual himself follows from a series of such definitions" (42). Parting company here with social, economic, and biological determinism, Thomas courageously theorizes that personality, and even the whole life of an individual, are the products of choice. Only one obstacle stands in the way of such a behavioral utopia:

76   But the child is always born into a group of people among whom all the general types of situation which may arise have already been defined and corresponding rules of conduct developed, and where he has not the slightest chance of making his definitions and

following his wishes without interference. . . . There is therefore always a rivalry between the spontaneous definitions of the situation made by the member of an organized society and the definitions which his society has provided for him. The individual tends to a hedonistic selection of activity, pleasure first; and society to a utilitarian selection, safety first. (42)

The theory discloses here its double nature. On the one hand, by postulating a culturally and socially defined subject Thomas provides the tools to free the individual from both Darwinian and Lamarckian forms of determinism. On the other, by positing a collective and more powerful subjectivity, Thomas is forced to deny the newly discovered freedom and to defer liberation to a near sociological future.

If the "wishes" and "the definition of the situation" provide the conceptual framework for Thomas's discussion, it is the narrative of how the old world declined and the modern world rose that, introducing time and history, illuminates the sociologist's program toward past and future.

Originally the community was practically the whole world of its members. It was composed of families related by blood and marriage and was not so large that all members could not come together; it was a face-to-face group. I asked a Polish peasant what was the extent of an "*okolika*" or neighborhood—how far it reached. "It reaches," he said, "as far as the report of a man reaches—as far as the man is talked about." And it was in communities of this kind that the moral code which we now recognize as valid originated. (44).

This is the once-upon-a-time of Thomas's narrative, the magic formula evoking a time and a place where the physical space occupied by kin completely contained the universe of the individual. Through this narrative form Thomas historicizes the dominant moral code of his time, implicitly denying its innate and everlasting validity and underscoring its precariousness in times of social change.

Resistance to change, repression of individual wishes, and, ultimately, power to uphold immobility are, according to Thomas, the primary traits of older communities:

In small and isolated communities there is little tendency to change or progress because the new experience of the individual is sacrificed for the sake of the security of the group. . . . In the small and spatially isolated communities of the past, where the influ-

77

ences were strong and steady, the members became more or less habituated to and reconciled with a life of repressed wishes. The repression was demanded of all, the arrangement was equitable, and while certain new experiences were prohibited, and pleasure not countenanced as an end in itself, there remained satisfactions, not the least of which was the suppression of the wishes of others. (70–72)

When the community successfully exercises control, upholds uniformity, and maintains order "as it does among savages, among Mohammedans, and as it did until recently among European peasants, no appreciable change in the moral code or in the state of culture is observable from generation to generation" (70). "Savages," "Mohammedans," "old Europe" and, elsewhere, even "rural America," all fall within the compass of Thomas's compact, premodern world, a world that stretches in time and space to include "primitive" and "rural" communities of different ages and continents. Primitive and rural worlds emerge as identical, held together by monolithic world views, one-dimensional norms, intolerant rules and standards. The dichotomy that splits human nature into a wish favorable to change and a wish opposed to it finds its sociological complement here in the polarity between individuals who desire change and a community that opposes it; it also finds its narrative complement in the polarities between immobile, traditional communities and historical, modern societies.

Several documents concerning the lives of immigrants both in the old world and in the new bring Thomas's model of social control in traditional societies to life. Two travelers are called in as witnesses of how communal decisions are taken in the old world:

25. We who are unacquainted with peasant speech, manners and method of expressing thought—mimicry—if we should be present at a division of land or some settlement among the peasants, would never understand anything. Hearing fragmentary, disconnected exclamations, endless quarreling, with repetition of some single word; hearing this racket of a seemingly senseless, noisy crowd that counts up or measures off something, we should conclude that they would not get together, or arrive at any result in an age. . . . Yet wait until the end and you will see that the division has been made with mathematical accuracy. . . . In the end, you look into it and find an admirable decision has been formed and, what is most important, a unanimous decision. (45)

28. It sometimes happens that all except one may agree but the motion is never carried if that one refuses to agree to it. In such cases all endeavor to talk over and persuade the stiff-necked one. Often they even call to their aid his wife, his children, his relatives, his father-in-law, and his mother, that they may prevail upon him to say yes. . . . It seldom occurs in such cases that unanimity is not attained. (48–9)[8]

These travel notes in tone and form are not unlike the ethnographic writings that had resulted from the observation of more "exotic" people. Sociologists, not just ethnographers, participate in the discursive practice of pushing peasant societies into a "prehistorical" past—incidentally, a contradiction in terms—with other "primitive" cultures.

The unanimity that prevails in the old world, Thomas points out, does not immediately break down upon immigration, even though such dislocation undermines and threatens to dissolve it. The classical example, not surprisingly, is the Romeo and Juliet-like fable of love across ethnic boundaries, of romantic love as a breakdown of traditional identities.[9] The letter of a Jewish woman of Hungarian descent who has secretly married a "gentile boy of German parents" recounts how she was cast out by parents and friends first, and by her own husband later:

29. I cannot stand the loneliness and do not want to be hated, denounced and spurned by all. My loneliness will drive me to a premature grave. Perhaps you can tell me how to get rid of my misfortune. Believe me, I am not to blame for what I have done—it was my ignorance. I never believed that it was such a terrible crime to marry a non-Jew and that my parents would under no circumstances forgive me. I am willing to do anything, to make the greatest sacrifice, if only the terrible ban be taken off me. (51–52)

Immediately below and in juxtaposition to this document, Thomas introduces the letter of a Jewish father whose daughter has married an Italian man, and who cannot solve the riddle between a belief in freedom and the rejection of a gentile son-in-law:

30. My tragedy is much greater because I am a free thinker. Theoretically I consider a "goi" [gentile] just as much a man as a Jew. . . . Indeed I ask myself these questions: "What would happen if my daughter married a Jewish fellow who was a good-for-nothing? . . . And what do I care if he is an Italian? But I can not seem to answer

79

these delicate questions. The fact is that I would prefer a refined man; but I would sooner have a common Jew than an educated "goi." Why this is so, I do not know, but that is how it is, of that there is no doubt. And this shows what a terrible chasm exists between theory and practice! (52)

Through the traveler reports and the immigrant letters Thomas composes a representation of the traditional community—both in Europe and in the immigrant colonies of America—as a society where the individual is controlled by the family, where situations and emotions are predetermined, where gossip is a powerful form of social control.

And even after the individual migrates to the modern world and to the American cities, the community continues, across the ocean, to exercise control. Stepping momentarily outside his sociological role to enter as a witness, Thomas asserts:

In examining the letters between immigrants in America and their home communities I have noticed that the great solicitude of the family and community is that the absent member shall not change. . . . And the typical immigrant letter is an assurance and reminder that the writer, though absent, is still a member of the community. (57)

In describing the old community Thomas projects onto it all that is opposed to change: permanence and stability, of course, but also conservatism and opposition to progress.

What could be more antithetical to this monstrous stasis than the fragmented and contradictory nature of the modern world?[10]

But by a process, an evolution, connected with mechanical inventions, facilitated communications, the diffusion of print, the growth of cities, business organization, the capitalistic system, specialized occupations, scientific research, doctrines of freedom, the evolutionary view of life, etc., the family and community influences have been weakened and the world in general has been profoundly changed in content, ideals, and organization. (70–71)

80 At the opposite end of the spectrum appears a world of change, novelty, and metamorphosis; the world of cities, industry, consumer capitalism, and, most importantly, science. Through a neomaterialist theory of evolution Thomas disrupts the immobility of the old world, introducing time and history. Material and technological develop-

ments mark the transition to this generic "modern" world; yet this world is clearly furnished with the industrial and urban develop- ments of early twentieth-century America.

As he condemns the past as irrelevant and hails material evolution as the agent of change, Thomas's prose breaks out of its scientific and objective disguise.

> The typical community is vanishing and it would be neither possi- ble nor desirable to restore it in its old form. It does not correspond with the present direction of social evolution and it would now be a distressing condition in which to live. . . . It represents an ele- ment which we have lost and which we shall probably have to re- store in some form of cooperation in order to secure a balanced and normal society—some arrangement corresponding with hu- man nature. (44)

Far from being a nostalgic reformer—the old community will not be restored—Thomas indirectly responds to those who looked back- ward in time, who yearned for the prelapsarian world of the village and who damned the city and industrialism for the sins and evil of human nature or modern capitalism.

Endowed with all that was missing in the village and more, the modern world signifies for Thomas free individual choice, social par- ticipation for women, sexual freedom for all. The process resembles the opening of a frontier where the barriers represented by commu- nal and kinship groups are finally torn down. Within this social pro- cess physical migration comes to overlap with social evolution, and both converge toward a "higher" modern world, one that promises the possibility of new individual identities.

> Young people leave home for larger opportunities, to seek new ex- perience, and from necessity. Detachment from family and com- munity, wandering, travel, "vagabondage" have assumed the char- acter of normality. Relationships are casualized and specialized. Men meet professionally, as promoters of enterprises, not as mem- bers of families, communities, churches. Girls leave home to work in factories, stores, offices, and studios. Even when families are not separated they leave home for their work. (71)

Once they step outside the communal boundaries, however, 81 young people find themselves in a world that is "large, alluring and confusing" (78), a world that contains both freedom and conflict, lib- eration and corruption. The modern world is also synonymous with "vagueness," "rival definitions," "indeterminateness" (82). Here clashing codes coexist to the confusion of the young girl, simultaneously influenced "by the traditional code . . . [and by] the passing show of the greater world which suggests to her pleasure and recognition" (82). The sociologist himself seems to become hypnotized, not unlike the people he is discussing, captured by a spectacle of glittering beauty and by the unceasing mutability of that world.[11] "Thus in a city the shop windows, the costumes worn on the street, the newspaper advertisements of ladies' wear, the news items concerning objects of luxury define a proper girl as one neatly, fashionably, beautifully, and expensively gowned, and the behavior of the girl is an adaptation to this standard" (82).

Emblem of innocence and sophistication, nature and culture, purity and corruption, the girl at once contains and defies these opposites. Precisely at this juncture the ambiguous nature of both the modern world and the modern girl become apparent. Along the elegant avenues of the city, in the theatrical character of its show, Thomas chooses to locate the central conflict of the modern world.

> [T]he modern world presents itself as a spectacle in which the observer is never sufficiently participating. The modern revolt and unrest are due to the contrast between the paucity of fulfillment of the wishes of the individual and the fullness, or apparent fullness, of life around him. All age levels have been affected by the feeling that much, too much, is being missed in life. This unrest is felt most by those who have heretofore been most excluded from general participation in life,—*the mature woman and the young girl*. (72, my emphasis)

These two figures are the archetypes of change that sit at the center of Thomas's sociological universe clamoring for a freer future. Somewhat like the other historical class, they have nothing to lose but an old system that excludes them from life.

II

The overall narrative of The Unadjusted Girl follows the paths of vanishing communities and disappearing families. Yet the literary substance of the text materializes where the existences of real people are introduced through letters, autobiographical sketches, and case histories. Women and girls, prostitutes and peasants, hoboes, and thieves give life to Thomas's mosaic of human behavior in times of change. "The Regulation of the Wishes," "The Individualization of Behavior," and "The Demoralization of Girls," the three chapters where most of the documents appear, reproduce even in the titles the narrative progression from traditional community to modernity. Underlying these titles are dozens of moving personal accounts, testimonies uttered by a multitude of modern marginals. Among them stand out the mature woman and the young girl. They symbolize the old world Thomas wishes away. Their life histories illustrate the control that the old community continues to exercise on its members even after they have migrated to America, to the city, or to modern society; at the same time they illustrate the dangers awaiting them in the midst of modernity.

The nature of the modern world and the changing norms that regulate the Gorgon of female sexuality in that world provide two recurrent themes in the stories of women and girls. The modern world, however, seems to inspire and cause different desires and behaviors in the woman and in the girl. For the mature woman modernity translates into a desire to participate in social life, to be free from Victorian conventions and domesticity; for the young girl modernity signifies a desire for clothes, movies, and all those objects that consumerism promises to make available to everyone. In the stories of women and girls, all in rebellion against dominant conformity, Thomas detects the signs—dissatisfaction, rebellion, deviance—of a relentless erosion that is consuming communal power.

Age is the most visible but least important mark distinguishing the mature woman from the young girl. Whether bourgeois or petit-bourgeois, middle-class or working-class, most of the mature women appear to live in fairly stable social and economic conditions. These documents recount stories of women who are dissatisfied with marriage; women who, unable to find fulfillment in marriage, have betrayed their husbands; women who have rejected marriage conventions and are now living in adulterous sin. The complexities of romantic love and the frustrations of conventional marriage receive here the sanctions of science. Unconventional and even "immoral" behavior is theoretically and sociologically legitimized on the basis of the four wishes that Thomas has posited as essential components of human nature.

Thomas introduces one such case as the "cry of despair . . . from a woman who limited her life to marriage . . . and is now apparently too old to have other interests" (87). The letter—like many docu-

83

ments concerning mature women—was written to the *Forward*—a New York Yiddish newspaper. It expresses in confessional form the tensions splitting a woman's consciousness between sanctioned role and unquenched desires:

> 37. There is a saying about the peacock. "When she looks at her feathers she laughs, and when she looks at her feet she cries." I am in the same situation.
>
> My husband's career, upon which I spent the best years of my life, is established favorably; our children are a joy to me as a mother; nor can I complain about our material circumstances. But I am dissatisfied with myself. My love for my children, be it ever so great, cannot destroy myself [sic]. A human being is not created like a bee which dies after accomplishing its only task.
>
> Desires, long latent, have been aroused in me and become more aggressive the more obstacles they encounter. . . . I now have the desire to go about and see and hear everything. I wish to take part in everything—to dance, skate, play the piano, sing, go to the theater, opera, lectures and generally mingle in society. As you see, I am no idler whose purpose is to chase all sorts of foolish things, as a result of loose ways. This is not the case.
>
> My present unrest is a natural result following a long period of hunger and thirst for non-satisfied desires in every field of human experience. It is the dread of losing that which never can be recovered—youth and time which do not stand still—an impulse to catch up with the things I have missed. . . . If it were not for my maternal feeling I would go away into the wide world. (73)

Two antipodal worlds loom over the letter: on the one hand is the world of settled domestic contentment, on the other the world of contingent human experience and social participation. The woman speaks to an audience that might misread her motives and compels her to emphasize "I am no idler whose purpose is to chase all sorts of foolish things, as a result of loose ways" (73). This audience might too readily conclude that she is dangerously leaning on the precipice of deviance and sin. To some extent this is the same audience Thomas is addressing in his book, the audience whose moral standards he is attempting to modify. To such an audience Thomas hopes to prove that the wish for new experience, a natural wish present in everyone, and not latent corruption is the source of domestic despair.

84

The restlessness and rebellion still contained within words in the previous case spills into actions in subsequent ones. A woman who has betrayed her husband recounts a touching experience of adultery and guilt. The letter narrates the story of a woman who has an affair with her husband's cousin, a house boarder. The central paragraphs of this long letter retrace the inner conflict leading to the adultery:

> 10. I almost never spoke to him, and never came near him. God only knows how much these efforts cost me, but with all my energy I fought against the diabolic feeling in my heart. Unfortunately, my husband misinterpreted my behavior as a lack of hospitality. His resentment compelled me to assume a more friendly attitude toward his relative, as I wished to avoid quarreling. What followed may easily be inferred. From amiability I passed to love until he occupied my whole mind and everybody else was non-existent for me. Of course no one was aware of my predicament.
>
> One day I decided to put an end to my sufferings by confessing all to my boarder and requesting him to go away or at least leave our house and avert a scandal. Unfortunately, my hope of a peaceful life was not fulfilled, following my confession. He remained in our home and became more friendly than ever towards me. I began to love him so intensely that I hardly noticed his growing intimacy with me and as a result I gave birth to a baby whose father is my husband's cousin.
>
> I am unable to describe to you one hundredth part of the misery this has caused me. I always considered an unfaithful woman the worst creature on earth and now . . . I am myself a *degraded woman.* . . . The mere thought drives me insane. My husband of course, knows nothing about the incident. . . . Everyday in the week is a day of utter anguish for me and every day I feel the tortures of hell. . . . I cannot stand my husband's tenderness toward the child that is mine but not his. When he gives the baby a kiss it burns like a hot coal dropped in my bosom. Every time he calls it his baby I hear some one shouting into my ear the familiar epithet thrown at low creatures like me . . . and every time he takes the child in his arms I am tempted to tell him the terrible truth. . . . And so I continue to suffer. (15–16, my emphasis)

The protagonist of this domestic drama constructs her sin as an evil fate, as a series of events that accidentally lead to her fall.[12] Stressing from the beginning that "as a child I conducted myself decently," and that "as a young girl I strove to marry some good young man and live contentedly" in the attempt to establish her moral and behavioral credentials, the author of the letter, like the previous one, evokes the

85

moral context surrounding her. To her potential judges she enjoins that her tale of betrayal is not to be discounted on the basis of innate corruption or youthful depravity. The guilt that she imposes on herself and her description of herself as a "degraded woman" measure the moral order she and her audience share. They measure, as well, the repressed desire released in the forbidden act. A sin committed and then represented as "real" rather than fictional: this is what gives the confession its quasi-cathartic quality. At once representing and forbidding, the letter articulates the fear-desire of becoming a "degraded" woman. In this case, as in many others, Thomas follows the advice of his patroness—Mrs. Dummer—who opens her foreword to *The Unadjusted Girl* by quoting Spinoza's "Neither condemn nor ridicule but try to understand" (v). In keeping with the exhortation of the philosopher Thomas abstains from judgment and points instead to the wish for response as explanatory of the woman's behavior.

A special case adds new elements to Thomas's gallery of middle-class deviance and illustrates how far the limits of unconventionality could stretch for the middle-class woman. This is the story of Margaret, related not in letter form but through a case history.[13] It illustrates what social landscapes were available outside conventional morality:

> 38. I had been looking for Margaret, for I knew she was a striking instance of the "unadjusted" who had within a year come with a kind of aesthetic logic to Greenwich village. She needed something very badly. What I heard about her which excited me was that she was twenty years old, unmarried, had never lived with a man or had any of that experience, had worked for a year on a socialist magazine, was a heavy drinker and a frequenter of Hell Hole, that she came from a middle class family but preferred the society of the outcasts to any other. Greenwich Village is not composed of outcasts but it does not reject them, and it enables a man or a woman who desires to know the outcasts to satisfy the desire without feeling cut off from humanity. Hell Hole is a saloon in the back room of which pickpockets, grafters, philosophers, poets, revolutionists, stool-pigeons, and the riff-raff of humanity meet. Margaret loves this place and the people in it—so they told me—and there she did and said extreme things in which there was a bitter fling at decent society. (73)

86

The narrator proceeds to quote the story in Margaret's own words and to fill in the details of a middle-class existence, which, after turning against its own class, has drifted toward the margins of society. From these moral outskirts Margaret's concluding words are uttered.

" 'I want to know the down and outs,' said Margaret with quiet, almost fanatical intenseness. 'I find kindness in the lowest places, and more than kindness sometimes—something, I don't know what it is, that I want' " (75–76). For Thomas, Margaret's is simply a case of "revolt." Thomas had already provided both the behavioral ingredients—the wish for new experience and for response—that combine in this type of life history, and the sociological ingredients—modern revolt and unrest, desire to participate, and rejection of the old system—that accompany it. Thomas does not notice that Margaret's is a romantic quest for the humble but ideally good transposed into the modern city. It is a Wordsworthian-Byronesque search for the lost self among the lowly or the exotic, a search that parallels Margaret's voyage from rejection of a "respectable, middle-class family," to discovery of "sex" and "hard street life," to embracement of "socialism," "poetry," and "anything which expressed a reaction against the conditions of my life at home" (75), and, finally, to the waterfront, to the saloon back rooms, to their prostitute and criminal guests. "And I liked them. They seemed human, more so than other people. And in this place were working men. One man, with a wife and children, noticed I was going there and didn't seem to belong to them, and he asked me to go home with him and live with his family; and he meant it, and meant it decently" (75). By the end of her quest Margaret has come full circle. Opening and closing with family images, the case history narrates both Margaret's symbolic adoption into the family of the "down-and-outs" and the success of her quest for a new self.

III

Not included in the documentary selection of *The Unadjusted Girl* yet central to its portrayal of middle-class deviance is an important episode of Thomas's own life history, an episode that mandates a short digression.

On April 12, 1918, just below the full-page title "FLANDERS LINE STIFFENS," and surrounded by more war news, the *Chicago Daily Tribune* carried on its front page the following headline:

EXTRA—DR. THOMAS AND WOMAN TAKEN
IN LOOP HOTEL

87

The article, several columns long, recounted how the manager of the hotel, suspecting a couple of not being married, had complied with a new law, alerted the FBI, and brought about the arrest on charges of violating the Mann Act and registering under false pretenses. The article went on to inform its readers that "Prof. Thomas is the author of the widely discussed book 'The Mind of the Woman.' His wife has been known as an ardent exponent of pacifism and was one of the supporters in the Ford peace ship enterprise."[14] During the following days it became known to readers of the press that Thomas was fifty-five years old and Mrs. Granger—the adulteress—only twenty-four; that Thomas was a professor of sociology at the University of Chicago and Mrs. Granger the wife of a lieutenant serving in France (this fact was reiterated every day for a week); that Mrs. Thomas had welcomed Mrs. Granger into her own house during the pretrial hearings. The heavy-handed symbolism of this scenario was unmistakable: fantasies of incest taboos, unspeakable sexual sins, betrayal of the country, and sexual triangles could be made out behind the daily news accounts.

Thomas's career suffered a sudden and irreparable rupture when this scandal broke out. In spite of his twenty years of service he was dismissed from the university—never again to hold a permanent professorship—amidst a fanfare of well-publicized remarks over his "eccentric" ideas, his "shocking" behavior, and, worst of all, his teaching "The History of Prostitution" to classes attended by *both* men and women.[15] The University of Chicago Press immediately interrupted the publication of *The Polish Peasant* "as if to complete the expunging of W. I. Thomas from the Chicago scene."[16] His next study, *Old World Traits Transplanted*, had to appear under the name of his colleagues Robert Park and Herbert Miller, for the Carnegie Corporation, sponsor of the study, would not have its name associated with that of Thomas. A proposed appointment to the Americanization Project was vetoed, and as late as 1928, when he was finally elected president of the American Sociological Society, voices were still casting doubts over his moral fitness.[17] From this point on Thomas became an academic "marginal," sharing directly—if on a different level—some of the experiences of the immigrants, women, and deviants he studied. In due time he issued a defense statement.

> I am therefore not guilty of this charge as it is understood, but I am guilty of the whole general charge in the sense that I hold views and am capable of practices not approved by our social traditions. Society should not interfere with the free association of mature persons capable of leading their own lives and seeking their own values.[18]

88

Labeling as "practices" actions that his contemporaries considered immoral and that the law treated as criminal and dismissing as "social

traditions" the moral truths of his age, culture, and class, Thomas subjected that reality to the estranged gaze that is often the mark of cultural, political, and historical outsiders—immigrants, minorities, and
ethnographers most typically; he was proclaiming himself outside
the moral jurisdiction of the tribe, that same tribe he tried to consign
to the past in his studies.

Some of the basic facts of this episode remain obscure. Janowitz
has suggested that it was perhaps in order to discredit Mrs. Thomas—
whose political activities were "under official surveillance"—that the
scandal was so vicious.[19] As Deegan and Burger have pointed out,
Thomas himself was closely associated with Jane Addams, Hull
House, and Chicago reform activities.

> Thomas's ties to Addams and her close associates were not only
> professional but also private. He frequently dined with Jane Ad-
> dams; his first wife, Harriet T. Thomas, was intimately involved in
> the Suffragist Movement in Chicago and an active member of the
> JPA and the Women's International League of Peace and Freedom, a
> controversial group of which Addams was one of the founders.[20]

Commenting on the almost complete absence of personal papers
concerning the most prominent figure of American sociology in the
archives of The University of Chicago, Janowitz has noted that it "appears to the intellectual historian as if there may have been an effort to
obliterate the record of W. I. Thomas as a man."[21]

The Unadjusted Girl loudly resonates with the scandal that brought
Thomas down from his academic seat. Viewed in this context *The Unadjusted Girl* yields one more element of its agenda: the attempt to confront from a scientific point of view—as objective, empirical observations—the system of power that oppresses many of the mature
women discussed by Thomas and that eventually caused his own fall.
More important than Thomas's theory or the minimal interpretations
that he provides, the case histories of restless and rebellious women
represent as many efforts to assert the reality and the existence of
such behaviors, to bring them back from the nether world of "deviance." *The Unadjusted Girl* is an attempt both to erase the line that separates deviance from normality, a line Thomas himself had become
caught on, and to modify the law of irreversible regression that gov- 89
erned the discourse of female deviance.

Exemplary in both respects is the long autobiographical document that closes the chapter on mature women. The opening lines,
surprisingly, announce that this is a story with a happy end. "54. I am a

college graduate, 27, married five years and the mother of a three-year-old boy. I have been married happily, and have been faithful to my husband" (93). The reasons for displacing the end of the story at the beginning soon become clear. Brought up well within conventional middle-class boundaries the woman recalls her childhood love for a boy whom, from age six, she has decided to marry but who dies in a fire, leaving her adolescence "dreary for a long time" (94). After a number of years she leaves home to go to college where her best friend initiates her into the secrets of sex.

> [My best friend] saw an upper classman [girl] falling in love with me, and she came to me with the news. Then she saw how innocent I was and how ignorant, and my sex education was begun. She told me of marriage, of mistresses, of homosexuality. I was sick with so much body thrown at me at once, and to add to the unpleasantness someone introduced me to Whitman's poetry. I got the idea that sex meant pain for women and I determined never to marry. (94)

Soon thereafter, however, her feelings begin to change as she falls in love with a girl and as a new world of experiences open up to her:

> She told me her ambitions, and I told her mine; it was the first time I had ever been a person to any one, and I was her loyal and loving friend. I kissed her intimately once and thought that I had discovered something new and original. We read Maupassant together and she told me the way a boy had made love to her. Everything was changed, love was fun, I was wild to taste it. I cultivated beaux, I let them kiss me and embrace me, and when they asked me to live with them, I was not offended but pleased. I learned my capacity, how far I could go without losing my head, how much I could drink, smoke, and I talked as freely as a person could. I discussed these adventures with the other girls, and we compared notes on kisses and phrases, and technique. We were healthy animals and we were demanding our rights to spring's awakening. I never felt cheapened, nor repentant, and I played square with the men. I always told them I was not out to pin them down to marriage, but that this intimacy was pleasant and I wanted it as much as they did. We indulged in sex talk, birth control, leutic infections, mistresses. (95)

90

Perhaps to the surprise of the contemporary reader, this protosixties hymn to sexual liberation turns out to hide sexual amusements that may appear relatively innocent by contemporary standards.

I could have had complete relations with two of these boys if there had been no social stigma attached, and enjoyed it for a time. But instead I consoled myself with thinking that I still had time to give up my virginity, and that when I did I wanted as much as I could get for it in the way of passionate love. (95)

The encounter with a man "fine, clean, mature and not seemingly bothered with sex at all" (95) prompts a second important shift in the life history. With this new companion the conversation shifts from sex to "music and world-views and philosophy." She is more experienced sexually while he is more experienced intellectually. When they eventually marry it is a happy marriage based on friendship, respect, honesty, frankness, a marriage in which, she writes, "I don't feel that I possess my husband, nor that he does me" (96).

Through this case history Thomas was scientifically proclaiming a new model for women's behavior, a model in which deviance would not be irreversible. The document sums up Thomas's reform program with regard to mature women and clarifies the reason for their inclusion in a study of juvenile female delinquents. It proves that women who have been "promiscuous" or who have experimented with nonheterosexual relationships are not necessarily harmed for life, condemned forever to drift among the "variants." It is possibly in reference to such unorthodox beliefs that, when the scandal broke out, the *New York Times* provided its readers with the following mean-spirited summary of "Thomas's teachings":

Women are better off for having had their flings as men do.
Dissipated women often make excellent wives.
Calvalry [sic] is the persistence of the old race habit of contempt
  for women.
Any girl, mentally mature, has the right to have children and
  the right to limit their number.
The morality of women is an expediency rather than an innate
  virtue.
Marriage as it exists today is rapidly approaching a form of immorality.
Matrimony is often an arrangement by which the woman
  trades her irreproachable conduct for irreproachable
  gowns.
Children are not the result of marriage, but marriage is the result of children.[22]

This summary hardly contains the outraged sneer of Thomas's censors.

IV

Thomas's portrait of the "unadjusted" girl begins not far from and indeed overlaps with that of the "restless" woman (and, one should add, of the "immoral" professor). Neither science nor morality drew fine distinctions between these types. They belonged to the same group: congenitally corrupt or perverted early in life.[23]

Most of the cases of juvenile delinquency appear in the chapter "The Demoralization of Girls." The social phenomenon here is much the same as before: girls who break away from norms and rules. This time, however, the focus is primarily on girls from the poorest classes, recent European immigrants or girls who have run away from midwestern farms and villages. While the mature woman is attempting to stretch or break open the domestic circle defined by the moral boundaries of love, sex, and marriage, the young girl is more precisely trapped in a circle of theft, prostitution, vagabondage, and drugs.

Neither confessions, nor cries for help or advice, nor outbursts of frustration, the personal documents concerning young girls generally contain factual narratives and detached "scientific" observations, the kind of narratives one finds in institutional case records. Most of these documents come, in fact, from the records of social agencies and institutions. The case worker is the primary author, the one who summarizes and orders the events and establishes causal connections between them. Sometimes the record includes long direct quotations or paraphrases of the girl's words, testimony, or reflections.

Two elements contribute to Thomas's portrait of the delinquent girl. On the one hand poverty, demoralization within families and urban lures, amusement, adventure, pretty clothes, etc., emerge as primary causes of delinquency, on the other social workers, social agencies, and juvenile courts emerge as agents of reform and ideal surrogate families.

Poverty and the degradation of families, or their absence altogether, is the opening theme in several case histories:

59. Helen comes from a large family, there being eight children. Her father is a miner and unable to support the older girls. She was

told at the age of fourteen that she was old enough to support herself and to get out. She came to Chillicothe because of the draftees from Western Pennsylvania. . . . In a few weeks she had developed from the little red hood and mittens with the stout shoes of the foreigner into a painted-cheeked brow-blacked prostitute. She had her name and address written on slips of paper that she passed out to soldiers on the streets. (102–3)

60. Evelyn claims to know absolutely nothing of her family or relations. Was found in a room in a hotel, where she had registered as the wife of a soldier. Seemed entirely friendless and alone. . . . Did not seem to feel that she had done anything very wrong. It seems to be a case of society's neglect to an orphan. She was taken to the Isolation Hospital for treatment for syphilis infection and escaped within 24 hours. (104)

63. Carrie is a colored girl, 23 years of age at the time of her commitment. She was sentenced for possessing heroin. She was born on Long Island—the illegitimate child of a notorious thief and prostitute known only as "Jenny." She was adopted when fifteen months old. . . . Her foster mother states that she was always a difficult child and very stubborn. When she was as young as nine years old the neighbors complained of her immoral conduct with young boys on roofs and cellars. She seemed to have no feelings of shame. (107–8)

This type of analysis—a version of Lamarckian sociology—posits families and communities as part of the social environment. Analogous to the deformation that the physical environment can cause to the body, the social environment can exercise a negative influence on the mind and eventually cause severe forms of "maladjustment."

The social environment includes not only the kinship group but also the modern urban world. A perceptive observer of that world, Thomas identifies in some of its manifestations more causes which ignite the process of deviance.

62. Catherine got acquainted with her brother's sister-in-law, Jennie Sopeka, a girl ten years older, with an exceedingly bad reputation. . . . Catherine said she knew nothing of this girl when she came to see her and proposed they go to Chicago "to have a nice time and nice clothes." (106)

68. "When I saw sweller girls than me picked up in automobiles every night, can you blame me for falling too?"

Pretty Helen McGinnis, the convicted auto vamp of Chicago, asked the question seriously. She has just got an order for a new trial on the charge of luring Martin Metzler to Forest Reserve Park, where he was beaten and robbed. The girl went on:

"I always wanted good clothes, but I never could get them, for our family is large and money is scarce. I wanted good times like the other girls in the office. Every girl seemed to be a boulevard vamp. I'd seen other girls do it, and it was easy." (114–15)

71. American girl, twenty-one years old, semi-prostitute, typical of a certain class one grows to know. Works as a salesgirl in one of the high class shops—a pretty girl, languid manner but businesslike.

Sex had been a closed book to her and, as she was naturally cold and unawakened, she was not tempted as some girls are. She did not care about being loved, but the wish to be admired was strong within her and love of adornment superseded all else, particularly when she realized she was more beautiful than most girls.

The department store is sometimes a school for scandal. Many rich women are known by sight and are talked over, servants' gossip sometimes reaching thus far, the intrigues between heads of departments and managers are hinted at and the possibility of being as well dressed as someone else becomes a prime consideration. (122–23)

Arguing in part against a vulgar Freudian view that sought in the abnormal or maladjusted sexuality of the individual the causes and effects of all major problems, Thomas turns his gaze, instead, toward the main symbols of consumer capitalism:

The beginning of delinquency in girls is usually an impulse to get amusement, adventure, pretty clothes, favorable notice, distinction, freedom in the larger world which presents so many allurements and comparisons. . . . Sexual passion does not play an important role, for the girls have become "wild" before the development of sexual desire. . . . Their sex is used as a condition of the realization of other wishes. It is their capital. . . . Mary (case No. 64) begins by stealing to satisfy her desire for pretty clothes and "good times." . . . Katie (No. 65) begins as a vagabond. . . . In the case of Stella (No. 66) the sexual element is part of a joy ride. . . . Marien (No. 67) treats sexual life as a condition of her "high life," including restaurants, moving pictures, hotels, and showy clothes. Helen (No. 68) said, "I always wanted good clothes." (109)

94

Fashion, money, amusement thus play a double role in Thomas's narrative. On the one hand they signal the birth of the modern world, the end of the era of repression, and the beginning of the era of titillation.[24] On the other they corrupt young girls and encourage them on the road of deviance. Not congenital sexual impulses out of control but that beautiful world of clothes, shows, and restaurants that liberates the individual and allows the expression of long-repressed wishes is for Thomas at the origins of theft and prostitution.

Central to this chapter is the record of Esther Lorenz, a young woman native of Prague, Bohemia, born to a family described by the case worker as "poor and very foreign and unprogressive" (172); "86. Statement from the Laboratory of Bedford Hills Reformatory for Women: Esther Lorenz was committed to the institution March 23, 1914, from Special Sessions, N.Y. Offense: Petit Larceny" (172). The case record consciously articulates the interaction between family poverty, theft, and desire for a "good life." More importantly, it exposes in a striking dialogue of voices, the relationships of power disguised under the label "deviance." The dialogue includes the voice of Esther, in the form of letters to a friend and to the parole officer; the voice of the case worker, sketching Esther's background and the events leading to her conviction; the voice of the parole officer, who is writing to the superintendent of the reformatory, recommending that she not be given another parole and that, possibly, she be deported; finally, Thomas's voice reinterpreting Esther's letters so as to show the "ideal human material" in a girl who was ruined by the penitentiary.

The letters included in the case record are part of an exchange between Esther Lorenz and Lillian Marx over a period of several months. The two friends were caught stealing clothes at Macy's. Convicted, they are sentenced to serve probationary sentences working as domestics in the households of two different families in upstate New York from where they correspond. Written in Bohemian, the letters have been translated into English, the parole officer informs the reader, by a Bohemian woman who has attempted to reproduce the style "of the few letters written in English by Esther" (174).

Esther's letters are characterized by two recurring themes: the harshness of work and life in the family where she is a servant and the desire for nice men, wealthy men, for the good times of dances and movie theaters. Her description of work could be part of a number of maids' journals, real or fictionalized:

95

October 1, 1914

Dear friend,

I apologize not to answer you right away. I have lots of work. I have two people and little baby girl. I have so much work; I haven't got even time to wash my face.

November, 1914

Dear friend,

if you could come with me to moving pictures, there we would meet nice mens [sic]. Wouldn't that be nice? I have my hand so hard like a man from hard work, so you can imagine how hard I am working.

Dear Friend:

I have such a cranky lady. If I stay here another two months with her I think I go crazy. I was very sick the other Sunday. We had 8 people and so you can imagine what work I had. Only if you would see me you would get frightened how I look; I am only bone and skin and pale in face. You would say that I go by and by in grave. Everybody ask me what's the matter with me but you know I can't tell everybody I come from Bedford.

February, 1915

I am crying so much—I have such a hard work. Everything hurts me; I am all broke down. If I can only come free I wouldn't mind to have not even a shirt. I would give everything if we can be free. (174–87)

Esther, however, unlike those servant girls who let themselves waste away from overwork and consumption, has strong and clear ideas about who, what, and where the fun is.

October 1, 1914

Dear sweetheart,

you ask me to come to see you but how can I do that; I haven't got no shoes and no money, I am very poor. If you can come over on Saturday evening and sleep with me. I got big bed. On Sunday . . . we go in a place where we can have a good time and lots of kissing. We going to look for some nice man but something better, not only working man; we shouldn't have to go to work.

My dearest friend:

If you want to marry one of the officers, you know what they are, they are ever the other [army] men. They can't marry only a poor girl. If they want to marry they got to have a girl with lots of money 20,000 Kronen, and they got to put the money down for guarantee. If happens something to your sweetheart officer, then you get the money back. Do you under-

96

stand me, Sunday School? But dear we havn't got the means yet, we have to wait for them. If we going to get mens [sic] like that, cause we not rich.

November, 1914

Dear friend,

I am going to moving pictures every Wednesday and every time when I going out I see the nice young mens [sic]. How they love them, the girls, and we can't help that. I met one nice man and he want to go with me for a good time but I realize maybe he some kind of detective. . . . Dear friend, if you could come with me to moving pictures, there we would meet nice mens. Wouldn't that be nice?

Dear Friend:

I received letters from my sister and they were so happy. . . . My sweetheart is not killed yet, so I going to take him when I get home. He always asks about me if I'm angry at him. I rather take him than America; they only want to have girl got to have money [sic]. The poor girl they don't want her and those which are not rich they are nothing worth. Don't you think so friend, I am right?

[March, 1915]

Friend, I go to school every Wednesday but next Wednesday I wouldn't go, I go to the dance. I have white dress under black skirt and long coat and she going to think that I go to school. I leave my skirt and my books in my friends house and I go to the dance, ha, ha, ha. Come with me [,] ha, ha, I have there lots of nice young boys and the man who brings me the eggs and lots of other young man, so I going to have nice time. . . . I be very glad if you can come with me, but don't tell on me that I going to the dance. My lady she don't know anything about it. She think I am innocent girl, No 1. I am, don't you think friend? When I think I have three years, I start to cry, I don't know what to do. But when I think of nice men, I start to jump in the kitchen and singing [sic]. (174–88)

More complex than most representations of servant girls, Esther is a suffering victim, a cunning schemer, an aspiring vamp, a pragmatist, and an expert on the laws that govern the marriage market.

Eventually Esther's letters are discovered by her friend's lady. Sent to the parole officer, their content brings Esther back to jail for breaking the parole. At this point the parole officer writes to the superintendent of the institution where Esther is incarcerated to express an overall opinion:

97

I think much of the subject's suspiciousness and deceitfulness is racial and there is small chance of her adjusting to American customs.

I remember that you considered deporting her in the first place and while I still think it would be very bad for subject to have the stigma of deportation added to that of her arrest, I do feel that her own country is the best place for her and that she will be far more apt to live a straight normal life there with the restraints of her family and their standards to help her than she will here. Do you think it may be possible to send her back on her own money when conditions of war permit? (192)

The officer invokes and juxtaposes two different sets of concepts. On the one hand is "racial behavior," presumably a behavior characterized by distrust, a recurrent trait in the stereotypes of peasants. On the other hand are "American customs," the opposite of distrust and, at any rate, something one is not born with but adapts to. Implicit in the officer's comments is the verdict that Esther has failed to pass the admission test into modernity; for this reason she must regress to the hypothetically stable and cohesive family of the old world.

Thomas's comments on Esther could not be farther from the parole officer's, nor could they be more revealing of the distance which separates the old school of deviance from the new one to which Thomas belongs. For Thomas Esther's desire for clothes, dances, and men signals a "strong and social" character. Her machinations to regain freedom and her fight against "organized society" reveal an intelligent and even imaginative mind at work. Esther needed stimulation through "creative work," participation in some "form of society," "recognition," "gratification," but the court failed to acknowledge these needs.

It is at this point that Thomas begins to unfold the agenda that he has in store for the reform of delinquent girls, an agenda that aims ultimately to transform this type of story into one with a happy ending:

But some years ago the juvenile courts were established. It had become apparent that numbers of disorderly children, mainly from broken homes, were being brought into the criminal courts for escapades and sexual offences, placed in jails with hardened criminals and thereby having the possibility of the formation of a normal scheme of life destroyed forever. Certain women were the first to protest and to act, and the result was the formation of a court for children which dispensed with lawyers and legal technicalities, and treated the child as far as possible *as an unruly member of a family*, not as a criminal. . . . Their service has been very great in checking the be-

98

ginnings of demoralization. The court is wiser than the parents of the children and incidentally does much to influence home life. (194–95, my emphasis)

Here the narrative, suspended for pages while the sociologist digresses through dozens of case histories, regains momentum as Thomas forecasts a future world in which juvenile courts and social agencies will displace families in regulating and shaping human personality. If the elimination of "lawyers and legal technicalities" euphemistically describes the elimination of the basic constitutional rights for a large class of people, the substitution of judiciary courts and social workers for families literally advances the power struggle between kinship group and state, and stages the victory of the latter.

The successful reform of several girls whose case histories Thomas reports provides a contrast to Esther's failed redemption. Two cases in particular exemplify the progression from deviance to reform that Thomas propounds. The first is the case of Helen Langley, nineteen years old in 1918, immoral daughter of an immoral mother and a drunkard father, depraved from age twelve, when, according to the record, "she began to 'go crazy over the boys,' to attend dance halls and to go out on motor trips with unknown men" (167); she was sexually attacked by a neighbor at age fourteen, "and since that time her life has been a series of immoral relations with sailors and civilians" (167). Her tortuous pilgrimage finally halts when she is confined to a tuberculosis hospital to be cured. Here, the case worker goes on to recount, the girl is finally adopted by a sympathetic physician and a motherly nurse:

> 85. Helen has gained several pounds and looks like a new person, is content and happy, *sleeps most of the day* and said she feels rested for the first time for years. She takes all the care of her own cottage, has become very tidy in her habits, *enjoys washing her dishes*, etc., and *keeping things in order*. Helen said that her plan when she is discharged is to find a good place where she can do housework. She intends to have nothing further to do with men, particularly sailors. *She loves to do sewing and handwork* and showed the most astonishing amount of embroidery which she has done for one of the nurses. (170, my emphasis)

99

Paradoxically, the oppressive domesticity that Thomas indicates as the cause of rightful rebellion in the case histories of well-to-do women emerges now, in the cases of deviant girls, as the sign of readjustment and normality. If Helen ever did find the desired job as domestic, she killed two birds with one stone: she cured herself of deviance and she also freed a wealthier sister of her domestic fetters.

The story of Mary even more clearly than Helen's shows in what direction Thomas was moving to find an appropriate ending for his narrative of deviant modernity. Daughter of a promiscuous mother and uncertain father, Mary grows up surrounded by a "complete lack of ordinary sex morality and social standards" (204). Her early experiences "break down completely any sex inhibition she might have had, aroused sex needs and accustomed her to the habit of sex expression" (206). Eventually discovered by a social worker, her life takes a turn for the better. First the psychological examiner "indicates the sex situation," next the psychometric tests "showed her to be well up to average in intelligence," and finally the social worker takes charge of Mary:

> 89. There seemed to be every basis for a satisfactory adjustment to life if the environmental opportunities could be provided so that her work and social interests would have a chance to develop and help to organize a more socialized sex expression.

> Meantime the case worker built up the social background, finally raised scholarship money and Mary went into the second year of the commercial course in a good High School.
> There was never any attempt to deal with the sex side by repressive methods, never any interference with her social life, nor any form of restraint. When she wanted to go to visit her mother, the whole situation was talked out with her and she was given the worker's attitude frankly and honestly but decision was left to her. She did not go. She has continued to associate with boys on an unusually free basis. She will go to see a boy friend at his home exactly as she would visit a girl. She could not be made to see why she should not accept a boy's invitation to go to New York City for a sightseeing excursion. . . . Her standards are changing rapidly with her developing tastes and interests. She has made good in her school work consistently. She has been rash and unconventional in the extreme but has never, apparently, overstepped the boundaries of morality on the sex side. For a year and a half she has made steady progress and there is no indication that she will ever again become a delinquent. (209)

If Helen and Mary's case histories can shift from Maggie-a-girl-of-the-streets to Little Women, it is because, unlike fictional literature, case records need not follow a particular style or literary mode with abso-lute strictness and consistency. Loaded with the authority of empiri-cal reality, sociological literature can afford to disregard the narrative laws of plausibility and to create, instead, new plots, causations, reso-lutions.

Thomas's tale finds the desired happy ending by proposing, first, a shift from authority to influence as the means to elicit conversion and readjustment, second, a view of deviance as a temporary phase rather than a permanent trait, and, last, the role of the social worker as hero. Commenting on juvenile delinquency and on the larger issues sur-rounding this "social problem," Thomas concludes that "the child should be taken in charge by society as soon as it shows any tendency to disorganization" (211). Quoting from "one of the most systematic proposals," he adds:

> Each city, probably each county would require an extension or re-organization of its personnel to include a department of adjust-ment to which teachers, policemen, and others could refer all chil-dren who seemed to present problems of health, of mental development, of behavior or of social adjustment. For good work this would require the services of doctors, nurses, psychiatrists, field investigators, recreational specialists.

> The ideal would be to have the school act as a reserve parent, an unusually intelligent, responsible and resourceful parent, using whatever the community had to offer, making up whatever the community lacked. . . . All neglected, dependent and delinquent children, whether of school age or not, would fall within the prov-ince of [the department of adjustment]. (211)

Having shifted to the subjunctive mood, Thomas's narrative closes with a ghastly sociological vision. What begins as a story of how the traditional family and community are declining and must disappear as modern society is born suddenly undergoes a striking meta-morphosis, emerging as an apotheosis of those same social institu-tions transposed into the state and its branches. In this Kafkaesque universe social workers, judges, and teachers will be the parents of a brood of citizens subsumed by way of adoption into a new mega-family: modern society.

Through the young girl and the mature woman Thomas carried out a scientifically encoded attempt to explain and posit a new era of "individualism" where individuals exist apart from their immediate surroundings. It is, in the last analysis, the behaviorist version of an old American myth: the (male) individual as his own class, community, and family—a myth born as the emblem of the western frontier and now reinterpreted to serve the purposes of an urban frontier. At the same time the wish for "security" and the wish for "new experience," earlier presented as antithetical elements of the individual personality, are now reformulated to become a dichotomy between individual and group. "Society desires stability and the individual desires new experience and introduces change. But eventually all new values, all the new cultural elements of a society are the result of the changes introduced by the individual" (234). This was Thomas's solution, in the sphere of social evolution, to the origin of variation, an unresolved riddle in Darwin's theory of evolution. With this reformulation Thomas comes very close to celebrating deviance—a behavioral variation—as the agent of social change. Thomas's apotheosis of individual deviance and rebellion, however, actually contains two distinct programs. One program speaks for the middle classes and preaches a message of liberation, the other speaks of the underclasses and preaches a message of social control. If social evolution is to progress, individuals must "derange the existing norms"; yet ultimately a sharp line separates prostitutes and criminals as "merely destructive of values and organization" from the unconventional woman, the scientist, or the inventor as "temporarily disorganizing but eventually organizing." Here, where unconventionality, sexual immorality, and delinquency meet, where the mature and middle-class woman is made to stand next to the young and lumpenproletarian girl, the previously questioned line separating deviance and norm is reestablished.

V

Thomas never discusses at length the methodology underlying *The Unadjusted Girl*. His instinctive empiricism and suspicion of abstract theorizing made such a self-conscious analysis difficult. However, in the last chapter of the monograph, "Social Influence," somewhat lost amidst the concluding remarks, Thomas did include the fragments of a methodological and poetic position. The unconventional form of the monograph rests on Thomas's belief that "the 'human document,' prepared by the subject, on the basis of memory . . . is capable of presenting life as a connected whole and of showing the interplay of influences" (250). In the personal documents, not in the physical body of the deviant, the former philologist and professor of literature proposed to discover the laws of human behavior. Not unlike the biologist who collects selected organisms, Thomas suggests, the sociologist collects personal documents for the purpose of studying selected personalities. "Ordinary and extraordinary personalities should be included, the dull and the criminal, the philistine and the bohemian. Scientifically the history of dull lives is quite as significant as that of brilliant ones" (253–54). Such documents at once measure social influences and reveal the interplay between internal and external factors, the interconnections of influences, values and attitudes. The first-person document, in the diverse literary forms it takes, is presented by Thomas as the ideal sociological source.

The literary documents that Thomas selects, edits, and arranges in *The Unadjusted Girl* proclaim the existence of people living on the outer margins of the physical and moral city: the restless woman and the deviant girl. These same documents, however, reveal strategies that are far from identical. The personal documents concerning mature women include a large proportion of letters written in the first person and only a small proportion of case histories written in the third. The ratio is inverted with regard to young girls. The written record of their lives is inseparable, in fact, from their arrest and institutional confinement. The mature woman writes herself into a confession, an outburst, a cry for help. The young girl, on the contrary, "is written" into either of two case histories: the unhappy ending of spiraling and everlasting deviance; or the happy ending of illness and cure, corruption and recovery, sin and redemption. Obviously critical of sociological "omniscience," Thomas asked social scientists to forego the practice of ventriloquizing their subjects' thoughts and words and, instead, to exercise their function by selecting, editing, and ordering the documents already in existence. Thomas was compounding into a sociological methodology and a literary practice the skills of journalists, fiction writers, social workers, with those of psychologists, ethnographers, and biologists. Imagined as a collector of literary fragments, the sociologist's task is to make these utterances intelligible through juxtaposition and sequence: such is the author in the age of montage and sociological observation. "I trace the origin of my interest in the document to a long letter picked up on a rainy day in the alley behind my house, a letter from a girl who was taking a training course in a hospital to her father concerning family relationships and discords."[25] More than simply an invitation to leave the safe aseptic walls of academia, Thomas uttered an injunction to go out and find sociological treasures among the urban debris.[26] As it emerges from the *The Unadjusted Girl*, the modern sociological author is an archeologist of the modern self who escavates the records of juvenile courts, girls' bureaus, probationary associations, charity organizations; who digs for fragments among discarded epistolary exchanges and hunts in Miss Lonelyhearts' columns. What he hopes to discover are the secret laws of human personality and behavior.

When Thomas lectured on primitive and modern people, a student recalled years later, a phantasmagoria of colored slips would flip in front of students' eyes. "He brought into the classroom materials from his research recorded on small slips of paper. Bibliographical items were on blue slips, extracts from books and articles on yellow slips, and his own comments on white slips. His custom was to read quotations from the literature upon a given topic, supplementing these by his own inimitable comments. Students in his courses were alternately shocked and thrilled by an extract on behavior widely different from our own or by a penetrating interpretation which showed among the great diversity of human behavior a manifestation of human nature akin if not identical with our own."[27] Montage—the basis of his lectures as of his writing—was inextricable from the nature of modern society; it was the aesthetic form that could both contain and convey the fragmented and dislocated nature of that reality. The colored slips of paper that he brought to his lectures represented the treasures that the sociologist had accumulated during his expeditions to the borders of urban civilization. Through these multicolored fragments Thomas familiarized the "strange," deviant behavior, and estranged the "familiar," middle-class morals, bridging the gap that separates the modern-urban-middle-class-male-self from the primitive, the immigrant, the woman, and the deviant.

VI

> The book is intended for social workers and students of criminology, but the layman will find it a major [sic] thrilling human document than the great majority of fiction. It is the raw material of which fiction is made.[28]
> Bookman, 1923

> This is an anthology of existences. Lives of a few lines or of a few pages, countless misfortunes and adventures,

gathered together in a handful of words . . . for such is
the contraction of things said in these texts that one does
not know whether the intensity which traverses them is
due more to the vividness of the words or to the violence
of the facts which jostle about in them. Singular lives,
those which have become, through I know not what acci-
dents, strange poems:—that is what I wanted to gather
together in a sort of herbarium.[29]

Michel Foucault, "The Life
of Infamous Men," 1977

By using the girl to represent the transition to the modern world as
dangerous but also inevitable and necessary, Thomas also redefined
the female "types" that could be recognized as legitimate and therefore "real."

[F]ifty years ago we recognized, roughly speaking, two types of
women, the one completely good and the other completely bad—
what we now call the old-fashioned girl and the girl who had
sinned and been outlawed. At present we have several intermediate types—the occasional prostitute, the charity girl, the demi-
virgin, the equivocal flapper, and in addition girls with new but social behavior norms who have adapted themselves to all kinds of
work (230–31).

He authorized new female types into sociological and literary existence by allowing their voices to be heard, their stories to be told, their
actions to be understood. Thomas's labeling the cases as responding
to this or that wish is often but a flimsy pretext to let suppressed behavioral discordances be heard. Scattered and, at times, hidden under a layer of "objective" scientific prose—"the sexual passions have
never been completely contained within the framework of marriage"
(68)—Thomas's corrosive strokes recur: "A clean and protected mo-
ron is not far from corresponding to the ideal woman of the Victorian
age" (166).

While ostensibly concerned with the sociological phenomenon of
female deviance, Thomas's study showed how deviance stands for
the "other" possibilities shut off to "normal" women by conventional
Victorian morality. In this study the image of the deviant provides the
weapon with which to criticize the moral order, to make visible the
constructed and constricted nature of its rules and, finally, to redefine

105

a new behavioral order altogether. A relationship of transference joins the unrest of middle-class women and the deviance of lumpenproletarian girls. The delinquent girl exists empirically as a sociological phenomenon to be studied, as a social problem to be solved, and as a social illness to be cured; at the same time she exists metaphorically as that part of the female self that bourgeois morality has ruled out. Around these two figures, as they foreshadow the impending doom of conventional domesticity and Victorian morality, Thomas wrote a double-edged gospel: on the one hand *deviance as freedom* for the middle-class rebellious woman; on the other *deviance as degeneration* to be cured by social workers and psychologists for the young lumpenproletarian girl. While the first will be saved through deviance from the prison-house of bourgeois domesticity, the second must be saved from deviance through a conversion to middle-class female morality. It is perhaps this remarkable ambivalence that has caused Thomas to be reclaimed as a protofeminist by some feminist historians and castigated as sexist by others, two contradictory positions that leave the task of assessing Thomas's work still largely unaccomplished.[30]

From a literary point of view Thomas's study of juvenile female deviance in modern society occupies a central position within the early urban literary tradition, whose most emblematic figure is precisely the girl who leaves the country for the city and there finds not only the excitement of freedom but also the danger of corruption. Stories of girls corrupted by the slum or by the wealth and sophistication of the city are the focus of a tradition that includes such well-known works as Stephen Crane's *Maggie, A Girl of the Streets* (1893) and Theodore Dreiser's *Sister Carrie* (1901). Suggesting at once the promise of regeneration and the threat of degeneration, this archetype of city tales embodies the hopes for freedom, culture, and refinement, and the fears of deviance and deterioration. With *The Unadjusted Girl* Thomas also foreshadowed some of the urban novels of the thirties and early forties and their stories of delinquent young men and women in the urban jungle. Among others, James T. Farrell, Nelson Algren, and Richard Wright would soon create a literature that made room for the subjectivity of the criminal, the delinquent, the prostitute. These novels would transform the prostitute or the delinquent, and by implication the larger class that each symbolizes, from helpless victim of heredity and the environment or passive recipient of social workers' benign intentions to active historical and existential subject.

106

Farrell, Algren, and Wright inherited and built upon the moral rela-tivism that underlies Thomas's theory of deviance. Farrell appropri-ated it to show that Studs' deviance is the product of a prosperous, lower middle-class, upwardly mobile, solid, and stable community. Algren used it to show that sexual "deviance" is freedom not just for the middle-class woman but for the young lumpenproletarian girl as well—freedom from a morality that becomes progressively stricter the more poorly paid the job is. Wright did the same by constructing his own story as a sequence of "deviant" experiences within the differ-ent worlds of the South and the North, the Black church and the Communist Party, and by showing that deviance within a social group is a form of rebellion against the codes and mores of that group.

5

Ethnographers at Home: The Trilogy of Studs Lonigan

The Pullitzer [sic] prize choices are just in today's papers, and they look quite agrarian, to say the least. But I refuse to read prize choices of anything, and in particular, I refuse to read the poetry of Robert Hill, i during the baseball season when I can read the box scores, and the batting averages, not to mention looking at the pictures of [B]abe Ruth and Jimmy Fox in the paper.
—James T. Farrell to Morton D. Zabel, May 8, 1934

The Studs Lonigan[1] trilogy is as much the product of James T. Farrell's personal experience of growing up in the South Side, a well-known Irish neighborhood of Chicago, as it is the product of his escape from it, biographically as a result of family necessity, intellectually as a result of his enrollment at the University of Chicago. The son of a poor Irish American teamster and a domestic servant already burdened with several children, Farrell was still a small child when he was sent away from his parents to live with his grandparents. This event had a clear influence on the writing of Studs Lonigan. Farrell never fully belonged to the wealthier neighborhood in which his grandparents lived and felt himself an outsider there, much as outsiders are the few characters in the novel who speak for the author. Had Farrell moved from one generic Chicago neighborhood to another the move might have been less significant. Instead, he moved from the Near Southwest Side to the South Side of Chicago. He left behind one of the poorest and most congested areas, a "port of entry" for thousands of immigrants, the home of Hull House, and the center of Jane Addams's reform movement. He found himself growing up in an area of second immigrant settlement, of middle class professionals and home owners, a community of Irish American immigrants who had escaped the slum. Farrell moved, in Edgar Branch's words, from poverty and cold, to heat and plumbing.[2] It was in part due to this family decision and to the more intellectual aspirations of his grandparents and uncles that Farrell was able to go to college and acquire the intellectual tools to articulate his personal experience and set it within the sociological and historical changes of his time. As we shall see, Farrell was thus able to do what the characters in *Studs Lonigan* consistently fail to do.

Moving from the urban slum to a residential neighborhood, the three-year-old Farrell was literally following the paradigm of urban mobility that the Chicago sociologists Robert Park and Ernest Burgess were to formulate into a theory of urban change only a few years later. Farrell himself would later encounter these theories in his sociology courses at the University of Chicago. It is precisely these theories that provide the historical backdrop for the events in the Studs Lonigan trilogy, and the intellectual backdrop for the characters' failure to understand the city, social change, history, and their own lives.

Contrary to what critics have stated and readers still tend to imagine, *Studs Lonigan* takes place in the middle-class neighborhood of Farrell's adoptive family and not in the slum of his biological one. This sociological misreading began with the first publication of *Young Lonigan* (1932).[3] That Chicago sociologist Frederic Thrasher should have written the introduction is not surprising given the affinity of concerns between the novel and the sociologist's recent study of gangs.[4] The field of juvenile deviance in the modern city has traditionally been the privileged terrain of the sociologist. Thrasher, however, did more harm than good to the novel as his introduction authorized a long line of misreadings whose influence still continues.

Thrasher placed the novel in "one of those heterogeneous and rap- idly changing neighborhoods of Chicago which have been described scientifically by sociologists as *interstitial*."[5] These areas, he explained, paraphrasing himself and his teachers Robert Park and Ernest Burgess, are "characterized by shifting populations, changing conditions of business and industry, miscellaneous collections of residential properties, successive invasions of varied racial and nationality groups."[6] Thus, Thrasher placed *Studs Lonigan* in the urban slum, the region he himself had but recently studied and labeled an "urban frontier," and framed the events within what Chicago sociologists were fond of calling a "transition" zone, a metaphor for the upward mobility soon to take immigrants elsewhere.

That reviewers should have welcomed *Studs Lonigan* as an exposé on the corruption of youth in the urban alleys is also not surprising given Thrasher's authoritative pronouncements and the rich literary tradition on the theme by the naturalist writers already in existence.[7] Accordingly, one reviewer described the novel as "a thousand-page story of the life and death of a slum boy in Chicago."[8] Another reviewer described the "deadly" environment surrounding Studs and his friends and emphasized "[t]he bleak wide streets, the roaring of the El, the spiritual and actual poverty of more than a million people crowded within a restricted area."[9] The most expressive among these horrified reviewers wrote for the *Saturday Review* that Studs Lonigan

> would have been a failure anywhere but in this cheap, shoddy neighborhood. . . . [Mr. Farrell's] descriptions of the cheap squalid streets of Chicago, the poolroom bums, the smells and sounds of the animal life of vicious children trying to be sports, are vivid and convincing. . . . The effect is of a tenement street on a muggy night in September, replete with body odors, curses, screams of hysterical children, dark dirty whispering in doorways, old women with teary eyes, old men with loosened belts.[10]

Implicitly expressing regret that the likes of Studs should waste their lives in dissipation, these reviewers followed a long tradition as they cast their vote with traditional urban reformers: programs were needed to clean up the slum, empty the poolrooms, and redirect the energies of the youth toward better activities such as the YMCA and the Boy Scouts.[11] In their reading of *Studs Lonigan* critics reproduced the sociological assumptions about the slum and juvenile deviance of their time. They missed the rather crucial detail that the novel is set in a middle-class neighborhood and not in the immigrant slum.

In order to reestablish the socioeconomic status of the Lonigans one does not need the most modern critical technology. In his essay "How Studs Lonigan Was Written" Farrell unambiguously proclaims that Studs is neither a child of the poorest working class nor of the lumpenproletariat.[12] Studs, he writes, is "a normal American boy of Irish-Catholic extraction" and his "social milieu . . . was not, contrary to some misconception, a slum neighborhood." By deciding to set the story in a well-to-do working-class neighborhood, Farrell's goal was to avoid the vulgar economic determinism his critics nevertheless saw in the novel. Had he set the story in the slum, Farrell explains, "it would then have been easy for the reader falsely to place the motivation and causation of the story directly in immediate economic roots." Instead, Farrell deliberately chose "a neighborhood several steps removed from the slum and dire economic want." Accordingly, the Irish-Americans of the trilogy have worked their way "into the American 'petit' bourgeoisie and the American labor aristocracy." Like Studs' father and most of his friends' parents they have dedicated their lives "to work, to advancing themselves, to saving and thrift, to raising their families." Many of them "[own] buildings and [conduct] their own small business enterprises." Some have become "politicians, straw bosses, salesmen, boss craftsmen."[13] Studs himself is "better off" than "many of the other characters in the novel"; he "has a future as his father's successor"; he "works steadily for a number of years." Studs is neither the victim of heredity nor of the environment that some critics have made of him. His economic decline—Farrell has emphasized elsewhere—has a collective rather than an individual origin, since when he loses his savings and his job the cause lies not in personal failure but in the catastrophe of the Depression.[14] Paradoxically, critics have eagerly imposed on the novel the vulgar determinism of heredity and environment Farrell took so much pain to avoid; instead, they have evaded the historical determinism Farrell tightly wove into the events.

If the sociological and historical reading of *Studs Lonigan* has fared poorly, the aesthetic analysis of this original novel has fared even worse. Critics who read the novel as the story of the title hero must fail to understand why the sparse events that comprise the narrative should take so long to unfold. *Young Lonigan* opens as sixteen-year-old Studs and his friends are graduating from St. Patrick Grammar School and covers the events of the summer and fall following their graduation. We follow Studs' aimless summer days with his friends in the streets near Indiana Avenue and Fifty-eighth Street, playing, talking, swimming, fighting, wandering, often bored and yearning for something to happen. The novel also recounts Studs' solitary wanderings,

111

and highlights through the interior monologues his dreams of growing up, his yearnings for fullfillment and self-expression, and, most
important, his inarticulate yet instinctive desires to escape the values
of his parents. At the end of *Young Lonigan* Studs has become a tough
gang youth. He spends his time at the local poolroom, has been suspended from the football team for his irregular school attendance,
and is skipping school more often than not. *The Young Manhood of Studs
Lonigan*, the second volume of the trilogy, focuses almost exclusively
on the tough gang of Prairie Avenue, their activities around the poolroom, their occasional expeditions to the brothel or the dance hall,
and their incursions against Blacks, Jews, foreigners, and other "inferi-
or" races whose members happen to cross their path. *The Young Manhood* also details Studs' physical degeneration through alcohol, smok-
ing, and syphilis, and his moral degeneration through racism and
violence. *The Young Manhood* climaxes in the New Year's party of 1929, a
party that leaves one of the women raped and in a coma and Studs
beaten and drunk in an alley, lying in his vomit. *Judgment Day*, the third
and last volume, dramatizes the results of Studs' profligate life and
amplifies its relation to the national economy. In particular, it follows
the parallel course of the Depression, which reduces the Lonigans to
poverty, and the gradual failing of Studs' health, which leads to his
premature death.

Whereas Farrell's philosophical leanings toward pragmatism on
the one hand and Marxism on the other have received some attention, his sociological debts and orientation has failed to engage the
attention of scholars in any sustained form.[15] As his biographer Edgar
Branch has made clear, Farrell was more than superficially acquainted
with the work of the Chicago urban sociologists.[16] As an undergradu-
ate Farrell went to the University of Chicago. At the university Farrell
concentrated on literature and the social sciences and took courses
with some of the most significant American social thinkers of the early twentieth century: Veblen, Dewey, and Mead, among others.[17]

Among the student papers Ernest Burgess was fond of saving there
remains one by Farrell. This is a term paper, written for the course
"Social Pathology, 1925–26" and entitled "The Dance Marathons."[18]
The essay is generally moralistic and censorious in tone and point of
view—"[the marathon dancer's] activity is the product of a chaotic
and anarchic society"; "a marathon is unqualifiedly stupid, degrading,
sordid"; "the dance hall, the brothel, free sexual experience, pool
rooms, movies and the like tend to provide the proper object of gratification . . . [for the] contestants [most of whom] are poor or mem-

bers of the petit bourgeoisie"[19]—and it contains the same clichés concerning popular culture and modern culture that were predominant within and without sociology—"the mechanistic life of modern times," "impulses have been mechanically chained." The essay is interesting as it illustrates in detail some of the forms of observation, thinking, and writing that contributed to Farrell's fictional work. Even more important, the document measures the distance that Farrell had to travel in order to depict Studs Lonigan and his friends, their poolroom and street corner bantering—a social sphere not unlike that of the marathon dancers—not just as "degrading, uncivilized, unwholesome, animalistic, disgusting" but as complex, ambivalent, sympathetic, and, in short, human. To what extent the Chicago sociologists themselves contributed to this more mature understanding is a question that should at least be raised even if it cannot yet be answered.

Farrell's own description of the experiments that led to the writing of *Studs Lonigan* indicates the methodological affinity between the novel and the work of Chicago sociologists. In his introduction to the 1938 edition Farrell recalls his attempts

> to describe dusty and deserted streets, streets corners, miserable homes, poolrooms, brothels, dance halls, taxi dances, bohemian sections, express offices, gasoline filling stations, scenes laid in slum districts. The characters were boys, boys' gangs, drunkards, Negroes, expressmen, homosexuals, immigrants and immigrant landlords, filling- station attendants, straw bosses, hitch hikers, bums, bewildered parents. Most of the manuscripts were written with the ideal of objectivity in mind.[20]

Years later, in a letter to his long-time friend Meyer Schapiro, the well-known art historian at Columbia University and a militant leftist of the 1930s, Farrell recalled that for him going to the University of Chicago had been like moving to "another city, another world, almost another continent."[21] Farrell had been fully aware of the originality of the work being done by Chicago sociologists. As he wrote to Schapiro, "[I]n sociology we were beginning to devise the Chicago method of going out and asking whores, with all due respect to scientific methods, why they were whores. It was, as you can see, a tremendous time for learning in the portals of Chicago."[22]

References scattered throughout Farrell's writings, especially in his nonfiction, also record the author's ongoing interest in sociology. Well into the 1950s, long after the sociological thirties and, in fact, in response to the New Critics' attacks against the "social" concerns and responsibilities of literature, Farrell was still paying homage to the Chicago school of urban sociology:

> University of Chicago sociologists were among the pioneers in shifting the course of American sociology from the plane of theory to that of empiricism. They embarked on a search for facts, and they sought these in many social areas, most of them marginal. Various sociologists, such as Frederick Thrasher, Nels Anderson, Paul Creecy [sic], and others, studied the Bohemian area, the rooming-house districts of Chicago, the taxi dance halls, the boys gangs of various neighborhoods, the West Madison or Bowery section of Chicago, and so on. They attempted to develop the technique of the interview and to rely rather heavily on case histories. Also, they went to newspapers for data. . . . Dr. Walter C. Reckless, a University of Chicago sociologist, in his book *Vice in Chicago*, attempted to establish a co-relation figure between the number of brothels and the number of roadhouses and taverns or saloons in a chosen "interstitial" area in the city of Chicago.[23]

The "search for facts," the focus on "marginality," the "interview" and "case history" methods, anyone familiar with *Studs Lonigan* must notice, are as characteristic of Chicago sociology as they are of the trilogy itself. They are, in fact, what is most original in the novel.

Critics who have discussed Farrell's sociological aesthetics appear divided in their evaluations. Many have condemned his work as "less than art" and his sociological perspective has frequently been their target. Representative of this group is Eunice Clark who, reviewing *Studs Lonigan* in 1935, remarked upon Farrell's "massed description," his use of "every detail, to the color of a girl's drawers and the most minute indecency of a boy's conversation." She concluded that "Mr. Farrell's artistic integrity is impeccable, but while his conscientious inclusiveness would be admirable in a *sociologist doing case histories*, it is old fashioned and bad fashioned in art, though alas, too common in the quasi-art of naturalistic fiction."[24] The overall assessment on this side of the critical fence has been, in the words of another critic, that Farrell might be "an earnest sociologist" but not "a good artist."[25] Aware of the antisociological prejudices filtering the evaluation of his work in the United States in the 1930s Farrell wrote to a friend: "I am sending you a copy of the French edition of *Young Lonigan*. No French reviewer has said well this is after all not art or a novel, but a note book so I have developed a high respect for la douce France."[26]

A few critics have actually praised *Studs Lonigan* for its sociological orientation, which, one of them argues, makes this work more "scientific" and therefore more "real" and "true." For Richard Mitchell, for example, *Studs Lonigan* is a "social document . . . of much greater value to mankind than the work of art, for the trilogy is what scientists would call a collection of observed data made with the intention of forming hypotheses."[27] This is praise that Farrell himself might not have found so acceptable.

Between the two extremes is the more ambivalent position of critics who at once acknowledge and deny the sociological quality of Farrell's fiction. Blanche Gelfant finds it necessary, in order to praise *Studs Lonigan*, to deny that Farrell writes "sociologically," even though, she perceptively admits, his novels are a kind of aesthetic correlative of the case history, since they collect data about an individual's past and show how he became what he is.[28] Ann Douglas notes, in a similar vein, that "a great deal has been made of Farrell's involvement with sociological theory and its visible effect on *Studs Lonigan*." She too admits that "sociology . . . helped to form Farrell's literary technique." And yet, she goes on to add, "it is less true to say that Farrell wrote sociological fiction than to say that he wrote about people so enmeshed and entrapped in the static stereotypes of their culture that their lives *are* sociology."[29]

There is more than a little truth in each of these remarks. Farrell's prose is indeed "a collection of observed data" and "details" in the spirit of the social sciences; Studs' story *has* the same uneventful quality as case histories; the dozens of characters that animate the trilogy, including Studs himself, *are* recognizable sociological types. The critical issue, however, is to avoid the easy recourse to cliché distinctions between science and art, facts and fiction, truth and imagination and to ask instead, first, in what sense does Farrell write "sociologically"? Second, in what sense is *Studs Lonigan* analogous to a sociological "case history" and what are the consequences? And last, to what extent are the weaknesses and strengths of the trilogy beyond Farrell's personal aesthetics and instead part of a "world view" that Farrell shares with a specific sociological tradition?

I

In a novel like *Studs Lonigan*, which is so reluctant to accommodate its material within a traditional narrative frame, it is important to take notice of those episodes, rare as they may be, that in spite of the novel's antinarrative posture do provide some kind of structure. The two monologues of Studs' father, Pat Lonigan, function as a beginning and an end for a story whose essential nature as the life history of an individual and the ethnography of a group defies narrative form altogether.

Old Lonigan's first monologue is a combination of semiphilosophical reflections over the nature of life and time and shuttle-like movements between his past, family, friends, the city and the present, personal success, his children, the neighborhood. As his family prepares for the graduation of Studs' class at St. Patrick's Grammar School Old Lonigan sits on the back porch of his house, lost in self-satisfied nostalgia. We learn how poor his family was when "he and his brother had to stay home from school because they had no shoes," and when they lived in a house that "was more like a barn or a shack" and "was so cold they had to sleep in their clothes" (YL 13). At the time Old Lonigan's family lived around Blue Island and Archer Avenue, in an area called Canaryville, not far from where Farrell himself was born and the center of one of Chicago's poorest immigrant slums. As he reflects on "Old Man Time" and on how "[t]hings just change," Old Lonigan's thoughts turn toward the city and the radical changes that have transformed it since his youth. "Chicago was nothing like it used to be, when over around St. Ignatius Church and back of the yards were white men's neighborhoods, and Prairie Avenue was a tony street where all the swells lived . . . and the niggers and whores had not roosted around Twenty-second Street, and Fifty-eighth Street was nothing but a wilderness." (YL 14) Carried away by the recollection, he also remembers his friends, his gang, his siblings. He remembers "[t]he boys that hung out at Kieley's saloon, and later around the saloon that Padney Flaherty ran, and Luke O'Toole's place on Halsted" (YL 13). The recollection of his "old gang" friends inspires a stream of elegiac thoughts:

> Many of them were dead, like poor Paddy McCoy, Lord have mercy
> on his soul, whose ashes rested in a drunkard's grave at Potter's
> Field. . . . There was Heinie Schmaltz, the boy with glue on his fin-
> gers, the original sticky-fingered kid. And poor Mrs. Schmaltz, Lord
> have mercy on her poor soul. God was merciful to take her away
> before she could know that her boy went up the road to Joliet on a
> ten-year jolt for burglary. And there was Dinny Gorman. . . . Din-
> ny had made a little dough, but he was, after all, only a shyster law-

yer and a cheap politician. He had been made ward committeeman because he had licked everybody's boots. And there were his own brothers. Bill had run away to sea at seventeen and nobody had ever heard from him again. Jack, Lord have mercy on his soul, had always been a wild and foolish fellow . . . and he'd been killed in Cuba. . . . And Mike had run off and married a woman older than himself. . . . And Joe was a motorman. And Catherine, well, he hadn't even better think of her. Letting a traveling salesman get her like that, and expecting to come home with her fatherless baby; and then going out and becoming . . . a scarlet woman. His own sister, too! (YL 16–17)

A prose poem in the style of the *Spoon River Anthology*, this passage projects Pat Lonigan's present success against the backdrop of his own past and of recent American history. In particular, it reveals Pat Lonigan's achieved American dream to be an exception at best. He has made it into the world of middle-class respectability, but he has left behind friends and family, some of whom became thieves, alcoholics, and prostitutes, and several of whom died in their youth. And those whose fate was less unfortunate did not climb high on the social ladder.

Coming from a family of poor immigrants and brought up in a slum neighborhood, Old Lonigan perceives his own success as the result of personal stamina and will. The connections between different forms of social change—urban change and personal success, urban decay and upward mobility, economic success and physical degeneration—are invisible to Old Lonigan. He can at once tell himself—after Peter Finley Dunne—"who will tell what makes wan man a thief, and another man a saint?" (YL 17) while he also reassures himself that only his own will is responsible for his success.

While change in his personal life is perceived as a source of wealth, change in the physical and social space that surrounds him is perceived as a threat to be resisted.

When he'd bought this building, Wabash Avenue had been a nice, decent, respectable street for a self-respecting man to live with his family. But now, well, the niggers and kikes were getting in. . . . And when they got into a neighborhood property values went blooey. He'd sell and get out . . . and when he did, he was going to get a pretty penny on the sale. (YL 19)

117

By separating social change from individual change, Lonigan can sit on his back porch and bemoan the changes that are transforming the city under his very eye even as he congratulates himself for the benefits derived from those changes.

His understanding of his own children and of youth in general is similarly split. For Old Lonigan, the girls who are playing in the street behind his house and telling each other to go "to hell" must be "poor little girls with fathers and mothers who didn't look after them or bring them up in the right home atmosphere; and if they were Catholic girls, they probably weren't sent to the sisters' school" (YL 12). The sight of a boy in the street, like his reminiscences of the past, triggers in Old Lonigan "a vague series of impulses, wishes and nostalgias" (YL 13) and the wistful reflection that "it would be great to be a kid again" (YL 13). Yet when a group of children in the street reminds him of Bill, he begins to wonder "what do kids talk about?" and finds himself unable to answer.

> He wondered, because a person's own childhood got so far away from him he forgot most of it, and sometimes it seemed as if he'd never been a kid himself, he forgot the way a kid felt, the thoughts of a kid. He sometimes wondered about Bill. Bill was a fine boy. You couldn't find a better one up on the graduating stage at St. Patrick's tonight, no more than you would see a finer girl than Frances. But sometimes he wondered just what Bill thought about. (YL 17)

More consciously than Old Lonigan and not much later Jane Addams reflected on the same questions and concerns that worried him. "Youth," she remarks, in her 1925 address "The Spirit of Youth Today," has become a "foreign region," especially for "those of us who go back to the Mid-Victorian or early Victorian in our experience."[30] The same sensations of estrangement inform Frederic Thraher's brooding, in *The Gang*, over the alienation of adults from youths:

> [I]t is hard for the grown-up with all his responsibilities, and practical necessities to retain an understanding of the boy's imaginative outlook on life. . . . He loses sympathetic touch with youth and becomes a scoffer at the precious dreams and sentiments which are such an essential part of boyhood. On this account he rarely has a complete understanding of the boy.[31]

118 Addams and Thrasher express the same preoccupation that Old Lonigan feels in the opening monologue. His anxiety about his oldest son Bill, his wondering "just what Bill thought about" resonate, as do Addams's and Thrasher's words, with a larger historical and cultural

anxiety about youth that is also characteristic of F. Scott Fitzgerald, Ben Hecht, Floyd Dell, the early Dos Passos, Hemingway, all of them, incidentally, midwestern modernists. The perception of youth as a mysterious and foreign region metaphorically expresses the perception of a somber and hazardous future, which youth obviously represents, and inevitably of the past, which Studs Lonigan insistently scrutinizes.

In the opening monologue of Old Lonigan Farrell compresses with great skill the complex facts of racism, economics, urban change, and history that constitute the essence of twentieth-century America. Crudely expressed in Lonigan's thoughts is the myth of the American dream and endless upward mobility, a myth that is made less out of hard work than real estate speculations. In racist and unsophisticated language Old Lonigan describes yet does not understand the same phenomena that the urban sociologists were studying at the University of Chicago at the same time. The city, sociologists were arguing, is an animated map of history whose secret codes people like Old Lonigan ignore, at their own expense. The reading that the city yields to them is a paradoxical mixture of nostalgia and amnesia: the past is either grim, marked by poverty, early deaths, privation, or the object of nostalgia; "Them was the days," Pat Lonigan repeats at intervals, "[a]nd now that they were over, there was something missing, something gone from a fellow's life" (YL 13). Likewise, his view of the present must remain split between complacency over his success—Lonigan is the proud owner of his house and business, has been a good father, husband, Catholic and American—and anxiety—Lonigan has no memory of his own childhood and now must sit in puzzlement wondering "just what Bill thought about." Old Lonigan's amnesia about his own youth, the second main theme of the monologue, correlates with his inability to understand his own life, his movement out of the slum and away from poverty, as part of the larger processes of history. Having obliterated the past, he has made of the present a mystery. As a result the city now appears to him as a mysterious space that changes for no apparent reason, and youth as an impenetrable stage of life. Having lost insight over what happened to the friends of his youth and to his siblings, Old Lonigan has lost the ability to understand both his children and the future.

Old Lonigan's blindness to the city and youth establishes a pattern that, in the course of the novel, turns out to be characteristic of the Irish American community. To that community the story of Studs

119

Lonigan is addressed. The narrator's detached, clinical observation of the city and the gang stands as Farrell's challenge to those who, like Old Lonigan, have surrendered the past to nostalgia and the future to false expectations.

II

After the title character himself and his gang, Chicago is the most pervasive presence in the trilogy of *Studs Lonigan*. Farrell's distinctive style in representing the neighborhood, his insistence on the details of that space being that style's most characteristic trait, should be labeled "topographic realism."

The spatial center of the trilogy is an area that, from the point of view of Studs and his gang, is a half-mile square, and has at its center Fifty-eighth Street between Prairie and Indiana Avenue. As even the most superficial reader must notice, the trilogy is saturated with topographic details about each corner, block, street, and alley. Charlie Bathcellar's poolroom, where the youths gather, is "two doors east of the elevated station," which is "midway between Calumet and Prairie Avenue" and across the street from the barber shop. The fireplug, the outdoor gathering place, is on the northeast corner of Fifty-eighth Street and Prairie Avenue, in front of the drug store and across the street from Sternberg's cigar store. A few steps west, between Prairie Avenue and Indiana, is Schreiber's ice cream parlor, and a few yards further, at the intersection with Indiana, are Levin's Drug Store and a vacant lot. One can sit down with pen and paper and, based on the information contained in *Studs Lonigan*, reproduce a quasi-photographic image of the streets and stores in Studs' neighborhood.

Events never happen just anywhere, nor do people just meet on any street or walk in some general direction. During one of Studs' many strolls around the neighborhood, to give a typical example, we first follow the boy as he walks "north along Indiana Avenue" and fantasizes about becoming a war hero. He then pauses "under the elevated structure at Fifty-ninth and Indiana" and, after reciting the pledge, turns "down the alley between Indiana and Prairie" as he continues to fantasize about war, heroism, violence, and death. Having just made his way into the history books of the yet-to-be-declared war, Studs proceeds to walk from the alley "down to the northeast side of Fifty-eighth and Prairie." Here he notices that "[a]t the elevated station, a half block down" many people are crowding around the

120

newspaper man. He begins to move in that direction when he is called by Red Kelly, who is standing "in front of Frank Hertzog's shoe repair shop, about fifty yards or so down from the corner" and so on (YM 5–8).

The Chicago of James T. Farrell is a living and intrusive presence, not merely through its macroscopic symbols, the Yards, the Loop, the Lake, etc., but in its microscopic details, the block, the street, the corner, the store.[32] The novels of Charles Dickens are also inseparable from a city that is unequivocally recognizable as London. And yet the identity of Dickens's London derives from its landmarks, never from the minute details of its neighborhoods. The neighborhood is the heart of the trilogy in a much deeper sense than even the Lower East Side in Abraham Cahan's stories or the Battery in *Maggie, A Girl of the Streets*. More than just a background presence, Chicago permeates *Studs Lonigan* not only symbolically but ethnographically, empirically, and microscopically as well.

Ann Douglas addresses the nature of Farrell's city when she writes that "Farrell's city, unlike Dreiser's, never functions as a metropolis; it is a collection of warring provinces, a conglomerate of uncongenial if similar suburbs."[33] Indeed, the metropolis around the neighborhood impinges on it yet never substantially alters its provincial insularity. The Chicago of *Studs Lonigan*, in fact, is composed of a myriad of Main streets; it is a cultural paradox: a metropolis made up of little towns. It is this fragmented Chicago that Farrell indirectly evokes when he writes, "The neighborhoods of Chicago in which I grew up possessed something of the character of a small town. They were little worlds of their own."[34]

Farrell's "little worlds," which are more than just a figure of speech, invoke two important literary traditions that have focused on the provinciality of the petit bourgeoisie, traditions whose influence Farrell has repeatedly acknowledged: the one exemplified by Sherwood Anderson and Sinclair Lewis's novels on this side of the Atlantic and the other exemplified by Balzac, Flaubert, Tolstoy on the opposite side. Heir of these important traditions, *Studs Lonigan* generously contributes to the novel's ongoing critique against the political and religious bigotry of the petit bourgeoisie, the intellectual narrow-mindness of the "provinces," and the cultural claustrophobia of small-townocracy. 121

Important as these literary referents are in locating Farrell in a context that is not restrictively urban-naturalist, and in highlighting the small-town neighborhood, as the cultural and spatial center of the novel, they still do not explain the obsessive insistence of Farrell's narrator on the topographic details of the city. Farrell's representation of the neighborhood as a self-enclosed "little world" is as much part of a literary tradition as it is part of a sociological one: a tradition that revolves around the theory that the city is a continent of little distinct worlds to be explored topographically and ethnographically. The empirically detailed character of Chicago in *Studs Lonigan* is inseparable from the theories and methods developed by the Chicago sociologists during the first decades of this century. The essence of the metropolis, its very structure, Park had explained, is to be composed of "cities within cities," to be a "mosaic of little worlds which touch but do not interpenetrate."[35] Articulating a view of the city as a cultural continent, these metaphors encapsulate ideas that inform both the content and the form of *Studs Lonigan*: first, the idea that sociologists should become the anthropologists of their own culture; second, the view that the city is a microcosm of modern society; and finally, the notion that the neighborhood is a microcosm of the modern city.

In true ethnographic fashion the narrator of *Studs Lonigan* proclaims that he has been there but also that he can write about that world because he is no longer there. Farrell's narrator with his "objective," detached, social scientist's gaze, stands as the antithesis of Old Lonigan. Like most other characters Old Lonigan moves within and observes the city without ever noticing it. When he does notice that the city is changing he misses the significance of those changes, lost as he is in his desire to bring back the past, and engulfed by his refusal to ever let go of it. Farrell's narrator, on the other hand, observes and records, and does so with a vengeance accomplishing what Danny O'Neill sets out to do in one of the interchapters when he decides to "destroy the Old World with his pen." Sitting alone at night in the gas station where he works, Danny vows that "some day, he would drive this neighborhood and all his memories of it out of his consciousness with a book" (YM 369–72). *Studs Lonigan* is that book, a book that both purged Farrell's memory of the neighborhood and rescued that same neighborhood from oblivion.

III

Studs Lonigan's debt to Frederic Thrasher's ethnography of youth gangs illustrates well the experimental nature of Farrell's work. Thrasher had claimed that gangs are culturally part of the surrounding community and had explained theft, for example, as in part justified and excused by the community around the youth. At the same time, and incongruously, Thrasher had divorced gang culture from the larger social environment by treating the gang as an aberration, as an illness to be cured, and as a social epidemic that from the slum threatens to spread over the city. Gangs had been understood as both "frontier tribes" within the city and a veritable "empire" that from the outside threatens to take it over.[36]

The trilogy of *Studs Lonigan* is as much a conventional novel, the story of Studs' dissipation and death, as it is a sociological novel, the ethnography of a youth gang in Chicago, of its culture, beliefs and activities, and the case history of one of its representative members, a record of his desires, thoughts, fears, frustrations. The reader who disregards the sociological intent and method of Farrell's novel must fail to understand why the gang receives as much attention as the hero himself and what kind of literary method Farrell was exploring in the dozens of sketches of gang life that form a substantial portion of the novel.

The depiction of the gang consists less of the youths' activities than of their dialogues and gatherings, their idle afternoons wondering what to do and asking what time it is. Farrell chooses to present the gang through the texture of these uneventful afternoons. Similarly the story of Studs is composed of few events—the fights, the walk in the park with Lucy, the drunks, etc.—and by a large number of undramatic episodes, his mental yarns, his solitary walks, his fears and fantasies.

In *Studs Lonigan*, much as in *The Gang*, gangs are ubiquitous to the urban landscape and to the world of the adolescent and young man. Thrasher had opened his discussion with the alarmed news that "No less tha 1,313 gangs have been discovered in Chicago and its environs!" and then claimed that "approximately one-tenth of Chicago's 350,000 boys between the ages of ten and twenty are subject to the demoralizing influence of gangs."[37] These twenty-five thousand youth belong to "childhood gangs" that meet "on the streets, in yards, or in other open spaces of the neighborhood;" they belong to "adolescent gangs" that tend to meet "on a special street corner, in a prairie, or in a cave shack, or barn"; they belong to "older adolescent gangs" that have their meeting place "in a poolroom, saloon or store of some sort"; finally, they belong to "adult gangs" that take the form of "a club" or a "criminal" organization.[38]

Every block of Farrell's fictional neighborhood has a gang. Indiana Avenue and Fifty-eight Street is the gathering place for the gang of "punks," with whom Studs' younger brother spends his time, and for the adolescent gang to which Studs belongs early in the novel. A gang of tougher and older adolescents and soon-to-be young men meets at the corner of Prairie Avenue and Fifty-ninth Street or at the local poolrom, where they eagerly rub elbows with a group of older men. These are men who, probably since their youth, have never stopped their drinking and carousing at the saloon. They belong to the generation of Old Lonigan, who in his youth also used to spend time at the poolroom with his gang. Instead of leaving the gang and poolroom for a conventional life of work, church, marriage, and family these men, those who survive, have chosen a life of permanent adolescent dissipation that slowly destroys them. The nearby blocks and neighborhoods are also populated with gangs with whom Studs and his friends occasionally collide. When the Lonigans move to a new neighborhood, there too, Studs finds a new street corner and a new gang, even though, he muses, "no other corner would ever be the same" (YM 382). And by the end of the novel, after most of the Irish families have moved out of the neighborhood, we discover on the old corners new gangs of Black children and young men doing precisely what Studs and his friends have done before them.

Gangs are not just spatially contiguous but also culturally interlocking. The neighborhood kids admire their gang peers; the older boys envy and imitate the tough young men; these, in turn, find their models among the older saloon men who probably remember as little as Old Lonigan of what it was like to be a kid. In Farrell's fictional neighborhood, then, as in Thrasher's sociological region, gangs are the main social group and space available to youth outside of their families and outside of the institutionalized spaces of dances and missions provided by the church and the school.

Studs Lonigan focuses on two main themes of gang culture, toughness and sex, as they find expression in the language and activites of the gang and in the privacy of Studs' mind. In the first part of the narrative Studs spends most of his time with the Indiana Avenue gang, which consists primarily of the unruly but healthy adolescents who attend St. Patrick Grammar School. It includes, among others, "Jim Clayburn who did his homework every night," "Dan and Bill Donoghue and Tubby and all the guys in his bunch, and you couldn't find a better gang of guys to pal with this side of Hell," "goofy young Danny

124

O'Neill, the dippy punk who couldn't be hurt or made cry, no matter how hard he was socked, because his head was made of hard stuff like iron and ivory marble," as well as Vinc Curley, TB McCarthy, Reardon, and Weary Reilly (YL 5–6).

Merely sixteen, these adolescents spend their time together looking tough and talking tougher. During the graduation ceremony they gather in the school lavatory to smoke, practice their tough poses, and remember how tough they have been with their teachers—" 'I'm glad I'm through with Battling Bertha. . . . You had to fight with her, didn' cha?' said Studs. 'Well, the old cow went to swing on me, and I told her hands off. No sir! I'm not lettin' no one take a poke at me and get away with it.' " Here they also imagine how tough they will be with their parents—" 'Are you going to high school? . . . Schools are so much horse apple,' said Weary. 'I don't want to go, but the gaffer wants me to, I guess,' said Studs. 'Well, I ain't goin', and my old man can lump it if he don't like it,' said Weary' " (YL 38–42). Behind the conventional and almost formulaic nature of their words is a genuine if unconscious impulse to reject authority, be it of the church, school, or parents.

If their claims to toughness are sustained by what the boys say, the hierarchy of toughness within the gang is strictly determined by the ability to fight. Central to the first volume is the confrontation between Studs and Weary Reilly. The fight illustrates both the gang's code of physical valor and Studs' excellent physical shape at the beginning of his sixteenth summer and of the novel.

The eventual victory over Reilly brings Studs renewed prestige. He becomes "the conquering hero," "the champ of the neighborhood," "the cock of the walk" (YL 86–7). This fills Studs with satisfaction.

> Studs told himself he had been waiting for things like this to happen a long time; now they were happening, and life was going to be a whole lot more . . . more fun, and it was going to make everything just jake; and he was going to be an important guy, and all the punks would look up to him and brag to other punks that they knew him; and he would be . . . well, in the limelight. (YL 87)

The gang is the main reference point of Studs' subjectivity, and it is the admiration of the other youths that makes his ego swell.

The youths' growing awareness of sex uneasily complements their cult of toughness. It is typical of Farrell's method that the youth's awkward sexuality emerges through routine and undramatic exchanges.

In one of these scenes Studs, who, as usual, has been haunting the neighborhood looking for some excitement, finally encounters his gang friends. The scene takes the form of a verbatim record of "kid trivialities" and the jargon of which their conversation is made. The scene opens with Danny O'Neill, one of the neighborhood punks, volunteering some gossip on Three-Star Hennessey, another neighborhood youth:

> "Spill it," said Dan Donoghue.
> "Well, it's funny; it's a good one," said Danny. Danny laughed like the goofy punk that he was.
> "Well, for Christ sake, out with it before we take your pants down," said Johnny O'Brien, who acted as if he were a big guy like Studs and Dan.
> "Well, Hennessey was under the Fifty-eighth Street elevated station . . . and gee, it's funny!"
> "Well, then, shoot it while you're all together," said Studs.
> "Well, he was under the Fifty-eighth Street elevated station. . . . lookin' up through the cracks to see if he could get an eyeful when the women walked up and down stairs.
>
> "Yeh, and we know what he was doing. That's nothing new," said Jonny.
>
> "But this time it's funny . . . You see, a dick caught him and shagged him down the alley. Three-Star got away, because nobody could catch him anyway, but the guys told me it was funny, him legging it with his stockings hanging . . . and he didn't even have time to button up," said Danny.
> They gabbed and laughed. Bill Donoghue interrupted the discussion on this latest of Hennessey's exploits to say:
> "That's a warning for you, TB."
> "Say . . . I don't do that," said TB.
> "No!" said Studs ironically.
> "What you got them pimples on your forehead from?" asked Johnny O'Brien.
> "Why, you're getting so weak that young O'Neill here can toss you," Studs said. (YL 89–90)

126   Within the gang the boys find room to express their shame-filled fantasies and prudish curiosities. And within the gang they can parody the messages of repression they receive in church and at home. When Studs' father decides to impart a lesson on sexual hygiene to his son, the result is catastrophic at best:

> The old man's face reddened. He started to speak, paused, blushed
> and said: "Bill, you're getting older now, an'. . . .I'm your father and
> it's a father duty to instruct the son, and you see now if you get a
> little itch . . . well you don't want to start . . . rubbin' yourself. . .
> you know what I mean . . . because such things are against nature,
> and they make a person weak and his mind weak and are liable
> even to make him crazy, and they are a sin against God." (YL 163)

Confronted with this mixture of "nature" and "religion," and with the
repressed sexuality of his father's inarticulate lesson, "Studs felt self-
conscious; he was ashamed of his body; he needed air and sunlight"
(YL 163). At home the youths are treated as innocent and asexual children and even the most indirect sexual reference is hidden behind a
veil of shame and blushing faces. In church their minds are filled with
hellish flames and truculent devils. Within the gang their sexual curiosity finds respite from the asphyxiation of their Catholic upbringing.

Studs' often discussed walk in the park with Lucy provides another
high moment of his sixteenth summer. Specifically, the episode dramatizes the conflict between the street and gang ethos of toughness
and the private world of romance. The scene climaxes in the park,
among the branches of a high oak.

> "It's so lovely here," she said, leaning toward him, puckering her
> lips. Studs looked at her. Without knowing what he was doing, he
> kissed her. It was swell to kiss Lucy. . . . And it made him feel . . .
> all-swell. . . . And he had a feeling that this was a turning point in
> his life, and from now on everything was going to be jake. (YL 112)

Studs' romantic ecstasy is interrupted when he remembers his gang
friends. "If some of the kids knew what he was doing and thinking,
they'd laugh their ears off at him. Well, if they did, let 'em; he could
kick a lot of mustard out of the whole bunch of 'em" (YL 113). Later
that evening, as Studs reminisces in his room, once more the gang's
ethos of toughness collides with his softer side and threatens to dissolve the romantic haze that still hovers over him. "He sat on his bed,
and contemplated the fact of Lucy. He told himself that he was one
hell of a Goddamn goof: he sat on the bed, thinking of her and becoming more and more of a hell of a Goddamn goof" (YL 115).

The fight with Weary and the romance with Lucy illustrate what is 127
at the center of many episodes in *Young Lonigan*: the conflict between
wanting to be tough and yearning for love. It also establishes the role
of the gang as Studs' primary social, cultural, and psychological universe. Within the gang Studs comes to life as a character. His con-

sciousness shapes and reshapes itself within the gang, just as through the gang the cultural precepts of the community are filtered into the youth's social outlook. Studs' perception of himself and of the world around him is molded within the gang rather than within his family, the church, or the school.

In Thrasher's discussion of the gang's role and function one finds sociologically expressed the motivation for what happens to Studs. Thrasher regards the gang as the boys' attempt "to create a society for themselves" and as a social group that, "supplanting home, school, church, and vocation, becomes the primary interest of the boy[s]."[39] He also emphasizes the gang's role as the natural attraction for the "active boy without an outlet for his energies," who as a result becomes "a restless boy."[40] Finally, Thrasher cites "the humdrum of routine experience" that enable the gang to become an "escape from, or compensatation for monotony."[41]

To a large extent *Young Lonigan* dramatizes these ideas. Studs' summer begins with great hopes "to grow up," "to become the white hope of the world," to "become a big guy," to be "independent." It turns into a succession of restless pacings around the neighborhood, yearning for something to happen, "feeling that he wanted something, and he didn't know what it was. He couldn't stay put in one place, and he kept shifting about, doing all sorts of awkward things, looking far away, and not being satisfied with anything he did" (YL 124).

The victory over Reilly and the conquest of Lucy's kiss temporarily fulfill Studs' desire for excitement but soon leave him yearning to escape the boredom and emptiness that the summer had promised to dispel. During one of these afternoons Studs runs into the youths of the nearby and tougher Prairie Avenue gang and after a successful fight with Red Kelly, the toughest one of the group, he is invited to join. Much as before Studs' moods soar high: "Studs felt pretty good again. He felt powerful. Life was still opening up for him, as he'd expected it to, and it was still going to be a great summer. And it was a better day than he imagined. A sun was busting the sky open, like Studs Lonigan busted guys in the puss. It was a good day" (YL 131). The chapter, which opens with Studs yearning for something unexpressed and unclear, closes with Studs happy once more, newly initiated into the world of tough gang youth, and no longer alone. "'What'll we do?' asked Davey. 'What'll we do?' asked Paulie. 'Let's do something,' said Studs. 'Let's,' said Davey. They walked along. Studs took a drag on Davey's butt. Paulie got between them, putting an arm

128

around each of their shoulders. *They were a picture,* walking along, Paulie with his fat hips, Davey with his bow legs, and small, broad Studs" (YL 131, my emphasis). The episode is a turning point in the life of Studs Lonigan as it dramatizes the end of his career as a neighborhood kid and the beginning of another as a tough young man. At the beginning of the next chapter we observe the results of Studs' new membership.

> Studs Lonigan, looking tough, sat on the fireplug before the drug store on the northeast corner of Fifty-eighth and Prairie. . . . His jaw was swollen with tobacco. . . . He sat, squirting juice from the corner of his mouth, rolling the chewed wad from jaw to jaw. His cap was pulled over his right eye in hard-boiled fashion. He had a piece of cardboard in the back of his cap to make it square, just like all the tough Irish from Wentworth Avenue, and he had a bushy Regan haircut. (YL 135)

"Portrait of the young man as a gang member" would be an appropriate caption. The image of the three youths at the end of one chapter, Paulie in the middle, Davey and Studs at his sides, and the image of Studs himself at the beginning of the next chapter are, in fact, verbal photographs in the ethnographic mode. They are the verbal equivalents of the photographs that generously illustrate Thrasher's *The Gang.*

The physical center of the Praire Avenue gang is the poolroom, that most castigated place of philantropists and social workers. Farrell's narrator, very much in the style of social observation, describes it as follows:

> The poolroom was two doors east of the elevated station, which was midway between Calumet and Prairie Avenues. It had barber poles in front, and its windows bore the scratched legend, Bathcellar's Billiard Parlor and Barber Shop. The entrance was a narrow slit, filled with the forms of the young men, while from inside came the click of billiard balls and the talk of other young men. . . . The poolroom was long and narrow; it was like a furnace, and its air was weighted with smoke. Three of the six tables were in use, and in the rear a group of lads sat around a card table, playing poker. The scene thrilled Studs, and he thought of the time he could come in and play pool and call Charlie Bathcellar by his first name. (YL 147–50)

129

Standing just outside the poolroom, Studs is midway between two worlds. As he looks toward the street "Studs noticed the people passing. Some of them were fat guys and had the same sleepy look his old man always had when he went for a walk. . . . Those old dopey-looking guys must envy the gang here, young and free like they were" (YL 152). In the poolroom Studs thinks he has found a haven from the boredom and conventionality of his parents' life. He has found vicarious parental figures among the poolroom men who drink, swear, and tell dirty jokes. When the men in the poolroom play a trick on Nate by filling up his pipe with manure, and Studs is allowed to help, he "felt good, because he'd been let in on a practical joke they played on someone else; it sort of stamped him as an equal" (YL 150). Studs' admiration expresses his desire no longer to be a kid; it is his rudimentary way of escaping the conventionality and conservatism of his family and of his Irish-American community. This yearning finds fulfillment when Studs can talk with and be like the poolroom men, when he participates in their heavy-handed jokes, when he can tell himself that "Well, it wouldn't be long now before he'd be the big-time stuff" (YL 155).

Studs' perception is of two diametrically opposite worlds. Inside is the exciting poolroom world, thick with smoke, heavy with alcohol fumes, and resonating with the older men's scabrous exchanges; outside are the people in the street, conventional, well-behaved, and for Studs hopelessly uninspiring and dull. Among the Prairie Avenue gang youths who spend their time in front of the drug store or around the poolroom Studs finds new models to imitate, new ways to be tough, new jokes to express his repressed sexuality. The Prairie Avenue gang, from this point on, becomes the magnetic pole of Studs' life.

The code of toughness among the Prairie Avenue youths finds expression not in athletic contests fought according to some rule of honor but in group violence against weaker boys and people of different color, religion, and sex. A typical afternoon around the neighborhood begins with Tommy Doyle's question "What'll we do?" and with Red Kelly's reply "I'm pretty tired of sockin' Jew babies, or we might scout a few." As nothing more engaging becomes available, the youths proceed to beat up and rob two younger neighborhood kids whose misfortune it is to cross the gang's path at the wrong time. Next they run from their victims and reassemble at "Joseph's Ice Cream Parlor at Fifty-fifth and Prairie" from which they flee leaving the bill unpaid. Again, "[t]hey wondered what to do." More time goes by as they smoke, box, recount dirty jokes; they tell each other how they hate school; they boast how tough they are with their parents, and they imagine that they will run away from home. The appearance of two new kids and the hope of some excitement distracts them from their talk. Upon questioning, they discover that the kids are from "an Irish neighborhood and all right, so they let the kids go." Again, "[t]hey wondered what to do." They decide to raid the ice-boxes of nearby buildings and, having completed the operation, they proceed to destroy the food they have stolen but that no one cares to eat by throwing it against walls and against a neighborhood kid who is just walking by. Finally, at the cry "[T]he Germans are comin'!" they choose as their target two janitors who have recognized them and are chasing them. They reassemble a few blocks away to brag that "they could have licked the lousy foreigners anyway." Here, they realize that they are now "in little Jerusalem," so they set out to "catch a couple of Jew babies." The first two "hooknoses" who happen on their path receive the standard treatment of beating and theft and are left "moaning in the alley." Next, the gang takes the direction of the park as they consider that "[n]ow it will be a perfect day, if we can only catch a couple of shines." As the option is not available, they spend some time in the park watching Danny O'Neill's skilled baseball play, a reminder for the reader of the healthy tough youth ethos that Studs has left behind. They conclude the afternoon by using Andy, the mascot of the group, as their last target. They accuse his father, who belongs to a union, of being a "kike," of being a "sheeny fox-in-the-bush," and they finally beat up Andy, one last victim of their empty afternoon. (YL 170–76)

The scene is representative of many others through which Farrell depicts the forms of toughness that Studs finds available with the Prairie Avenue gang. Here, as elsewhere, one notes the author's deliberate aesthetic choice. Through this long afternoon sketch the narrator captures the youths in some of their most undramatic moments, in the microscopic details of their steps around the neighborhood, and their racism in the texture of their daily existence as they search for something to do. Behind this strategy is the author's unwillingness to sensationalize, his refusal to depict racism only through its spectacular but isolated moments. And behind this aesthetic is a militant strategy. Farrell documents microscopically and ethnographically in order to force his readers into physical proximity with the most disturbing aspects of their little world; readers are led to recognize the often abstract and apparently distant phenomena of violence and racism in the texture of their own surroundings.

The new gang like the earlier one is the focus and center of sexual

131

remarks, tensions, codes. Stud's initiation into adult sexuality takes place through the young men's visit to Iris, the neighborhood prostitute. We reencounter Studs and his gang later that evening around the corner where they are bragging about the experience, worrying about their parents and their souls:

> "But, hell, what's a guy gonna do? If he doesn't get a girl now and then, well, he's liable to put himself in the nut house," said Paulie.
> "Yes, I guess a guy does. I guess it's a sin . . . " said Studs, shrugging his shoulders.
> "But, gee, I don't see why it's a sin if a fellow has to do it. I think the priests and sisters tell us this because they think we're a little too young. Maybe they don't mean it is a sin if you're a little older," said Paulie.
> "Maybe," said Studs, who was having a time with his conscience. (YL 188)

At home that evening Studs is still troubled by the recollection that "[n]inety-nine per cent of the souls in hell were there because of sins of the flesh," and by the feeling that "[h]e wasn't even worthy of Lucy now," but finally resolving that "he'd had to do it." When he is summoned at the dinner table, "[h]e walked into the dining room, acting and feeling like a man" (YL 189–91).

Around the tough youths of the Prairie Avenue gang, Studs' grudging attendance of high school turns into a routine of cutting school, which eventually results in his expulsion from the football team for irregular attendance. With the gang Studs becomes a heavy smoker and drinker; with them he is initiated into commercial sex; around them he is socialized into racism, sexism, political conservatism. The gang, in short, much as Thrasher had argued, is the primary agent of Studs' moral and physical decline and of his eventual destruction. In this important respect *Studs Lonigan* bears out Thrasher's thesis that gangs are the primary agents of juvenile corruption. On a deeper level, however, one finds Farrell a more complex sociologist than this statement would suggest.

For Frederic Thrasher as for other Chicago sociologists gangs were sociologically of interest because they were viewed as symptoms of social disorganization resulting from the loss of control suffered by the institutions of family, church, school, and, more generally, by the community after the upheaval of migration. However, it is not as a result of weak parental or communal control that Studs drifts from the Indiana Avenue gang to the Prairie Avenue gang and from the playground to the poolroom and street corner. The priestly vocation that Studs' mother has in store for him and the house painting vocation that his father is imagining for him denote not a lack of control but rather a lack of imagination. That he is sent to high school at all is the result of a compromise between his parents rather than a conscious decision. The impulse to escape what is ahead of him, at home as in school, the need to find an outlet for the impulses that his cultural environment denies, the yearning for something he can only articulate as a desire for adventure all lead Studs to join the Prairie Avenue gang. Farrell himself was to remark that the youth like Studs "drift into the poolroom and its complements as the only outlet of their impulses for the romantic and the adventurous."[42] He was echoing Thrasher's perceptive reflection that "[t]o understand the gang boy one must enter his world with a comprehension on the one hand of this *seriousness* behind his mask of flippancy or bravado and on the other, of the role of the *romantic* in his activities and in his interpretation of the larger world of reality."[43]

The *Young Manhood of Studs Lonigan* records Studs' life in his twenties and is the part of the trilogy that most emphatically focuses on the tough gang. The events take place against the backdrop of World War I and the onset of the Depression and close on the symbolic New Year's eve of 1929. Rather than centering on a dramatic turning point the narrative builds upon a series of episodes that constitute a crescendo of dissipation. In particular, while *Young Lonigan* explores the mysterious realm of adolescence and dramatizes a boy's healthy desire to escape his petit-bourgeois environment as the primary impulse that leads him to the gang, *The Young Manhood* is a dramatized demonstration of how misled Studs has been in adopting the poolroom as a valid place of escape.

The gang's racism and hatred of Blacks, Jews, foreigners, reds, and homosexuals emerges in *The Young Manhood* as the controlling motif of their talk, much as beating up non-Irish kids from nearby neighborhoods provides their main form of entertainment and diversion from boredom, drinking, and "whoring."

The gang's racism finds climactic expression during their participation in the race riots of 1919.[44] We find Studs and his friends armed with "clubs and sticks," "a straight razor," "a twenty-two revolver," "a pair of brass knuckles," "a baseball bat," "a hunting-knife," and thirsting for blood and violence; the riots provide but one more occasion for them to give vent to their racism:

> Tommy Doyle said the niggers were never going to forget the month of July, 1919. Studs said that they ought to hang every nigger in the city to the telephone poles, and let them swing there in the breeze. Benny Taite said that for every white man killed in the riots, ten black apes ought to be massacred. . . . Fat Malloy started telling how the Regan Colts were marching into the black belt and knocking off the niggers. Andy said well the Fifty-eight Street guys were going to do the same thing.
>
> Young Horn Buckford suddenly appeared and breathlessly said that there was a gang of niggers over Wabash Avenue. Studs, Red, Tommy, Weary, Kenny, and Benny Taite led the gang along Fifty-eighth Street, over to Wabash. For two hours, they prowled Wabash Avenue and State Street, between Garfield Boulevard and Fifty-ninth Street, searching for niggers. . . . They were joined by other groups, men and kids. The streets were like avenues of the dead. (YL 73–74)

The race riot episode inserts this insignificant little gang of toughs into a horrifying but far from isolated chapter of modern American history. Surrounded as it is by many and lengthy scenes of routine racism, the episode brings into focus the class matrix of this historical event. Among these parochially educated children of well-organized families, Farrell's dispassionate narrator asks us to note, originates real racism, a racism that seldom makes the headlines and yet without which the riots themselves would remain but a freak of history.

The Young Manhood minutely records the forms, slurs, and variations of the gang's racism. For Studs and his friends, a man who talks about racial migration and urban change is a "nigger-lover Irishman," and someone who "would let a nigger jazz his sister" (YM 313); Balzac is a "Frenchman" who "wrote stories that are so filthy they make you want to puke," but "the French are a pretty filthy race anyway" (YM 315); "niggers" are "worse than Polacks" or more precisely, as Red Kelly expostulates, "[t]he Polacks and Dagoes, and niggers are the same, only the niggers are the lowest" (YM 306). The "greed" of Jews is the main analytical tool upon which the gang has learned to rely in order to understand the profound social changes that are transforming their neighborhood against their will and in spite of their obtuseness. As one of them puts it, " '[I]t's a lousy thing, if you ask me, Jews ruining

134

a neighborhood just to make money like Judas did. It's all greed all over again, the greed of the Jews' " (YM 347).

Much as the narrative places the race riots within the racism of a specific class, the racism of the gang is itself contextualized within that of the surrounding community. This may be more extreme in its language and actions, yet it is qualitatively not unlike that of the youths' parents. From the very beginning we hear Studs' father worrying about "the niggers and the kikes" moving into the neighborhood (YL 19). As people begin to sell their houses, we observe Old Lonigan and others in the neighborhood clinging to the expectation that "the niggers will be run ruggedy if they ever try to get past Wabash Avenue" (YM 138). After the Depression has destroyed his business, and after the deterioration of the neighborhood has forced him to sell and lose money on his buildings, Old Lonigan becomes more indiscriminate against the "Jew international bankers," against "all those foreigners [who] came here to take jobs away from Americans," against "the Polacks and Bohunks squeezing the Irish out of politics" and against the Reds "agitating to overthrow the government. . . . [and] exciting the niggers down in the Black Belt, telling them they're as good as white men and they can have white women" (JD 306–8). One might safely say that the worst traits of the gang's culture are little more than extreme repetitions of their parents', teachers', and priests' words. Under the bohemian, unconventional, and illicit surface of the gang's activities hides an indigenous product of the community around it.

The gang's views on women appear to be the antithesis of their parents'. Women are all "broads" with the exception of sisters and mothers. Wives should be "trained right" so as to make them "meek as a lamb" (YM 70). Their sisters however are "pure as lily" (YM 182) and generally "the finest and most decent girls are Irish Catholic girls" (YM 331). At the bottom of the gang's epistemology of inferiority, lower even than all "inferior races," the gang places the lesbian. When the gossip comes out that Helen Shires, once Studs' good childhood friend, is lesbian, Red Kelly, as usual the most vocal of the group, loudly remonstrates,

> "That's worse than having a nigger. Think of it, a girl comes from a self-respecting family, with a decent old man and an old lady. She had a decent home, a chance for an education, an opportunity to meet decent fellows, and to become a fine, decent girl. And what does she do, but become worse than the hustler of a nigger pimp?

135

And you try to say she can't help it! Why girls like that ought to be made to live with pigs." (YM 330)

Ironically, these very words will soon be said of Kelly himself after he is arrested and sentenced to jail for raping and nearly killing a woman at the New Year's party that closes *The Young Manhood of Studs Lonigan*.

The gang's views on women are not so much the antithesis as the obverse of the Catholic church's teachings. Father Shannon's sermon is a corrosive attack on "forward looking women" and birth control or what he defines as "the legalization of sin, disease, promiscuity." His sermon is an attack on all the forms of behavior that most typify the gang: "wild parties," "drinking," "animalistic dancing," "brothels." The sermon is a call to the young men to protect their sisters. Instead of birth control Father Shannon proposes "self-control," which, judging from the gang's behavior, is no control at all. It is an appropriate commentary on this kind of teaching that at the end of the mission, having just purified their souls, after the papal blessing, the plenary indulgences, and the benedictions, Studs and his gang go first to a saloon and then "to a new can house" (YM 349–60).

The violence that lurks below the surface of the gang's remarks on women finds fullest expression in the New Year's party. Punctuated by the drunken racism of its participants and by the verbal and physical violence against the women present, this party dramatizes the youths' view of women as objects over which to assert their superiority and virility. The gang's celebration of the last day of 1929 and a reunion for many of them who have moved to new neighborhoods, the party closes this infamous year with its own infamy by leaving one of the women raped and in a coma and Studs drunk in an alley, lying in his vomit.

IV

Set against the racism and blindness of almost every character in the trilogy, Farrell interpolated an episode that both highlights that blindness and reveals the pedestal on which the narrator has been standing all along. Halfway into *The Young Manhood of Studs Lonigan* Farrell takes Studs and his gang to the Bug Club—a famous center of debate in Chicago during the 1920s and the 1930s. Here, while engaged in jokes and rowdy behavior, they hear the crazy and the sane deliver lectures on relativity, God, political corruption, and more. One of the speakers is a John Connolly, "king of the Soap Boxers," who proposes to talk on "certain aspects of urban growth which were relevant to the question of race prejudice in Chicago" (YM 312). The facts he is going to describe, Connolly promises, are based not on rumors but on ideas formulated "by members of the Department of sociology at the University of Chicago" and are drawn from "the work they have already done on a community research programme" (YM 312). From Connolly, Studs and his friends hear that Chicago consists of "three concentric circles, the "business or downtown district," around this central area the "manufacturing and wholesale houses, slums, tenements, can houses and other haunts of vice," and finally still further out are the "residential districts." Connolly closely paraphrases Burgess's essay on urban expansion, "The Growth of the City," and reproduces the sociological model for which Burgess is still famous.[45] Connolly closes his lecture stating:

> When the city expanded, it expanded from the center. In Chicago, thus, expansion spread out from the Loop. The inner circle was pushed outwards causing corresponding changes in the other concentric circles. The Negroes coming into the situation as an economically inferior race, had naturally found their habitation in the second circle. Since they had located in the slums of the black belt, the city had been growing into bigger and better Chicago. The pressure of growth was forcing them into newer areas . . . and resulted in a minor racial migration of Negroes into the white residential districts of the south side. . . . It was an inevitable outgrowth of social and economic forces. (YM 313)

Connolly's lecture is a synthesis of the changes we have been observing in the course of the novel. The lecture sociologically frames the Irish-American neighborhood in space as a subregion of the third urban circle and in time as an area which is in the process of changing or, according to the ecological metaphors so popular among the Chicago sociologists, of being "invaded" by families from the nearby Black Belt. Ernest Burgess, like other Chicago sociologists of his generation, was concerned with the invasion of Chicago by large numbers of rural immigrants from the Mid-West, Europe, and the South. Far from abstractly speculative, the sociologists' attention was ultimately directed at the social problems they felt were the result of such large scale migration—"disease, crime, disorder, vice, insanity, and suicide."[46] The originality and success of Burgess's model was to a

137

large extent due to its ability to read the city dynamically, in time as well as space, and as an image of endless outward expansion and of American upward mobility. Farrell borrowed Burgess's model of the city as a system of concentric circles activated by a teleological progression and grafted onto it the pessimism that he inherited from the Depression on the one hand and Marxist philosophy on the other. A downward spiral replaces the ladder of upward mobility and of the American dream. Against this telos of urban change, progress, and history we are meant to read the story of Studs Lonigan, the story of a progressive and eventual total paralysis set against urban change and history.

The episode is important not merely as it reminds us of the socioeconomic status of the Irish-American community in question. Another speaker after Connolly takes the stand to lecture on anthropology, "a new science they were studying at the University of Chicago" that states that "no one race is superior to any other race." Both represent the social sciences and the sociological claims to truth and objectivity which authorize and authenticate Farrell's novel.

In the chapter following this, we find ourselves in a Greek restaurant listening to the communist waiter Christy, who sententiously states:

> "Silly boys. They have no education. They go to school to the sisters. . . . Sisters, sanctimonious hypocrites. They pray and pray and pray. Fear! Crazy! What can they teach boys? To pray and become sanctimonious hypocrites too. Silly boys, they grow up, their fathers want to make money, their mothers are silly women and pray like the sanctimonious sisters, hypocrites. The boys run the streets, and grow up in pool-rooms, drink and become hooligans. They don't know any better. Silly boys, and they kill themselves with diseases from whores and this gin they drink." (YM 336)

And shortly thereafter, almost at the end of *The Young Manhood*, we find Danny O'Neill in the service station where he works, studying for his courses at the University of Chicago. Suddenly realizing "that all his education in Catholic schools, all he had heard and absorbed, had been lies," Danny feels overwhelmed by "loneliness," "rootlessness," and "nostalgia," and has a vision of his future. "He, too, he would destroy the old world with his pen; he would help create the new world. He would study to prepare himself. He saw himself in the future, delivering great and stirring orations, convincing people, a lead-

138

er, a savior of the world" (YM 369–71). Richard Wright closes the second volume of his autobiography, *American Hunger*, with almost identical words, the same gesture of self-creation, the same sense of loneliness.[47] For Farrell, writing at the beginning of that decade, this gesture expressed his self-exile from a community entrenched in dogmatism, that of the Catholic church and of the American dream, a self-exile that was to lead many to look for a new community in the Left in the years to come. For Wright, who was writing at the end of the Red Decade, it was the self-willed isolation of the writer in the face of the Left's increasing dogmatism and loss of direction.

In the words of the three authorial speakers, Connolly, Christy, and Danny, one sees sociology, Marxism and Farrell's personal experience merge. These are three "marginal" men, each one an outsider who speaks for the author and indicates where Farrell found the source and inspiration for his autobiographical self-exile. Farrell himself, sounding very much like the speaker Connolly, would later explain that in writing the trilogy he had used the "sociological formulations which have been made by the University of Chicago sociologists."[48] Farrell's objective narrator was writing from the vantage point of the sociologist.

V

The story of Studs Lonigan unfolds between Old Lonigan's two monologues. The second of these takes place in the final chapter and is historically framed by the 1929 economic collapse. As his son is dying and his economic and social status has collapsed, Old Lonigan finds himself driving through the city, even though "[t]here was really no place to go, and it didn't matter where he went or why" (JD 423). This drive literally recapitulates the trilogy.

First he stops at St. Patrick Church, in his old neighborhood, and tries to make sense of what he perceives as personal misfortune rather than the relentless wheels of history and economics: "It wasn't right. It wasn't fair. He had done nothing to merit this punishment. Why, why was it? . . . Why was he, and not others, being ruined?" (JD 424–25). Finding no relief in prayer, Lonigan walks out of the church to find his old neighborhood transformed. "He stood on the church steps looking at the drab row of three-story apartment houses across the street. Looked old, not worth much. Probably run down inside, too. Nigger buildings now" (JD 427). Lonigan once again observes the social processes he had noticed many years earlier, as he sat on his back porch at the beginning of the novel. At the time, his main response had been to reflect over the profit he would make at the sale of his buildings.

Back in his car, he drives on, Fifty-sixth Street, Garfield Boulevard, Fifty-first Street, Wentworth Avenue, Forty-seventh Street, Thirty-fifth Street. Through the haze of his thoughts Lonigan notices the closed banks, the dilapidated neighborhoods, the unpaid firemen sitting idle "because the city was broke" (JD 428); he sees street corners crowded with men out of work and "[i]t made him suddenly realize something of what this depression was beginning to mean in people's lives" (JD 429). This is the first time that Old Lonigan has an insight that people exist in a larger social world. As he drives on he finds himself on Halsted Street, the main street of his childhood neighborhood. Here "he understood why he had come to this neighborhood" (JD 429):

> He was going back to an old neighborhood, to look at places where he had lived and played as a shaver. He remembered his Irish father and mother, his sister who had become a whore, Joe, getting old and tired, working still on the street cars, plugging along, Joe's oldest son Tommy in the pen for sticking up a store. Ought to see Joe. Joe, poor fellow, had had a hard life. . . . And Joe's wife Ann, she was sick, not much life left in her. . . . He felt kindly toward Joe, toward Ann, even toward the memory of Catherine [his sister]. (JD 429)

The self-satisfaction and narrow pride that had marked his earlier recollections are gone, and for the first time Old Lonigan feels sympathy for those he has left behind in the slum.

When he finally parks the car, Lonigan finds himself surrounded by a slum neighborhood, the one in which he grew up and at this point a mirror of the destruction in his own life:

> He parked the car by a vacant lot that was thick with weeds and littered with rocks, refuse, papers, tin cans. . . . He caught a whiff of stale garbage from the prairies. . . . He glanced down a block-paved street, with tumbling and sinking wooden houses stacked between old brick buildings of two and three stories, most of the houses appearing uninhabitable in a pall of gray smoke. The neighborhood still looked something like it had in the old days, only worse. He slowly moved down a narrow cracked sidewalk, unable

> to recognize most of the houses. He halted before a boarded, untenanted structure that was weather-worn and lop-sided, as if threatening to fall into a heap of junk at any minute. He noticed that the windows were broken, black with dirt and soot, and the grass-less plot of dirt in front of the house was messed with papers, small broken pieces of board and rusty tin cans, and the steps dropping into the cellar entrance were barricaded with refuse. (JD 430)

Lonigan is unable to remember which family used to live here be-cause nostalgia, the only form of historical consciousness he has culti-vated, has left him with no memory. All he can do is wonder, in a voice reminiscent of Edgar Lee Master's poetic persona, "where were they, and what had happened to them?" (JD 430). He also notices a few boys who are playing in the vacant lot across the street:

> Golly, he had played ball like that and so had his brothers, Jack and Mike and Joe, and so had Bill and Martin around Fifty-eight Street. And now here were these boys.
> "Go on, you sonofabitch, I'm safe."
> He laughed. Tough kids, all right. A whole new generation, going through the same mill that he had. Going through the same kind of a mill that Bill and Martin had. No. Bill and Martin had been given advantages that he'd never had, and these kids weren't get-ting them either.
> "If I'm a sonofabitch, you're a . . ."
> Swearing like teamsters. Well, when he was a shaver he'd done the same thing. *What would become of these lads?* They'd scatter like the kids he'd known. Some go to jail. Some just go nowhere. Some pull themselves up by their own bootstraps just as he had done. . . . Most of the kids hadn't turned out so well, and they had come to no good end. . . . *And how many generations of kids had come and gone since his time, and how many more would follow after those kids cursing and play-ing ball in the lot across the street?* (JD 431, my emphasis)

This prose poem reveals a Pat Lonigan who, in contrast to his previ-ous reverie, finally does recall his youth, his swearing, and his drink-ing. Old Lonigan, and Farrell through him, now asks questions; much the same questions that Thrasher had asked with his study. Some-where in Lonigan's mind dawns the realization that his personal es-cape from poverty and the slum cannot act as guarantee for his chil- 141 dren against the tragic destiny that befell his brother and many of his friends.

Between Old Lonigan's opening monologue and his final one unfolds the story of a community whose members blind themselves to the inevitability of social change and perceive it only as a threat to be resisted. It is the story of a neighborhood where people try to circumvent historical change through either passive nostalgia or aggressive assaults against those they perceive as agents of that change. Old Lonigan's drive through the city recapitulates the trilogy, the old man's past, and recent American history.

Studs' story is a clinical diagnosis directed at Old Lonigan and at the class he represents rather than a sermon directed at the children of this class on the wages of sin. In *Studs Lonigan* the gang may be on the "frontier" and at the "margins" of the community as far as the parents' understanding of the youths' needs and activities goes. Yet the novel's complex representation of the gang rests on the understanding that the gang is far from an aberration of that community. For Farrell the point of this epic-size chronicle of degeneration was not to chastize the boy but to critique the world around him. The target of Farrell's attack was a specific part of the Irish American community and, more generally, the American petit-bourgeosie that community typified; it was a class whose members, having "pull[ed] themselves up by their own bootstraps" and made it out of the slum, now sit self-satisfied on the porch of the buildings they own oblivious to the economic and spiritual destruction surrounding them, proud of the sacrifices made and the privileges acquired for their children while those children destroy themselves in dissipation.

In sociology Farrell found a theoretical framework that allowed him to recognize this process and understand why a Studs remains trapped even as he appears to be defying the norms of his community. Sociology revealed to Farrell the forms of that entrapment. Farrell juxtaposed the world of the university, of science, of enlightenment to the world of Catholic dogma, white chauvinism, and petit-bourgeois complacency. This is the same set of dichotomies operative in the sociologists' studies as well as in Richard Wright's autobiography. To the enlightened world belong the speaker Connolly, the waiter Christy, and the third-person narrator, and soon Danny O'Neill will also be a part of that world.

142   Sociology gave Farrell a perspective from which to observe and judge the world he had left behind. The trilogy is at once an extended therapy session about his past and an act of self-enfranchisement from his Irish American petit-bourgeois upbringing. The aesthetic of estrangement of the *Studs Lonigan* trilogy is the complementary oppo-

site of another favorite one of the 1930s, the "let the people speak for themselves" aesthetic, whose goal was to create empathy with the poor, the unemployed, the inarticulate. Farrell took his middle-class audience on a countervoyage through their own backyards and alleys; through an aesthetic of militant defamiliarization he prevented that audience from identifying and sympathizing with its own fictional representatives. The detachment of Farrell's narrator follows a strategy of cultural estrangement that forces readers to become outsiders of their own class and milieu.

Following Robert Park's invitation, Farrell quite literally subjected a white middle-class neighborhood to the estranged gaze of ethnography, a discipline born among foreign cultures and subsequently brought home to observe the urban poor. As he rewrote Thrasher's study in fictional form, however, Farrell also challenged some of the sociologist's assumptions, ultimately reasserting the radical potential of sociology as cultural critique over its more conservative version as social medicine. In this important novel Farrell borrowed the point of view of the stranger and used it to produce a defamiliarized and critical portrait of both his ethnic and his national culture. *Studs Lonigan* is the tragedy of a youth who attempts but fails to abandon his narrowminded, provincial, and bigoted community. Studs escapes from his family, the church, and the school by joining a youth gang, an institution that, he fails to realize, epitomizes and reproduces the essence of the petit-bourgeois values he unconsciously rejected in the first place. The gang, it turns out, is but a prosaic bohemia whose only message of liberation is self-destruction. Studs' life comes to stand for a society and a time—the United States during the 1920s—becoming a narrative metaphor for the destruction of youth and the future that came to fruition during the Depression. At the center of the novel the gang functions as an ethnographic device, a revealing human observatory from which Farrell could observe the ideology and culture of the American petit-bourgeoisie, the class that most closely embodied the values, myths, and ideology of American capitalism. Farrell used urban sociology and ethnography in the spirit of the radical social questioning that, George Marcus and Michael Fisher remind us, inspired such different movements as surrealism, the Chicago school of urban sociology, the WPA arts projects of the 1930s, and the Frankfurt School.[49] This is what makes the *Studs Lonigan* trilogy a portrait of a whole society in the best vein of the realist tradition.

143

6

Footnote
Fellows: Cold
Wars of
American
Letters

*He was born in South Chicago, the offspring of a Finnish
grocer and a Hungarian Jewish mother. He was twenty
when the great depression struck and for several years he
lived the life of a hobo, crossing America hidden in
freight cars, in turn peddler, dishwasher, waiter, mas-
seur, ditchdigger, bricklayer, salesman, and, when necessary, burglar. In some forgotten roadside lunchroom in
Arizona where he earned a living washing glasses, he
had written a short story which a leftist magazine accepted for publication. Then he wrote others.*
— Simone de Beauvoir, The Mandarins

Lewis Brogan, the character in question, is the
fictive name Simone de Beauvoir gave to her former lover Nelson Algren in her autobiographical novel *The Mandarins.* "At first," de Beauvoir recalls of their first encounter, "I had found it amusing meeting in
the flesh that classic American species: self-made-leftist writer."[1] The
love affair between Algren and de Beauvoir intermittently spanned
the period between 1947 and 1951 and ended bitterly. He had wanted
a permanent relationship, while she had imagined an indefinitely
protracted affair; she had loved him as her modern imaginary American Virgil, her guide through the lower circles of American capitalism—the slum, the burlesque show, the boxing match, the opium
den; Algren, attracted though he had been by this Parisian "engagé"

intellectual, came to resent the portrait of Lewis Brogan as "a preposterous proletarian stud in clean shirt" and "Madame Yackety-Yack" for ignoring "the old-fashioned puritanical idea that some things are private."[2] But, most of all, Algren resented de Beauvoir's use of their romance to articulate her concept of "contingent love," expounded a few years later in Force of Circumstance.[3] "Anybody who can experience love contingently," he huffed, " has a mind that has recently snapped. How can love be contingent? Contingent upon what? . . . What she means, of course, when stripped of its philosophical jargon, is that she and Sartre erected a facade of petit-bourgeois respectability behind which she could continue the search for her own femininity. What Sartre had in mind when he left town I'm sure I don't know."[4] Bluntly, Algren broke off the affair and delivered his verdict on the whole intellectual milieu to which his former lover belonged: "Procurers are more honest than philosophers."[5] Closer to the truth than these public pronouncements are Algren's private words in his letters to de Beauvoir, some of which she reprinted in Force of Circumstance. "I am stuck here, as I told you and as you understood, because my job is to write about this city [Chicago], and I can only do it here . . . [whereas] your life belong[s] to Paris and to Sartre."[6]

Herself an exemplar of a classic European cultural species, bourgeois leftist intellectual, Simone de Beauvoir's perception of Nelson Algren as a typical American phenomenon captures an important aspect of American literature, specifically of Chicago literature. In the United States the literary establishment had historically been more open than in Europe to writers born outside the traditional elites; Chicago, at a safe distance from the more Waspy and upper-class Boston and Europhile New York, had carried that tendency further than any other city, becoming for a time the true capital of American literature. "Find me a writer"—H. L. Mencken proclaimed in 1917—"who is indubitably American and who has something new and interesting to say, and who says it with an air, and nine times out of ten . . . he has some sort of connection with the abbatoir by the lake." He added, a few years later:

> From Ade to Dreiser nearly all the bright young Indianians have
> gone to Chicago for a semester or two, and not only the Indianians,
> but also the youngsters of all the Middle western states. . . . Go
> back for twenty or thirty years, and you will scarcely find an Ameri
> can literary movement that did not originate under the shadow of
> the stockyards.[7]

145

What exactly distinguishes the American from the European writer, Algren would himself explain in a 1955 interview with the *Paris Review*, is that "here you get to be a writer differently. I mean, a writer like Sartre *decides*, like any professional man, when he's fifteen, sixteen years old, that instead of being a doctor he's going to be a writer. And he absorbs the French tradition and proceeds from there. Well, here you get to be a writer when there's absolutely nothing else to do."[8] In his well-known prose poem, *Chicago, City on the Make*, Algren would later define the character of American literature by contrasting New York, with its "cocktail-lounge culture," or Hollywood, "where directors go on all-fours begging producers," with Chicago, where "a literature bred by hard times on the river, hard times on the range and hard times in the town once became a world literature" and where "the anti-legalistic tradition toward society . . . distinguished [its] writers since the early years of the century."[9] A similar comment has been made recently at a roundtable entitled "The Writer in Chicago:"

> Chicago is robust. It's less academic, precious, and mandarin—less Byzantine. . . . It's not just a place, local color, but an attitude. For instance, there's a premium placed on a certain kind of savvy—not urbane sophistication—more like street smarts. That Oak Park writer, Hemingway, called it having a good crap-detector. . . . It's in Algren, a kind of compromised laughter, a survivor's cynicism. And mixed in with it is . . . a certain sentimental streak. . . . No matter what qualities of toughness or alley-wiseness one ascribes to writers like Algren or Farrell, they never cross the line into obliterated human feelings. . . . Hanging onto feeling, how it manages to survive, has been more of a Chicago concern.[10]

In America and in Chicago, that "most American of cities," one becomes a writer, Algren realized, after encountering both the New York and the French mandarins, not as a result of being at the center of a literary culture but by virtue of being at its margins or even outside of it, not by absorbing the national tradition but by pretending to know nothing of it. A close friend of both Wright and Algren, Jack Conroy both invoked and parodied the self-conscious lack of sophistication of this "other" tradition when, announcing to Algren that he had just been awarded a Guggenheim Fellowship, he wrote: "Dear Will and Walt . . . A Guggenheim Fella is now addressing you, fellas! Yessir, the ol' Missouri hillibilly done gone clean ahead o'them smart city guys and collitch perfessers."[11] Years later Conroy invoked the same contrast to describe the internal factionalisms of the Left in the 1930s and to distinguish the political culture of the Midwest and the East Coast when he recalled: "Out in the Midwest of penny auctions and burning corn we were far from the ideological tempests raging in New York coffee pots. How many Marxian angels could dance on the point of a hammer and sickle?"[12] Within this uncouth, defiantly unintellectual and politically committed tradition Nelson Algren placed himself deliberately.

Simone de Beauvoir's appreciation of Nelson Algren as a special type of American novelist is representative of other European intellectuals who, before and after the Second World War, came to admire American novelists for their close ties to the social conflicts of their time and culture. While many American authors have become favorites in France, Nelson Algren is one of a handful whose fame abroad seems to have grown in inverse proportion to their popularity at home. By 1963 Algren had become acutely aware of that discrepancy. In his preface to the new edition of *Never Come Morning* he wrote,

> [T]he novel that the rear-echelon patriots and Sunday-morning Forgive-Me-Lords failed to understand strangely has found understanding on the bookshelves of Europe. *Le matin se fait attendre,* Jean-Paul Sartre's translation, was the first of a dozen translations. It is now available in every large city from London to Tokyo, Rio to Zagreb.[13]

Algren's cutting words still hold true. If James T. Farrell is not an academic favorite, the name of Nelson Algren is frequently met without a nod of recognition, even by students of American literature. Such ignorance goes hand in hand with the sparse critical attention Algren has received from recent scholars and, more important, with the attacks carried out against this author by the preceding generation of critics.

I

From the beginning the critical reception of *Never Come Morning* divided into two distinct camps. Critics who disliked the novel described it as a portrait of "shame and vileness and cruelty and ugliness" and a picture of "a slum world where life is at its most degraded and only money counts."[14] They questioned the value of focusing on

147

the poorest of the urban poor and implicitly denied to this class the symbolic and social resonance that guided Algren's choice in the first place.

Those who praised the novel, on the other hand, praised it precisely because they shared with the author such an underlying premise. Milton Hindus welcomed Algren as a "powerful storyteller of the Chicago school of realism."[15] Malcolm Cowley praised him for overcoming the "starved and stunted prose" of earlier naturalists and appointed him "poet of the Chicago slums."[16] Benjamin Appel, in a review that still deserves to be read, found at the center of the novel "one of our big industries—the crime racket:"

> In general, the crime industry shapes up about as follows. At the center are the millionaire receivers of the take. Revolving around them are the important satellites, the brokers, politicians, corrupt judges, the little-shot bigshots who gear into every wheel of American life. Around the satellites spin the mob leaders, ward captains, madames, fences. And way out in space, a million million dollars away from the center are the industry's bread and butter strong-arm lads, the poolroom sharks, the whores, the bookies. These are the little people of crime who live in the slums of the cities. They are recruited from the garbagey tenements to take their obscure places in the brothels and in the stolen cars.[17]

Equally illuminating is the original introduction written by Richard Wright, whose *Native Son* had been published only two years earlier. Wright found at the center of the novel a sociologically specific referent: "that stratum of our society that is historically footloose, unformed, malleable, restless, devoid of inner stability, unidentified by class allegiances, yet full of hot, honest, blind striving."[18] Responding in advance to critics who, like Clifton Fadiman, would see "the Poles of Chicago's West Side" as "a focus for social and political infection," Wright characterized the same group as "an unharnessed, unchanneled and unknown ocean" and vouched for the novel as an accurate portrayal of "what actually exists in the nerve, brain, and blood of our boys in the street, be they black, white, native, or foreign born."[19] Having found in *Never Come Morning* another segment of the class to which Bigger Thomas belonged, Wright closed off his powerful summation with a direct appeal to the audience. "I say this for the public record, for there will come a time in our country when the middle class will gasp and say (as they now gasp over the present world situation): 'why weren't we told this before? why didn't our novelists depict the beginnings of this terrible thing that has come upon us?' Well, Mr. and Mrs. American Reader, you are being told: the reality of the depths of our lives is being depicted."[20] Among these sympathetic reviewers, appreciation for the novel went hand in hand with understanding of both the sociology and the symbolism of the slum. For them as for Algren poetry and sociology were complementary rather than antithetical.

The remarks directed against Algren's work during the fifties deserve special attention. They succinctly evoke the critical landscape during the cold war, one dominated by a conservative ideology whose formulations may no longer be fashionable but whose effects are still with us. In them one finds not merely the specific contentions that marginalized Nelson Algren but, just as important, echoes of the larger dispute that exiled the whole urban sociological tradition from the hall of fame of American letters.[21]

William Bittner's was a lonely voice when in 1956 he praised Algren, comparing his "melodic" prose to the poetry of Dylan Thomas and warning that the "Wild Side is not merely the result of our social order; it is that social order growing wild."[22] More numerous were the ranks of Algren's faultfinders, who wrote for prestigious magazines and had famous names. In the politely polemical tone of the *New Yorker* Norman Podhoretz wondered "why [Algren] finds bums so much more interesting and stirring than other people."[23] A most vehement member of the group was Leslie Fiedler, writing for the *Partisan Review* and the *Reporter*, both of which by 1956 had a conservative liberal outlook. Deriding Algren as "the bard of the stumblebum," Fiedler assembled a long list of charges against him, which included those of "sentimentality pretending to be politics," surrender of the "imagination" to "information," creating "Ultima Skid Row" where "all [is] grotesque and titillating in the lurid light of Algren's 'poetic' prose." Finally cataloguing Algren away as a "museum piece, the last of the Proletarian Writers," Fiedler closed with a warning to the reader: "What final pleasure we find in his novels we find, alas, as *voyeurs*."[24] The anonymous reviewer of *Time* magazine passed the same verdict and gave it even wider coverage. He wondered whether Algren's "sympathy for the depraved and degraded has not carried him to the edge of nonsense" and judged that "in supposing that human virtue flourishes best among degenerates, novelist Algren has dressed his sense of compassion in the rags of vulgarity."[25]

These statements found an eloquent response in Lawrence Lipton's "A Voyeurs' View of the Wild Side."[26] Lipton notices how the critical assault against Algren after 1950 ran parallel to the "firings, jailings and blacklisting" of radical intellectuals within the media. These critics, he suggests, "[feel] like slummers," and like "*voyeurs*" as a result of their own conversion from radicals to "breast-beaters"; their "guilty pleasure," in reading Algren's novels is much like a "respectable citizen's at a peep show." "In Fiedler's case," Lipton goes on,

> it is complicated by another sort of guilt, the guilt of former association. [Fiedler] loses no opportunity in print to confess the guilt of "innocence" during the New Deal "United Front" thirties. . . . If Algren would confess to the political innocence of which Fiedler, too, confesses himself guilty he would cease to be "isolated from the real life of his time," that is he would forget all this nonsense and sentimentality about bums, tramps, whores, and pimps, all this wild talk about the losers on the wild side of the street, the gamblers and the junkies and the lost people, and see the real life of his time as one of Permanent Prosperity, the New Capitalism, the Highest Standard of Living in the World, in short, the world of Cash McCall and the Man in the Grey Flannel Suit.[27]

Lipton's incisive remarks are still suggestive of the cultural trenches during the cold war era.

On the more academic side the debate was often as fierce as in the magazines. Cutting across ideological alignments altogether, Algren was castigated not only by conservative critics but by liberal ones as well. Thus Charles Walcutt complained that Algren offers no solution, Alfred Kazin that he fails to "point an accusing finger" and that his novels are merely "picturesque," Chester E. Eisinger, immediately after extolling the virtues of Richard Wright's *Native Son*, that Algren's novels are a "truly cloacal vision of the American experience."[28] Edmund Fuller's *Man in Modern Fiction* extended Fiedler's treatment to all "modern writers"—Nelson Algren, Saul Bellow, and Norman Mailer, among others—who instead of "casting stones at the sinner" prefer the motto "[n]either do I condemn you—go and sin some more." Fuller charged them with authorial "self- pity," with confusing "identification with compassion," with "depravity"— "[t]hey take murder, rape, perversion, and say, belligerently, 'What's wrong with it?' "—and finally dismissed them as "destroyers of the social order."[29]

150

Reviewing *Man in Modern Fiction* for the *Nation*, Algren himself took the stand in defense of that literature, and, while responding to Fuller, responded to the larger critical establishment that was expunging the literature he believed was the true heritage of American letters:

> Edmund Fuller is an Ivy-League Calvinist whose specialty appears to be the divination of the wellsprings of True Compassion in recent American letters.
>
> "There is no true compassion in these modern works" is his final verdict, "the degraded, the criminal, the anti-social are sentimentalized over, wept over, identified with."
>
> "You have to be a pervert or a savage," [Fuller] decides, "to elicit sympathy."
>
> Now we're getting somewhere: compassion is too good for some people. It's not for the unloved, the lost or the badly-mannered. It's a dividend distributed to the well- adjusted, those who sleep safe from the beetles and the rain, who rise to tote the brief case that earns respect, down to the office space occupied by the righteous.

> "What I object to," he objects to, "is the writer who offers me the world's horrors and offers no solution."
>
> Actually, I don't recall offering this fellow either horrors or joys. Others may have, but I have not yet, written a novel in the explicit hope of pleasing him. . . . Fuller flatly refutes an old friend of mine, Frankie Machine, because he is a frightening character, without alternatives, without a larger frame of reference. "I declare," Fuller declares, "I declare these to be false implications of society. . . . You see," he explains, "the question of whether a writer's picture of life is true or false, is very important to me."
>
> I declare Fuller to be a false implication, period. How in the name of sense is a gingerbread boy popping out of a ribbon-bound cookie-box, a jack-in-the box with a beard, to tell what is true and what is false of any aspect of American life? What can he know of the millions who live out their lives behind numbered doors, in the nation of furnished rooms?

> Of course Frankie had no alternatives: that was the very reason I wrote about him. His frame of reference was the street he worked on, the army he served in and the needle he died by. Yet, being dead, he has more life than Fuller walking around breathing.
>
> I think that Frankie would be pleased to know he had finally frightened somebody. It doesn't take much, it appears, to frighten a

151

Fuller. Yet actually, if Fuller walked into the bar where Frankie and his friends once drank, with his beard, his degree and his true or false questionnaire, he'd be easily the most sinister party in the joint. They were men and women like men and women everywhere, with a little less luck than most. But they knew a fink when they saw one.

"But doesn't Christ preach forgiveness of sins?" he is asked. "Why shouldn't the modern artist forgive too?"

"Compassion and mercy, if they mean anything at all, *follow* judgment," is the answer to *that*. He throws the book at the accused, tells the next of kin "I'm sorry," and says: "call *that* mercy."[30]

The fissure between Nelson Algren and the literary critics became and has since remained an abyss, its depth sounded by Algren's lifelong harangues against the literary establishment, its width by Algren's virtual disappearance from the literary horizon. Writing to request a recommendation for a Fulbright fellowship at the height of that political period, Algren ironically pleaded with Malcolm Cowley: "All that would be entailed on your part would be the assurance to the Fulbright Committee, upon inquiry, that I am a poet of the Chicago slums beneath whose ragged exterior beats a heart of gold. If that doesn't fetch them nothing will."[31] A few weeks later, presumably in reply to Cowley's acceptance, and even more sardonically, Algren added: "Thanks for letting me have your name for a Fulbright. Actually, my qualifications for one are dubious. Over and above that, I've done everything I shouldn't have in the State Department's view, including such felonies as voting for Wallace, poor brute."[32] The literary polemics were but fragments of a larger political and ideological realignment within American culture after the Second World War, one that Algren saw and understood with full clarity.

Recalling the takeover of what he called the "New York literary bench" by a new breed of critics, Algren wrote at the end of that era:

> By the middle forties . . . [n]ew owners moved in. They arrived directly from their respective campuses armed with blueprints to which the novel and the short story would have to conform, were a passing grade to be awarded. For they were footnote fellows mostly, a species of public boy that talked like a head on a stick.
>
> Prewar mottoes still hung on the walls, ancestral homilies offering obsolescent mysteries: "No Man Is An Island." "I Have Always Depended Upon The Kindness Of Strangers." "While There Is A Soul In Prison I Am Not Free." . . . It was plain the old mottoes would have to come down.

152

So they made criticism the focus of American writing and that was a pretty shrewd move right there as neither Elvis nor Leslie nor Lionel nor Justin could write fiction. Yet at footnoting they were really skilled. In fact, it was said of Justin that he would rather write a footnote than ride a passenger train. . . . They formed a loose federation, between the literary quarterlies, publishers' offices and book review columns, presenting a view of American letters untouched by the life of America.[33]

It would be a serious mistake to dismiss this as the private quarrel between Nelson Algren—the "Grand Odd-Ball" of American literature, to use Norman Mailer's words—and a few conservative critics. Although a favorite target, Algren was not the only victim of this aesthetic and idelogical inquisition. The primary target of the attack was less Algren himself than that long tradition of politically engaged novels which European intellectuals so admired, the tradition to which Simone de Beauvoir alludes and that Algren hails. This tradition peaked during the 1930s and had found in Algren one of its most gifted interpreters. By the same token, Algren was not simply aiming at a few ill-disposed critics. He was attempting to stall the takeover of the literary institution in the United States by aesthetic formalist critics.

The analysis of Algren's work by recent scholars has exibited none of the hostility but also little of the enthusiasm that characterized the early reviews. By and large contemporary scholars read *Never Come Morning* as a naturalist novel on the evils of the slum and cast Bruno as a ghetto youth who is doomed by the evil influence of that environment. Typical comments are that Bruno Bicek's "selfish ethic [is] determined by existence in the urban jungle"; that Bruno lives in a world "where to be ruthless and selfish is to survive—a *West Side Story* jungle of alleys and mean streets"; that "Bruno 'Lefty Bicek' . . . is a Huck Finn with no wilderness to strike out for. . . . This is the world of post-agrarian America. The real antagonist . . . is the city itself"; or that the novel is "a study of first and second generation urbanized Polish people . . . trapped and doomed by the intricate cultural and economic machinery of the vast city."[34]

Beneath the surface of these comments are a number of familiar clichés. Nelson Algren emerges from this critical literature as a social determinist and an amateur sociologist, a twentieth-century muckraker and a belated romantic who, near the mid-twentieth century, still denounces the well-known evils of the city and yearns for a lost pastoral America. Elliott Podwill is the only critic who has actually referred to Chicago sociology as an important intellectual source for

153

Never Come Morning. "Many of [Algren's] first-hand observations of the cultural isolation felt by Polish immigrants and the rootlessness of their Chicago-born children were confirmed by early studies by University of Chicago sociologists during the 1920's and 1930's. . . . Robert Park and Ernest W. Burgess . . . Clifford R. Shaw . . . Louis Wirth."[35] Podwill's perceptive remarks tamely retreat, however, to the conclusion that though Algren "knew his subject well," his "static" vision of the city is in contradiction to Ernest Burgess's and Louis Wirth's theories of urban and social mobility, and thus is, in this respect, "hardly a sociologically realistic one."[36]

The most serious flaw in the critical literature on *Never Come Morning*, inseparable from the mechanistic and determinist epistemology of the critics, is the lack of understanding of what the slum and its inhabitants stand for and of what place these occupy within the fictional and social order. Traces of these sociological connections occasionally become visible yet they are left unrelated to or more often in contradiction with the main reading of the novel. The same critics who interpret *Never Come Morning* within a vulgar determinist framework also perceptively state that "Chicago and New Orleans are meaningful only because they are true microcosms";[37] that the slum is "a symbol of Chicago and ultimately of America";[38] that at the "bi-weekly police lineup [is] symbolized . . . all of America";[39] that Algren's "Skid Row is merely the ugliest manifestation of tendencies embedded in all strata of city life";[40] or, finally, that Algren's world of crime reproduces a "perverse hierarchy of connections in American society, from the card-dealing, dope pushing, outcasts at the bottom to the respectable 'hustlers' at the top."[41] These insightful remarks remain, however, unexplored, since they might threaten a naturalist reading altogether and lead one to acknowledge not merely an indictment of the slum but one of the larger city and by extension of the economic and social system that the city embodies.

The critic who has most fully explored the close ties between the sociological and the poetic in Algren's fiction is R. W. Lid, in an essay that remains to this date the most valuable discussion of this author.[42] Lid has taken his colleagues' erratic remarks on Algren's novels and has made them the heart of his discussion. Central to his analysis is 154 the understanding that for Algren the criminal and the righteous man are inseparable, much as corruption and power are inseparable.[43] Lid has thus acknowledged both Algren's depiction of the weblike nature of power, corruption, and authority and Bruno as an individual and a type rather than a stereotype, a representative rather than a degenerate American.[44]

To this date only two book-length studies and a few full-length scholarly articles have been published on Algren.[45] The author whom Ernest Hemingway once described as second only to Faulkner ("Mr. Algren, boy you are good," he wrote in a blurb for *The Man with a Golden Arm*) and whom Kurt Vonnegut recently described as yet another modern writer exiled from his Chicago homeland has thus become an exile of American literature as well.[46]

7

A Walk on the Other Side: Never Come Morning by Nelson Algren

Pourquoi choisissez-vous de vivre à Chicago?

Si je vivais dans une autre ville, même si la vie là-bas était plus fasteuse, je perdrais mon métier. A Mexico, je ne pourrais pas écrir sur Chicago, parce que ma manière de décrire cette ville n'est pas tant celle du souvenire qu'un reportage en plein jour; come si l'on attendait un cachemar qui revient à la même heure chaque nuit et se poursuit jusqu'à l'épuisement.

Parfois je me lève tout endormi et poursuis mon cauchemar en prenant soin de ne pas le déranger: c'est une espèce de poésie de l'horreur. Je suis sûr que le vers de Baudelaire:

> Le coeur content je suis monté sur la montagne
> D'où l'on peut contempler la ville en son ampleur,
> Hôpital, lupanar, purgatoire, enfer, bagne,
> Où toute énormité fleurit comme une fleur.

. . . ont influencé ma passion pour cette ville.

—Nelson Algren

Reportage and nightmare, journalism and surrealism, sociology and poetry: these are not forms one tends to associate with one another. Contradictory as they may appear in the light of prevalent aesthetic and epistemological distinctions, Nelson Algren chose to be both the Dickens and the Baudelaire, the Dreiser and the Dostoyevsky of Chicago, a city, he insisted, that "runs from coast to coast."[1] In other words, he refused to give up either the empirical legacy of the realist and naturalist traditions or the poetic legacy of symbolism and surrealism.

This ambitious poetics has found few sympathizers among critics, both in times of infatuation with "the real"—his brand of realism is hardly realistic enough—or in times of metaphysics and self-reflexivity—his skepticism toward "the real" is too specific, aimed as it is always at a specific class and its vision of reality. Algren's poetics of "reportage" and "nightmare," social observation and "poesie de l'horreur" may appear a contradiction to us especially, surrounded as we are by a philosophical atmosphere that has appropriated the radical skepticism of the 1960s toward "facts" as ideologically and politically tainted and transformed it into an ideology of relativism and nonassertion or, as Barbara Foley notes, into an apology of "impotence proclaimed as privilege."[2]

And yet, Algren's depiction of himself as both a city reporter and a poet *maudit* would have struck a familiar note during the 1930s, when social and economic distress made the confrontation of intellectuals and artists with the reality of poverty and inequality less a matter of will than of necessity. In the tensions between "reportage" and "poetry" one finds the best products of an era, from William Faulkner to James Agee, from Ernest Hemingway to John Dos Passos, from James T. Farrell to Richard Wright.[3] Moreover, while the 1930s epitomize the legacy of "poetic reportage," this legacy is part of a long tradition in American letters, one that speaks loudly for a "poetry of facts."[4] Nelson Algren's debt to sociology is part of that tradition, a tradition that, critics' prejudices against sociology notwithstanding, deserves and clamors to be recovered.

Some suggestive remarks concerning Algren's first encounters with sociology have come from the author himself. In his long interview with Donohue Algren recounts how in college at the University of Illinois-Urbana he was "moved by a course given by a sociologist named Taft," and how after this course he "decided to become a sociologist."[5] Going on to graduate school, however, was difficult during the Depression, and besides, "there weren't any openings for sociologists." He decided therefore to become a journalist, since in that field the chances of obtaining a job were better.[6]

> Between 1936 and 1939, I turned out some short stories and a couple of poems. . . . It was all Chicago stuff. It was about the old-time Black Sox, and I started a whole series about the cheap hotels on South State Street and I went to a walkathon, one of these three-days . . . everlasting dance marathons. I spent a couple of days there. . . . My real interest was in the dance marathons and the whorehouses and the old-time ballplayers.[7]

157

Algren's attraction to urban culture, and especially to the culture of urban deviance, and his preference for ethnographic methods of observation are strongly reminiscent of Chicago urban sociology. The fiction that he started to write soon thereafter belongs to a genre one is tempted to label "sociological sketches." As he prepared to write "Design for Departure," a short story about a young prostitute, his homage to Stephen Crane's *Maggie: A Girl of the Streets*, Algren recalls, "I slept in bum hotels and talked to prostitutes, and I knocked around State and Harrison streets, tried to hear conversations going on in the next room—picked up, you know, bits of actual conversation."[8]

For each of the social worlds that young Algren went out to explore one can find a study on the shelves of Chicago sociology: *The Hobo* by Nels Anderson (1923), *The Gold Coast and the Slum* by Harvey Zorbaugh (1929), *The Taxi-Dance Hall* by Paul Cressey (1932), *The Jack-Roller* by Clifford Shaw (1930), and so on.[9] Some of these books were called sociology, others literature, some ethnography, others journalism. The difference hardly mattered when sociologists found in novels the human and social material that concerned them and in sociological studies novelists did the same.[10] Robert Park himself had been a journalist for many years before becoming a sociologist and emphasized the analogies between journalism and sociology. What mattered to both novelists and sociologists was a belief in knowledge as first-hand experience. As Algren explains, "[M]y kind of writing is just a form of reportage, you might call it emotionalized reportage, but—as you know—the data has to be there. . . . You have to know how do the law courts work. You have to know how many bars there are in a jail cell. You can't just say 'the guy's in jail.' You've got to know."[11] This was the same imperative urged by Robert Park on his graduate students. Park recommended to all of his students, "[W]rite down only what you see, hear, and know, like a newspaper reporter," and once he ordered a student who spoke too pretentiously about his subject, "[Y]ou go down to Cedar Street, and keep your eyes open, and you come back and tell me what you've seen and heard down there. And I am the one who gives you the high-falutin' words about it."[12]

One can also guess that empirical sociology was in the air during the Depression and was especially so in Chicago. Algren was a close friend of Richard Wright, who, in turn, was a close friend of Chicago sociologists Louis Wirth and Horace Cayton and knew several of their colleagues. And Algren may have known some of the members of the sociology department as well, through the events that the liberal and

158

radical intellectuals of Chicago, a physically large but intellectually compact city, attended together, which occasionally featured lectures by Chicago sociologists on various aspects of urban politics and social conditions.[13]

Algren's novel *Never Come Morning* is representative of a literary tradition that found in sociology what nineteenth-century novelists found in history, psychology, and biology: a way to question the reader's perceptions of "reality" and "unreality" and to authenticate their representation of the world.[14] *Never Come Morning* typifies Algren's life-long commitment to challenging the perception of "reality" and "unreality" of middle-class America. The slum and its inhabitants are more "real," he insisted—authorized by the sociologists—than what he called "the gadget-infested middle-class."[15]

> There is no way of convincing or even making the slightest impression on the American middle class that there are people who have no alternative. . . . The world of the drug addict doesn't exist. The world of the criminal doesn't exist. The world of the murderer doesn't exist. . . . [They] said, "It doesn't exist, they aren't there, we know that they aren't there, and if they are there, it doesn't matter, because we're here and we don't live in that sort of world."[16]

More critically than any other author during the 1930s, Algren borrowed from sociology and used it to show his readers that their cozy and protected world is "unreal."

I

Never Come Morning takes place during the Depression, approximately at the same time as the last volume of *Studs Lonigan*. It recounts the life of Bruno Bicek, a Polish-American youth who, like Studs, grows up in an immigrant colony of Chicago. More compressed than Farrell's trilogy, *Never Come Morning* concentrates on a few crucial years: at the beginning Bruno is not yet eighteen; by the end as he prepares to go to the electric chair he has yet to turn twenty-one. As the narrator puts it, the novel traces Bruno's growth from "boyhood to manhood," from "vandalism to hoodlumhood," recounting the main episodes in his life history before the death sentence (50). Loosely structured, the narrative is divided into four books. In the first book Bruno is initiated through his gang into the world of petty mobsterism and commits his first serious crimes—a murder and the rape of his girlfriend Steffie—

the one against the law, the other against Steffie and his own conscience. Books 2 and 3 follow Bruno in jail and Steffie in the brothel.
The narrative captures the viewpoint of the two main protagonists in
their separate worlds. These sections also record Bruno's growing
guilt toward Steffie and his eventual decision to free her from the
brothel with the money he will win in a boxing match. The boxing
encounter provides the material for the last book, a long fight that
brings together in dramatic form some of the main themes of the novel and, most important, brings to a climax Bruno's redemption.

The influence of sociology on Never Come Morning—which Algren
described as a "thinly fictionalized report on a neighborhood"—is
tangible in the topography of the physical environment as well as in
the life histories, case records, speeches, and other ethnographic
documents through which the characters are depicted.[17]

Never Come Morning, like Studs Lonigan, is set neither in a generic city
nor a generic neighborhood. Chicago as a tangible city is the space in
which the story unfolds. Yet it is not simply Chicago in general—with
its well-known connotations of violence, exploitation, ruthless capitalism, crime, lack of tradition, and refinement—but a specific tile of
the city that Robert Park had appropriately likened to a mosaic. The
setting is a sociologically recognizable neighborhood, authenticated
by its streets and boulevards, its corners and stores, its parks and
churches. The gang's hideout is "in a shed under a Noble Street sidewalk" (8). On Division Street are the "gospodas" where "beer [is] a nickel
a glass and the big bass juke [plays] only Polish songs" (32). By the
northwestern tracks is the brothel where Steffie is a prostitute and
Bruno the house bouncer. "[A]round Grand and Halsted are the work
agencies" and on Green Street is the homeless shelter (34). Bruno regularly paces the familiar walks of Division Street, Chicago Avenue,
Milwaukee Avenue, Noble Street, and Walton Street. Within this precise if limited area the characters move and the story unfolds.

At the center of the narrative is "the Triangle formed by Chicago,
Ashland, and Milwaukee Avenues" (8), which reproduces in its geo-
metric finitude the enclosed nature of what Park had described as
"cities within cities" (19): what lies outside its borders is literally
"abroad" for the neighborhood youths. When Bruno drives with his
gang outside the neighborhood to commit a robbery and begin his
adult criminal career, he "had never been this far west of the Triangle
before" (20). In an alien ethnic colony the youths steal a slot machine,
knock down the owner, and return home. As the narrator comments,

"[Bruno] had been out of the Triangle and into the world" (25). The "world"—for the nineteenth-century hero some faraway territory in which to acquire fame, wealth, independence—for Bruno and his friends begins at the end of the block, wherever there is a change of accents, skin color, and faith. Later, when Bruno boasts of having been in "Stickney. Hammond. St. Paul. E. St. Louis. Gary" the cop questioning him is justly outraged at his lie. He retorts, "'You don't even get as far south as Lake Street 'cause you're scared one of them Lake Street boogies 'll take after you with a shiv. . . . These Polacks figure the South-side is out of town'" (105). For Algren, much as for Park and the protagonists of the novel, the city is a mysterious expanse of small worlds out of which, in the case of his characters, and into which, in the case of the ethnographers, one ventures at one's own risk.

The characters' identities find their sources within this complex and precise landscape. People's last names may indicate their kinship within a family but their long nicknames indicate their location within the city. We have, therefore, "Catfoot N. from Fry Street," "Bruno B. from Potomac and Paulina," "Playboy Pinsky from Roosevelt and Lawndale," "Cowboy Okulanis from by the Nor'twestern viaduct," "the caseworker from the Sangamon Street Relief." Steffie talks about her "girl friend Okulanis from Moorman Street" and her "girl friend Masurczyk from Ellen Street." Through a sort of Cartesian principle, "I belong to a neighborhood therefore I am," the neighborhood is essential to each character's identity and to her or his sense of being at home in the world. In jail, Bruno addresses the silent rows of cells through a solitary monologue that echoes another more famous one. " 'Call me 'Lefty,' fellas. . . . The triangle's my territory. . . . They call me Biceps in my neighborhood too—you fellas c'd call me that, 'r 'Iron-Man,' 'r just plain 'Lefty' if you want. I got lots of names'" (87).

Much as the city occupies a central position in *Never Come Morning* as the physical setting of the story, the gang and the brothel play a central role as the social settings for Bruno and Steffie, the juvenile delinquent and the prostitute. Algren's portraits of the gang and the brothel conceptually resonate and methodologically overlap with Frederic Thrasher's study *The Gang* and with W. I. Thomas's *The Unadjusted Girl*, with their use of case records and personal narratives.[18]

161

As Farrell does for Studs Lonigan, Algren sets the protagonist within his youth gang, a type of social group that Chicago sociologists explained as the organized product of social disorganization, an expression of the youths' natural need for a society of their own, and a major shaping force of their personality, outlook, and social behavior: "There were forty-odd youths, from every corner of the Triangle . . . who claimed membership in the Warriors S. A. C." (8). A "shed beneath the walk" (38) provides a meeting place for the Warriors and a "warehouse basement served for a wall on one side and the sidewalk for a roof; the dirt wall facing the street had been reenforced with planks and the alley side was of dirt. The side away from the street was open, but lay in a warehouse shadow. . . . A dozen youths huddled about the dice" (38).

The precision with which Algren captures this underworld of shadows matches that devoted to its patrons. They are the young men of the Polish neighborhood, most of whom have "already seen the inside of the Potomac Street Station" before they even come of age (50). Their childhood was spent and their friendships were formed in the alleys or under the El, away deliberately from both their families' crowded rooms—"they were in the way in the rooms" (36)—and from social workers' inane attempts to supervise their games. They avoided "the policed safety of the playgrounds and settlements" (30).

One of the older members is "Casimir Benkowsky from Cortez Street, called Casey by the boys and *kasimierz* by the girls" (5). He had been "a bicycle thief when he was ten, a pimp when he was fourteen, and a preliminary boy at sixteen" (4). Now at "almost thirty, he'd been kayoed twelve times in his last fifteen fights, his strength was gone and his kidneys were gone and his heart was gone and his memory was going" (10). The protagonist, Bruno Lefty Bicek, is "the Warriors' first-string pitcher and cleanup man. . . . A slouch-shouldered, slow moving sixteen-year-old who could slug with his left hand as well as throw with it" (6), and was therefore "divided in his ambitions between being a big-league hurler and becoming a contender for the heavy-weight championship of the world" (11). Finger Izdikowski is "so-called for his reputed ability to jinx anything, from fighters to race horses" (16). Catfoot Nowogrodski, whose name reflects that "he walked as soundlessly as he rolled" (39), is a "narrow face [youth], like a pale alley cat" (66), who walks around "with red dice hanging for luck from his belt and his hatbrim turned up in front" (39). Fireball Kodadeck, another prominent member, is "six feet and five inches, and a bare one hundred and fifty pounds" (38); "sick in his lungs and sick at heart, [he] longed for one last summer of being alive" (41); he "never became drunk [because] the more he drank the thinner he got,

the soberer he became, and the more desperate in his hopes and jeal-
ousies" (41).

These are the older boys, young men who are taking the reins of
the gang and will lead its younger members through both legal and
illegal activites. Age differences aside, the gang consists of several categories of members: those whom Bruno identifies as "screwloose
sprouts" and scornfully describes as "farmers [who] still [match] nick-
els on the steps of St. Bonifacius" (40); there are the toughs who play
"fifty-cent poker" with the barber, the local small-time mobster, or
play "silver-dollar blackjack with the precinct captain" (40), the next
one up in the ladder of local mobsterism. The gang also includes "the
five-and-dimers, the penny matchers, the yasheks who'd never come
closer to going on a job than to lean against the same newsstand that
Bruno Lefty leaned on" (118).

The youth gang, much like Studs Lonigan's gang, and the hundreds
of gangs studied by Thrasher, is Bruno's main instrument of socializa-
tion into petty crime first and more serious crime later. The robbery
of a slot machine and the transformation of the "Twenny-six Ward
Warriors Social and Athletic Club" into the "Baldhead True-American
S.A.C." (50), both secretly directed or supervised by the barber, for-
mally ratifies the transformation from what Thrasher had called the
"conventionalized" gang into a "criminal" gang, the shift from occasional theft to petty mobsterism.[19] As the narrator puts it, "[T]wo brief
days had brought [Bruno] from dependence to independence. From
boyhood to manhood. From vandalism to hoodlumhood" (50).

The same combination of case record and literary sketch characterizes the portraits of the girls in the brothel of Mama Tomek in the
section entitled "The Hunted Also Hope." With the exception of the
older matron, these are all young women whose perdition, explained W. I. Thomas, had its sources in the clash between the old-
world culture of Europe or rural America from which they invariably
came and the modern culture of the American city to which they invariably escaped.[20] This cultural clash is reflected in Steffie, over
whose face mingle "old world" traits and "new city light[s]" (60); it is
embodied in the juke box of the brothel, half of whose selection is
made of Polish songs, the other half of American songs (165), and in
the decor of the parlor, where "the old-fashioned European stove
looked oddly out of place between the American juke and the slot
machine" (167).

Sitting around the parlor are Fat Josie, "who had just come to Chi-

cago from Warsaw by way of West Virginia" (165), and Jockey, who
"spent hours yanking the slot machine's lever" (166), but soon became "disappointed in a world that didn't go whirling after all" (106).
Then there is Chickadee, who "had been an acrobatic dancer in East
St. Louis' taverns" (195) and whose "mother in East Alton assumed
she was working a swank Chicago night club" (196); Chiney-Eye
Helen, who "had become a prostitute through a man with whom she
had lived only a few months . . . [but] had lacked money for a meal
on the very day she had first met him" (200).

Waiting for their clients, the women recall over and over the events
that have led them to the "life" and to Mama Tomek's; they imagine a
future as the matron of a home; they dream of the arrival of a savior
prince or of retiring in "a little chicken farm somewhere" (198); they
follow "the marital fluctuations of screen stars" (196). In moments of
painful insight and often through Steffie's voice they reflect on "[t]he
enormity of being accessible to any man in the whole endless city"
(190) or realize the "terror" hiding behind their clients' faces, "that
they went to work and joked and lived sensibly with their mothers
and saved their money and married and grew conservative and cared
for their health by day while practicing all their lives by night, the
madness of the street" (216). When all else fails they console themselves by reflecting that "[i]t was all so much easier, so much simpler,
so much more sensible" here, for here "you didn't even have to take
insults" and "you always had change in your slipper"; for after all "the
hard way didn't work for the women of the poor" and as it turns out
"the lower the wage the greater the morality demanded" (210–11).

II

The longest "sociological" document in the novel concerns Mama
Tomek, the matron of the house and a heroin addict. After inhaling
"five neat rows" of "white powder," she begins to tell what she has
clearly told many times before, the story of her life. "When you live
like I done you don't believe *nobody,*" she states in the course of the
narrative.

In the Federal Writers' Project files of the WPA one can find several
164 manuscript documents signed by Nelson Algren, material he produced when he worked for the project and that miraculously was
not destroyed. One of these documents is an interview with a pros-

titute entitled "When You Live Like I Done." Dated July 17, 1939, and eighteen pages long, it reads like a dramatic monologue addressed to a silent listener. The speaker recounts her experiences as a prostitute in Chicago, her beginnings during the "prohibition years," her life in the brothel, her hopes for the future as a matron, her reflections on the type of women who "end up in the street," considerations on the clients' expectations and attitudes. Lacking a strong narrative direction, the monologue reproduces the verbal rhapsody of a speaker who over a few beers remembers her life and philosophizes about the world:

> All at once I owed everybody and I couldn't figure out why. They charge you four times over for everything. You got to pay for the towels, for the music, for the lifebuoy, for the guys who stay overtime, for guys who lose money somewhere else and think they lost it in your outfit, for the high-school kids who come with two dollars even and carfare and then forget and put a nickel in the slot machine. Then you got to give them carfare, you got to pay off the doc who finds out you're sick, a sawbuck just to let you off, a fin to the bondsman when the house is pinched—and still you aren't really sure you *want* to get out.[21]

> This 19th and Dearborn territory, that's been my territory for years, even before I got on the bum. Say, I know every window, every alley, every bust-out lamp, every car-line, every newsboy, every cigar store, every cop, every Chinaman—say, I even notice where somebody tossed out a cigarette against a wall and the next day the wind has blew the snipe into the middle of the street. I've walked this corner at 4 A.M. and 4 P.M., summer and winter, sick and well, blind drunk and stone sober, sometimes so hungry I'd have to walk slow so as not to fold up on the pavement and get pulled in, and once with a month's rent paid in advance and thirty dollars in a purse under my arm.[22]

The monologue of Mama Tomek in the novel contains more than a few phrases from the interview Algren had conducted for the Federal Writers' Project. Two examples will have to suffice.

> "Then come the money years, 'n I got in the big one on Twenny-Second n' Wabash, the Four Deuces they called it then. All a sudden I owed ever'body in the syndicate, I couldn't figure out why. They charge you five times over for ever'thin.' You got to pay for towels

you never used, for music you're tired of hearin', for Lifebuoy 'n potash 'n dates who stay overtime 'n drunks who been rolled somewheres 'n start hollerin' they lost it with you. For high school sprouts who come upstairs with two soldiers even 'n carefare 'n forget theirselves 'n put a quarter in the slot machine. You got to pay off the doc when he jabs you 'n sees you're sick, a sawbuck to let you off till Sunday mornin.' That gives you the chance to get it back. And a fin to the bondsman when the house is pinched 'n still you aren't sure you want to get out." (179–80)

"You know, this railroad beat been my territory for years. I know every window, every alley, every bust-out lamp, every car-line, every newsie, every Polack cop, every cigar store with a bookie in the back—I even notice where somebody tossed out a cigarette 'r bust a milk bottle against a wall 'n the next day the wind has blew the glass into the street. I've walked these corners at 4 A.M. 'n 4 P.M., summer 'n winter, sick 'n well, blind drunk 'n stone sober, sometimes so hungry I had t' walk slow so's not to fold up on the pavement 'n get pulled in, 'n once with a month's rent paid in advance 'n thirty soldiers in a spanty- new blue bead bag under my arm." (182)

A similar genealogy connects Ralph Ellison, his novel *Invisible Man*, and his folklore collections for the Federal Writers' Project. "I had a two hour interview with Ellison," Jerre Mangione reported to Conroy, "and was surprised to learn that he had been on the Project for five years. He says he owes his start as a writer to the Project."[23] Ellison himself has described his experience as folklore collector on the dole and his strategies in approaching informants, highlighting the broadly ethnographic experience that writers were exposed to within the Federal Writers' Project:

I hung around playgrounds; I hung around the street, the bars. I went into hundreds of apartment buildings and just knocked on doors. I would tell some stories to get people going and then I'd sit back and try to get it down as accurately as I could. Sometimes you would find people sitting around on Eight Avenue just dying to talk so you didn't have to encourage them too much.[24]

166   For Ellison as for Algren, at least two extant documents attest to the contribution of urban ethnography to American letters. This link has recently been discovered and rightly celebrated in the case of Zora

Neale Hurston. It deserves to be explored more broadly. The first interview signed by Ellison begins, "Ahm in New York but New York aint in me. You understand? Ahm in New York, but New York aint in me."[25] This in turn became Mary Rambo's admonition, in *Invisible Man*, to the hero, who is periodically warned "Don't let this Harlem git you. I'm in New York, but New York ain't in me, understand what I mean? Don't git corrupted." A second interview begins with the words "I hope to God to kill me if this aint the truth. All you got to do is go down to Florence, South Carolina and ask most anybody you meet and they'll tell you its the truth."[26] The speaker narrates the story of Sweet, a "wicked" man who could make himself invisible by taking the heart of a black cat, climbing a tree backwards and cursing God. In this way he could defy the police of Florence, "one of those hard towns on colored folks." The legend became the controlling metaphor in Ellison's novel and eventually a central trope in African-American literature, one that captures the experience of African-Americans in their discovered invisibility in the eyes of white America and in their search for a historical identity.

Jack Conroy's folklore experience in the Chicago Federal Writers' Project was not unlike that of Ellison. "My first assignment was collecting and setting down a group of industrial folk tales—the sort of stories factory workers tell among themselves." Later on, with Arna Bontemps, he was put in charge of the Federal Writers' Project unit working on the study "The Negro in Illinois." They inherited this study from the dancer and anthropologist Katherine Dunham, whose goal had been to "[gather] material on storefront churches, self-styled 'muslims,' and other unorthodox religious bodies." Recalling his encounter and collaboration with Arna Bontemps, Jack Conroy has explicitly reflected on the importance of the Federal Writers' Project for American literature:

> It was Dr. Frederick [head of the Illinois FWP] who set me to work on the Industrial folklore tales which sent me on the folklore trail I've been pursuing ever since. And there for the first time I met my long-time friend and colleague Arna Bontemps. Out of our Negro in Illinois study grew our book on Negro migration, *They Seek a City*. With Arna, too, I adapted two of the industrial folk tales into juveniles. . . . Both projects widened my horizons. . . . Much of the material we gathered has been lost, I know. I know that great reams of it were burned because some WPA supervisors who considered

167

the projects some sort of bondoggling joke saw no reason for preserving it. But for most of those who gathered it, some benefits linger. They have been reflected in books, plays and other cultural manifestations to whom the projects brought a new hope and impetus.[27]

The Federal Writers' Project remains justly famous for its guide books. Less known are the large collections of folklore, interviews, life histories, ethnic and neighborhood studies completed in the process of doing the research for the guide books. The project was most original, folklorist B. A. Botkin would explain at the end of the decade, as "a synthesis of anthropology, sociology, psychology, and literature." Through its "Living Lore," "Industrial Lore," and "Urban Folklore" research the Federal Writers Project "trained writers to record what they heard as well as what they saw with an ear for the characteristic phrase and rhythm of the vernacular."[28] Virtually unknown are the dozens of manuals produced and distributed across the country to all the Federal Writers' Project offices. Consisting of hundreds of pages when gathered together, these manuals constitute a veritable ethnographic sourcebook for the study of American culture, written with the collaboration of and sometimes fully authored by the most prominent contemporary social scientists. The names of Chicago sociologists appear in many of the manuals that instructed writers on research procedures and interview techniques in the fields of immigrant and urban history.[29]

In exchange for their research Federal Writers' Project writers received a meager salary, yet it was a salary that allowed them to survive as writers through the Depression. As Algren put it at the time, "[I]f it wasn't for the Writers' Project I'd either be starving to death or working for a living."[30] Most important, they received training in sociology as they learned to conduct interviews, record dialogues, depict ethnographic settings. The estimated ten to fifteen thousand writers who worked for the Federal Writers' Project between 1935 and 1942 learned, at the expense of the federal government, what many graduate students in sociology learned at the University of Chicago at their own expense.[31] The documents signed by Nelson Algren and similar ones signed by Jack Conroy, Arna Bontemps, Richard Wright, Ralph Ellison, among many others, suggest the impact that this project and the urban ethnographic methodology it fostered must have had on American letters.

168

III

Algren's depiction of the immigrant family and community, much as that of the delinquent boy and the prostitute, is framed by and against the sociologists' formulations about those institutions. A representative of this world is Bruno's widowed mother, who "had the peasant faith in work as a cure-all," or as she puts it in broken English, "'[D]o a little work, feel better'" (15). Somewhat like the sociologists she too feels that "[i]f they had stayed in the Old World . . . her son would have been a good son. There a boy had to behave himself or be put in the army" (16). Steffie's mother, who observes the youths like Bruno from behind the counter of her poolroom, also reflects "that long working hours kept good boys out of trouble with bad girls" (71). Not only is this wisdom hardly relevant in a time of mass unemployment such as the Depression, but it is even more irrelevant in a neighborhood and generally a society where theft is more functional than full employment from an economic point of view, and certainly more remunerative from the boy's point of view. Pathetically insignificant at best in the modern urban world in which their children grow up, these families, the sociologists felt, were defaulting on their role as guides and teachers: their children were abandoned to their own devices, to be educated by the street and by older and already corrupt boys. For both Thrasher and Thomas, social workers were to step in as substitute parents because, as the caseworker for Bruno's family thinks to herself, "[p]erhaps all [Bruno] needed was Social guidance" (12).

The lack of understanding towards the youths exhibited by the families in *Never Come Morning* turns out, on closer inspection, to be not dissimilar from that of the caseworker herself.

> Bruno had never taken advantage of the fact that he was a year younger than the woman credited him with being. He enjoyed being taken for eighteen. "At least you don't lie about your age," she had once assured him.
>
> "You didn't show up Wednesday morning," she apprized him now, "Why not?" . . .
>   "I'm in trainin.' Had to go to bed early 'n sleep late. That was orders."
>   Seeing the full-grown slouch of his shoulders, she found herself hoping that he'd lie more outrageously than ever before. But she kept that out of her voice.

169

"Training for *what?* Orders from *whom?* . . .

She jotted something in the book, and he took time out to fancy himself climbing through the ropes at the City garden. Then she'd see his picture in the paper the next morning and would write him a letter of apology addressed to "*Mister* Bicek" . . .

"What do you earn when you fight?"

The boy had no one to whom he could boast freely but an underage girlfriend, and she didn't count.

"I wouldn't pull on a glove fer less n' a hunerd," he heard himself saying. . . .

The implication, that he lied as fast as a dog can trot about everything else, was true as far as she was concerned. Why he lied to her the boy didn't know. Perhaps it was, in part, distrust of her notebook and pince-nez, perhaps it was partly her consistent failure to regard him as the Warriors' mainstay; perhaps it was chiefly his realization that she came from the same world as did detectives and truant officers and park policemen. Perhaps too he had sensed that she stopped to question him chiefly in order that she might leave feeling she had been most deliberately, brazenly and wantonly betrayed by a client she had trusted completely. (13–14)

The caseworker's periodical interviews with Bruno reveal as little understanding of the boy as his mother's old world maxims.

The immigrant community, moreover, turns out to be not so uniformly foreign in relation to American customs as one would gather from the sociologists' monographs. In Algren's Polish ghetto immigrants are of two kinds: those who still live by their old-world truths—pathetically obsolete in the new world and oblivious to the surrounding reality—and those who have adapted to the dominant values of the new world—exploitation, cheating, theft, corruption—and of the city—the law of the jungle, the survival of the fittest.

Bonifacy Konstantine, also known as the barber, is representative of the second group. His outward appearance is strangely surreal. An old man with a leg badly twisted by measles in childhood (4), he often sits alone in his barbershop "dealing a hypothetical game of seven-card stud to five hypothetical players. He himself wasn't playing. He was just cutting himself in a hypothetical five per cent for dealing" (3); he always imagines that one of the players "was cheating" (5) because "[t]hey were always trying to cheat him in this country" (10). The barber also seems an evil father figure lifted from the folktale tradition; he approves of "[b]aseball and boxing that paid money" but disapproves of "young Poles with a purely amateur enthusiasm for a wop outfielder or a Jew welterweight" (3); he recommends "snuff for old-country Poles like himself, but felt that the young men born and raised in America should stick to cigarettes" (5); he stages the transformation of the Warriors into the Baldheads—"a fellow could hardly belong to a mob called the Baldheads without getting clipped by the barber regularly, summer and winter" (9); he also fixes boxing matches for gang youths who will take a fall and a bad beating for a few dollars. Like the other old-world people, he has a favorite motto—"when the thunder kills a devil . . . then a devil kills a Jew"— which he is fond of telling the youths in Polish. The main refrain in the novel, this motto remains obscure until the last scene, for which it reads as epigraph.

The barber, however, turns out to be more than just a folktale figure. While the novel is the story of Bruno's sin against Steffie—of her confinement to the brothel, a captivity tale set in the modern city, and of his attempt to free her—it is also the story of how the lives of Bruno and Steffie become increasingly trapped in the web of power relations that the barber controls within the immigrant slum. The barber's true role and the nature of his power over the boys is first suggested by Catfoot:

> "Benkowski's washed up. Barber's just giving him kid stuff t'do to keep him from messin' around the big stuff. I know where you was with him 'n Finger last week. You pulled out a slot machine in Stickney 'n got a sawbuck apiece 'n now any time the barber wants he can put a finger on you fer the syndicate –"
> "It wasn't no syndicate machine –"
> "There ain't no slot machine in Stickney that ain't." (67)

The barber's role is also to "[get] twenty cents off every two dollars that Mama Tomek's women earn" (36) in exchange for protection from the police. From within his "West Division Street TONSORIAL PALACE OF ART AND BARBER SHOP" (2) and in spite of his broken English, the barber directs the activities of both the gang and the brothel, acts as a link with the larger world of urban corruption, machine politics, and mobsterism, and most importantly oils the circuits of protection that keep the boys and girls out of jail—most of the time—by getting a cut on their activities and by sharing part of the dividends 171 with those above him. The police represent—in their relationship to vice and crime—the next layer of power in the submerged political economy of the slum.

> Money. They wanted money. They were by turns friendly and
> threatening, but either way, it was for money. Any kind of money.
> The Heat took anything. A dollar. A half dollar. A quarter could get
> you out of spending a night in a cell as often as not. . . . Arresting
> [the girls] taught them the lesson that it was cheaper to pay off to a
> patrolman than to a bailiff; they were envious of the bailiffs. (164)

The web spinning out from the brothel, the youth gang, and the
slum has its proximate conceptual sources in the tradition of Chicago
empirical sociology, yet, one begins to see, reaches well beyond that
discipline. The empirical boundaries of representation begin to give
way as the city, in the course of the narrative, increasingly takes on the
role of an invisible yet active presence. The city evokes not just the
identity but the subjectivity of Bruno, his past and present experiences, his states of mind. In one of these scenes Bruno is walking under "the shadow of the El" when he recalls his childhood as a street
urchin.

> As a child he had learned that the safest place to play was beneath
> the El. For the streets belonged to streetcars and walks to people
> who lived in houses and not behind stores or above pool-
> rooms. . . . That was the safest part. Nobody came there to make
> you play in the sun; nobody could find you when you slept, an un-
> derfed, shoeless six-years-old of the cageworked city's curbs and
> walks. (29–30)

The tracks of the El, once the shelter for a poor boy, are now the vehicle for his memory, which expands into a long recollection of his family, of other children, of the cold. And it is again the train, that most
ubiquitous presence in American literature and in the literature of the
Mid-West especially, that triggers in Bruno's mind the moving picture
of his own American dream, the dream of a slum boy:

> The single-car local to Humboldt Park slowed up overhead and
> clattered lamely west; to the boy's ears the clatter became a crescen-
> do of applause. He jabbed with his right and threw the left—that's
> the hand they were cheering. A right to the heart and a left to the
> jaw. He bobbed, ducked, covered, swung and straightened up: the
> applause was faint and far away and then it was gone. He shoved his
> hands down his pockets and shuffled on. (37)

172

Personified into an applauding audience, with the regularity of its
rhythms the train also inspires a poem: the boxer poem.

Algren's recurrent shifts between empirical detail and poetic image defines the urban landscape of his writing and the poetic program that sustains it. This is a landscape dominated by an urban geometry: the "tunnel of the El," the "narrow streets," the "web of the tracks," "the river," the "viaduct," "the city wires." It is also brought to life by the pulsation of its parts: the "contracting" and "expanding" ties of the El, the "rising bridges," the "red lightning of the express," "the moving river." And finally it beats with the cacophony of sounds that fill the nights: "[t]he clatter of the locals," "the beat of the powerhouse," "the iron rocking of the bells of St. John Cantius," the "rush of city waters," "the low moan of river horns," the "clanging of engines from the Northwestern yards."

The city is ever-present, intrusive, impossible to forget or shut off. Even within a padded cell—where he is later placed, as the "lockup" explains, in case "they might take a notion t'turn the hose on you some night" (97)—Bruno can hear the city's ubiquitous presence. "At night he listened again for the murmur of the powerhouse. But he could not hear it through the padded walls. He heard the iron rocking of the bells of St. John Cantius above him, the tinny clang of the Chicago Avenue trolley below, and the smooth splash-splash of gas into the squad cars in the station yard" (99). In jail and no longer able to walk and see the city, Bruno repeatedly hears its sounds, tangible reminders of its presence, of his own being alive and, most important, of the jail's location in the *center* of the city. And from the brothel, that other place of seclusion, one can also hear the city's sounds even after its images have been shut off by walls, blinds, and curtains. "When [the juke box] paused the rainbows moved only down one side, and then their voices sounded unnaturally loud, there was a faint clanging of engines from the Northwestern yards, a chirr of crickets beside the tracks. . . . The drone of the power house all down Chicago Avenue to the river" (185).

If the sounds, lines, and colors of the city suggest a landscape of interconnected parts, the bird's eye view that Bruno has of it from a roller coaster translates that impression into a tangible experience through a picture that combines Baudelaire's view of the city from the mountain top with Park's mosaic of "little worlds."

173

He forced himself to look: thousands of little people and hundreds of bright little stands, and over it all the coal-smoke pall of the river factories and railroad yards. He saw in that moment the whole dim-

lit city on the last night of summer; the troubled streets that led to
the abandoned beaches, the for-rent signs above overnight hotels
and furnished basement rooms, moving trolleys and rising bridges:
the cagework city, beneath a coalsmoke sky. (62)

Algren's "cagework" city, much as Park's "mosaic" city, defines a space
composed of fragments, each one isolated yet never fully separate; it
conjures up a landscape that is also claustrophobic, scarred by num-
berless tracks, streets, rivers, trolleys, bridges. In another bird's eye
view Bruno sees one of these urban fragments as he waits to be placed
in an identification line-up at the police station:

Bruno Bicek, waiting beside a barred window for the last line of the
evening, watched the moving locomotive lights and saw, across the
valley of the tracks, the lights of the low-roofed village between
Halsted Street and the river; a village in the city, like his own low-
roofed streets. Clamorous, like his own, with old-world markets
and mid-American saloons, murmurous with poverty, filled with
old-world faces and mid-American cries, bound by the laced steel
of the railroads and the curved steel of the El. And covered, like his
own, with a slow pall of locomotive smoke. (136)

What Bruno sees from the window of the police station is similar to
the view Robert Park must have had from some other window when
he realized that these exotic inhabitants were as interesting to study as
the North American Indians. And Steffie's wakeful recollection of the
neighborhood from which the brothel has shut her off expresses
much the same idea.

On rainy nights she thought of the absurd habits of the poor, of her
mother's faded underskirts hanging out to dry back of the poolroom, hanging there through the rain and sun, four or five days before being taken in; of the washings hung on fire escapes, of laborers who tried to keep a sheep in a tenement basement, or chick-
ens in a kitchen, or a goat in a two-by-four lot. (213)

What most distinguishes Algren's city from Park's or from other sociologists' is less the use of poetic images than his use of the city and of
the slum as the estranged consciousness of society. Emblematic in
174 this respect is the episode of Bruno and Steffie's first date. In Steffie's
apartment above her mother's bar Bruno forces her to have sex with
him in what will turn out to be the first but not the last of Bruno's
crimes against his girl friend. As Bruno is about to commit the violence, time comes to a halt.

Outside, the evening's first arc lamp came on. Someone in the street was roller-skating on a single skate; and the single clack of a billiard ball sounded from below. He saw her dimly before him and sensed the city outside waiting for them both. Saw the green-plumed flash of a Chicago Avenue trolley a block away and heard the girl begin to plead indistinctly in Polish. He raised the chair then, Steffie and all, and slung both onto the disheveled couch. (28)

The omnipresent city is indifferent to the violence that is being consummated. Its sounds and flashes of light create an estranged distance between the violence and the perpetrator, a moment of stillness when the reader is forced to stop and look, to think. Such a still moment forces upon us the realization that violence does not happen effortlessly and cannot be put behind as one reads on.

A second episode, the main turning point in the novel, illustrates even more clearly Algren's Brechtian-like use of the city. It occurs after Bruno and Steffie's second date at Riverview Park, where he has taken her to free himself of the guilt produced by the first violence. "I'll make it up to her," Bruno had told himself after the rape, "I'll take her to Riverview" (29). After he gets her drunk, however, Bruno leads Steffie to the gang's hideout with the intention of repeating the sexual violence. Here he is soon joined by two other gang members—Catfoot and Fireball Kodadeck—whom they met at the amusement park and to whom Bruno had inadvertently confided his plan. The two demand that Bruno share his "prey." His refusal and attempts at negotiation are finally turned into acquiescence under the threat of a knife and of being turned in for the robbery. The most convincing argument comes when the two begin to make fun of Bruno for being in love—"'what's eating you, Left'—'you in love?'"—in other words, when they wave the flag of the gang code. What follows is one of the most horrifying scenes recorded in literature. As Bruno leaves the dark shed, a "pit gouged under the wooden walk" (64), and emerges onto the sidewalk above, trying to drink the horror and the guilt out of his consciousness, he discovers the rest of the gang members waiting in line for their turn: Knothole Chmura, John from the Schlitz joint, Sheeny Louie, Coast-to-Coast, Punch-drunk Czwartek, Corner-Pockets, Bibleback. This time too it is the city's role to be the indifferent witness: "[A] two-car local came clattering past, its lights moving downward, in yellow squares, across the warehouse wall" (69). At the same time, the sounds of the city force Bruno to hear what he will never forget. "Beneath them, once, between the passing of the El

175

lights on the wall and the chimes for early morning Mass at St. John's, he heard her struggling desperately to raise beneath someone and again he waited, hoping to hear her weep or cry out. And heard only a muffled whimpering" (70). When a Greek who does not belong to the gang tries to stand in line, Bruno challenges him to fight. As the man is taking off his coat and his arms are trapped, Bruno again hears Steffie's drunken voice and reacts to the guilt by killing the man in another brutal scene punctuated by Bruno's attempts to hear Steffie's voice. This time the city intrudes not with its usual sounds but with an unnatural stillness. "There was no sound from below. There was no sound from above. As though the last El had crashed and the last trolley had finished its final run. Only the beat of the powerhouse, the heavy throb through the city wires: and the blind wall waiting before them. Then they ran" (74). Always intruding in the moments of greatest tension, the city emphasizes with its sounds the violence silence cannot hush, with its flashes the horrors darkness cannot hide.

When Bruno is eventually arrested it is for neither the murder of the Greek nor the gang rape of Steffie but for a robbery committed earlier. Although the months he spends in jail fail to lighten his guilt, they actually function as a retribution of sorts. Over and over Bruno is haunted by the sounds of the outside city, which remind him of Steffie and the fatal night:

> "Tell us more about yourself while the officer gets your clothes," Tenczara asked. . . .
>
> Roller skates! The snow must be melting! The skates sounded for a moment, the way skates did over the wooden walk above the shed by the warehouse. Then like they did over cement, across the rink at Riverview –
>
> "Next!"
>
> Had someone called or had he spoken it himself? They were all looking at him a little oddly. (115)

By the end of his jail term, after several such scenes, Bruno is ready for repentance, a repentance that has nothing to do with the time spent in jail and one that the law cannot acknowledge:

176

> Had she called "next!" because she was mocking herself with the whisky in her? It seemed now that she had been mocking only him. If only they had killed her outright down there. If only that bullet had really bounced. If only the old man had been killed. Regardless of who held the gun, Bruno B. would have been guilty; it wouldn't

have been necessary to mention a woman then at all. Tenczara would have had him by the throat and who, in Tenczara's mind, he would have burned for, could have made no difference. For all his guilt was for Steffie R. Whatever happened to him now was on her account. He alone had killed her. (156)

The interior monologue of the juvenile delinquent flatly refutes the Polish Catholic cop of the precinct—"The kid don't feel guilty is the whole trouble" (131). More generally, it undermines the myth that the city may be a source of enlightenment and growth for the middle-class hero but is only a source of corruption for a lumpenproletarian youth, who must reform through the agency of a social worker, a priest, or some other representative of authority. From this point on the city becomes for Bruno a constant reminder of a guilt that no jail term can redeem, its sounds the embodiment of a consciousness that no priest can absolve. As the crime for which the police have arrested him and the one for which his soul actually aches merge into one larger sin, Bruno reveals in his interior monologue a man who is actively if unconsciously looking for punishment, a man who finally realizes his responsibility not to the law, for that law cares little for either Steffie or himself, but to his own conscience.

The second half of the novel follows Bruno's growing realization that he must save Steffie from the brothel where she was sent by the Barber after the rape and put to work as a prostitute. Through Steffie's eyes, now a permanent recluse of the brothel and of the night, we move one step further from both the empirical and symbolist sociology of the city discussed so far in the direction of what one might call surreal sociology. Often sitting at the window and observing the outside city through the permanently closed windows and curtains of the brothel, Steffie sees a world "of empty schoolrooms and abandoned churches and darkened bars with the chairs on the tables, boarded windows, for-rent signs on deserted streets, weed-covered walks and windowless places" (188). When she walks from the brothel to her room just across the street, in a scene that vividly evokes the figure of Maggie, the landscape around Steffie is part of the same world but not the same reality as that evoked until now through Bruno. "She left by the family entrance and turned down the rutted street, that went forever narrowing, down to the moving river. On either side great mounds of trash and garbage smoked and smoldered all night long. All night, and in the valleys between each mound sunflowers crowded, slender and bent; their petals glinting, in the dull

177

copper light, like petals of wetted metal" (189). Finally back in the safe enclosure of her room, once more behind a window, Steffie, like Bruno, captures a bird's eye view of the city:

> A copper-red shimmering ran down the rails, she looked up to see what arc lamp cast such a glow, and it was the moon. It was the moon, as large as a sun and crossed twice by city wires, glowing sullenly in the coal-smoke sky; and so motionless in the heat that its stillness was part of the sleeping city's stillness. Beneath it stood the abandoned hotels and boarded fences of the river front. She looked farther, at all the houses and all the factories all the parked cars and all the darkened dime-a-dance halls; and there was no one, nothing left alive, not a man nor a woman nor some forgotten child to waken and cry fear of the night. (192)

When observed through the eyes of the prostitute, the urban landscape is a surreal still life, the only style appropriate to her nightmarish existence. Relying more frequently in the last part of the novel on the use of dream material, Algren's vision of the city climaxes in one of Steffie's dreams:

> She dreamed one night that she walked, as a child and alone, through Lincoln Park; saw flames above the trees and, running toward it, saw the small-animal house ablaze. All manner of strange animals scurried past her toward the safety of the trees about the lagoon; they brushed past her legs, half monkey and half dog, pale catfaced things that limped as they ran, blind bird-faced rodents that wriggled like lizards as if in pain, and white-bellied, hairless things that leaped like frogs. As they passed she saw that some had tiny faces, like some tiny young man's face, pale and unshaven, the lips half-open and the eyes ablaze.
>
> When she wakened she held a picture in her mind of another place: a great stone penitentiary with all the exits barred and no sign of smoke or disorder without, no sound of crackling flame; but only the steady murmur of the machine shops within. Guards paced the wall steadily and regularly so that no one in the whole outside world could guess that the cells within were blazing, tier upon tier within the very stone, that the smoke was in the lungs of a thousand chained men. That the very bars they grasped were melting with the stone. (217)

178

Through Steffie especially Algren taps his most surreal vein to produce a vision that is at once a synthesis of and a departure from all he has expressed so far. The jungle connotations of the slum, the most popular trope for urban poverty and difference in the language of social workers, journalists, and sociologists alike, is here associated with Lincoln Park—"nature" inside the city, or the "garden" inside the "machine"—and therefore with the larger city. The inhabitants of this hybrid garden-jungle-zoo turn out to be themselves hybrid monstrosities and associated with the monstrous nocturnal drives of Steffie's respectable clients. The stone penitentiary evokes not only the brothel and the jail, the two main structures of confinement within the novel, but the factory as well, the three heads of the capitalist Scylla. Behind the bars of this infernal pit, Steffie hallucinates, the guards and chained men are imperceptibly burning toward destruction, undetected by those outside.

How can one assert that empirical sociology is a primary source of inspiration for a novel that is so far from anything one might confidently call realism? Algren's claim that his art is both "reportage" and "poetry" articulates that tension without really addressing it. After arguing for the empirical factuality of the novel, one still must notice how often the ethnographic material paradoxically disrupts rather than reinforces such an assertion. The surrealistic dreams are but one in a network of such disruptions. Lines of songs, inscriptions on the walls of bars, of cells and offices, letters to magazines, advertisements, labels on whiskey bottles, prayers, calling cards, all forcefully remind the reader of the historicity and factuality of the story, much as the topographic details about the neighborhood do. Yet, at the same time, like the poetic intrusions of the city within *Never Come Morning* and like the songs and the chorus sections in Brecht's epic theater, they force the audience to detach itself from a simplistic referentiality. They guard both audience and text from the dangers of vulgar empiricism looming large in any novel that so loudly proclaims its "veracity" and allegiance to the empirical slum and to social observation.[32]

Most revealing of Algren's poetics is the closing scene of the novel. This is a boxing match, fixed as usual by the barber, which Bruno will be paid to lose. His decision to fight, however, and his determination to win develop as his final act of redemption from the sin committed against Steffie and thus as an act of consciousness. If he wins he will receive the prize and cut out the barber from the deal altogether. On 179 the boxing stage are Bruno Bicek and Honeyboy Tucker, "[t]he sons of a Polish baker and a mulatto pigsticker" (260), but on a larger fictional stage is the audience of the match, "[a] North Side crowd and a white man's evening" (260), and the racist violence that is sublimated in the encounter. "Seven thousand whites in the dark, watching a single brown one in the pitiless glare of the lights. . . . It was good to feel the house behind him, the whole white man's house" (267, 272). Never for a second does Algren allow us to forget who is observing whom and that the observer must himself be observed.

This metatheatrical scene is one of several that punctuate the novel. Other audiences include the reporter at the police station, the captain and the cops at Bruno's interrogation, the relief worker, the jail inmates, the retarded janitor of the brothel, the doctor who periodically visits the brothel to certify the good health of the women, the crime victims at the police line-up who sit in the dark, "half a hundred men and women seated comfortably as though for a double feature" (137), and observe suspects who in turn stand behind a one-way window under the glare of spotlights and come forward to respond to the captain's circuslike questions. Complementing Algren's vision of the city as a system of interdependent worlds, the metatheatrical scenes bring together the worlds Algren labored to reveal as inseparable, entangled, and hopelessly compromised.

The sequence of staged scenes in which the words or actions of a criminal or a prostitute are observed by a fictional audience provide the novel's epistemological infrastructure. They weave into the text a critique of empirical sociology Chicago-style and of the stereotypes that that tradition ultimately fails to demolish. In all of the staged scenes Algren deliberately shows the criminal and the prostitute within a specific context, observed by a specific audience. Staged as "veracious" voices, to use Foley's crucial formulation, much as the documents used by the sociologists in their monographs do but, unlike the latter, framed against specific audiences and settings, these narratives, dialogues, case records succeed where the sociologists fall short: they represent individuals who are at once subjects and objects in their own lives and in the representation of those lives. These voices and performances articulate Algren's critique against all who would reduce the criminal and the prostitute, and following Foley's lead minorities, women, the poor, the "other," to stereotypicality. Through their voices the criminal and the prostitute who inhabit *Never Come Morning* challenge the objectification of which they are the victims. More important, they challenge the sustaining epistemology that condemns them to stereotypicality and denies them the privileges of individuality and typicality.

Bruno and Steffie ultimately come to resemble pieces—the smallest perhaps but fully homologous ones—in a set of Russian dolls, which includes the immigrant community, the slum, the city, and the larger society. When Bruno finally manages to rebel against the code of the slum through the boxing match in order to rescue Steffie from the brothel, it turns out he has broken not only the code of the slum but that of the law as well, two supposedly antithetical systems. In the final revealing scene of Bruno's boxing victory the police captain and the barber merge into one figure who comes to arrest Bruno ostensibly for the murder of the Greek, yet in fact for having broken the rules of compliance that bind the slum and the city, the delinquent and the prosecutor, corruption and power. " 'Go ahead. Put [the manacles] on,' Bruno challenged him, 'that's how we both want it. That's how you'n me always been wantin' it. We'll go right down the middle aisle.' " (284). The captain and the delinquent boy, manacled together and marching down the aisle in a parody of a wedding ritual, provide the appropriate closing image for this novel.

The political and economic structures of inequality and difference that the progressive Chicago sociologists hoped to erase as they envisioned a city of homogeneity, harmony, equilibrium, and synthesis—Park's mosaic city, Burgess's concentric city, Redfield's peasant-urban continuum and Wirth's telos of urbanization—Algren's novel has shown, are to society what the manacles are to the captain, the web of the tracks to the physical city. An indictment of the pathology of capitalist society, *Never Come Morning* reveals not just the marginal and mysterious slum but the much more mysterious social contradictions that paradoxically make the slum and the criminal both *margin* and *center* of the city.

8

Decentering
and
Recentering:
Richard Wright,
African-
American, and
American
Literature

Richard Wright's two-volume autobiogra-
phy, *Black Boy-American Hunger*,[1] demonstrates in remarkable detail the
theoretical and methodological tools that the author borrowed from
Chicago sociology, indicating at the same time some of the broader
consequences of using an interdisciplinary methodology for the literary criticism of his work. In the past critics have raised a number of
questions: why Wright wrote his autobiography at thirty-five; why he
included events that his biographers claim did not happen to him
personally; why the impersonal titles. More recently critics have
questioned his representation of the African-American community,
asking whether he can continue to be a founding figure of African-
American literature given what some perceive as scathing remarks
about African-American culture.[2]

When one approaches *Black Boy-American Hunger* as a life history of migration from the South to the North, from rural to urban society, from folk culture to modern civilization, some of the questions become substantially clearer.

An episode from *American Hunger* will illustrate the conjunction between literary autobiography and sociological life history. Wright recalls that during his years in Chicago he had decided to draw a series of sketches of Negro Communists. The story of Ross, a fellow comrade, would be the first:

> Southern-born, he had migrated north and his life reflected the crude hopes and frustrations of the peasant in the city. Distrustful but aggressive, he was a bundle of the weaknesses and virtues of a man living on the margin of a culture. I felt that if I could get his story I would make known some of the difficulties inherent in the adjustment of a folk people to an urban environment; I would make his life more intelligible to others than it was to himself. I would reclaim his disordered days and cast them into a form that people could grasp, see, understand and accept. (*AH* 78–79)

If Wright's view of Ross's life rests on the sociological view of the individual as representative of a group and on the notion of narration as a search for meaning; it relies specifically on the Chicago sociologists' view of migrants as "peasants in the city," and as "marginal men" living between cultures.[3]

Wright's plan eventually fails after the Communist Party becomes suspicious of his numerous questions to Ross. The episode, however, is important as it reveals Wright's reason for and method in becoming himself a sociological informant. He eventually discovered in his own life all the tiles of the mosaic that he was trying to compose. "I sensed that Negro life was a sprawling land of unconscious suffering, and there were but few Negroes who knew the meaning of their lives, who could tell their story" (*AH* 7).[4] He now had to make himself into a type—a migrant, a peasant, a marginal man—and he had to make his story a representative case history. As an informant, Wright would tell his story as "few Negroes" could; as a participant-observer he would capture "the sprawling land of unconscious suffering" of "Negro life"; finally, as a kind of sociologist he would give meaning to his own life 183 and to the lives of other Black migrants. This material is, strictly speaking, extraneous to both the "ex-slave narrative" and the "portrait of the artist" genres after which Wright's autobiography is largely modeled. It is, however, central to the sociological genres and methodologies of participant observation and life history that characterized Chicago sociology during the 1920s and the 1930s, genres the subtitle of *Black Boy*—"A Record of Childhood and Youth"—explicitly acknowledges.[5]

While literary critics have devoted little attention to Wright's exchange with urban sociology, it has been recognized as important by his biographers.[6] Michel Fabre and Edward Margolies, among others, have detailed some of the facts of Wright's readings and friendships. Robert Park, Louis Wirth, Horace Cayton, and Franklin Frazier figure prominently in these accounts. Their names also spell out the very earliest theories of migration, deviance, family breakdown, and urban change that came out of the department of sociology at the University of Chicago during the first half of the century, theories that for a time made the department synonymous with American sociology and world famous. Their studies were pioneer efforts to confront both the large-scale migration from rural to urban society of southern Black migrants and southern European immigrants and the family and community breakdowns sociologists saw as concomitant with that transition.

Wright himself has repeatedly acknowledged his debt to the sociologists. In *American Hunger*, he explains: "[m]y reading in sociology had enabled me to discern many strange types of Negro characters, to identify many modes of Negro behavior; and what moved me above all was the frequency of mental illness, that tragic toll that the urban environment exacted from the black peasant" (*AH* 26). He also cites sociologists in his introduction to *Black Metropolis: A Study of Negro Life in a Northern City* (1945) by St. Clair Drake and Horace Cayton.[7] Here Wright describes himself as a migrant to Chicago, where he had gone "to tell [his] story." And yet, he explains,

> I did not know what my story was, and it was not until I stumbled upon science that I discovered some of the meanings of the environment that battered and taunted me. . . . The huge mountains of fact piled up by the Department of Sociology at the University of Chicago gave me my first concrete vision of the forces that molded the urban Negro's body and soul.
>
> It was from the scientific findings of men like the late Robert E. Park, Robert Redfield, and Louis Wirth that I drew the meanings for my documentary book, *12,000,000 Black Voices*; for my novel, *Native Son*; it was from their scientific facts that I absorbed some of the

184

quota of inspiration necessary for me to write *Uncle Tom's Children* and *Black Boy. Black Metropolis*, Drake's and Cayton's scientific statement about the urban Negro, pictures the environment out of which the Bigger Thomases of our nation come.[8]

In short, Wright wanted to tell his own story but did not know *what* his story really was until he discovered the sociological "facts" that allowed him to see the links between his personal experiences and those of other Black migrants.

To Wright's own statements, one should add Michel Fabre's study, *The Unfinished Quest of Richard Wright.*[9] Fabre explains that Mary Wirth—the wife of Chicago sociologist Louis Wirth—was the case worker for the Wrights' household when they had first moved to Chicago, that Louis Wirth repeatedly provided Wright with reading lists of sociological material at the graduate level, that Wirth introduced Wright to Robert Park and Robert Redfield, and that as a result he collaborated with Drake and Cayton on his own 12,000,000 *Black Voices* (1941) and on their *Black Metropolis.*[10]

With few exceptions, literary critics have yet to make these autobiographical and biographical details relevant to the interpretation of Richard Wright's work. One of the first who raised this issue was John Reilly, who has focused on 12,000,000 *Black Voices*, Wright's seldom examined and powerful prose poem about the Great Migration and an outstanding example of the documentary tradition of the 1930s.[11] Reading in this work the encounter of Wright's experiences as a Black migrant from the South, his sociological readings, and his theories on African-American writing, Reilly finds that Robert Park's theories on nationalism and migration more than the Communist Party's position on nationalism shaped Wright's theories on African-American culture. Reilly rejects the idea that Wright may have "stumbled" fortuitously upon social theory. Instead, he suggests, this intellectual encounter resulted from an active search for "explanatory concepts," which enabled Wright "to tell not only his own individual story, but also the story of other Blacks, whose experiences, the Chicago school assured him, were his own."[12]

In another essay, by Robert Bone, Wright emerges as the central figure of what this critic terms the "Chicago School of Afro-American writing," among whose members Bone includes Margaret Walker, Willard Motley, Arna Bontemps, Gwendolyn Brooks, Waters Turpin, and Alden Bland.[13] Many of these writers "wrote repeatedly of the

Great Migration . . . of the pathology that was too often the price of adjustment to the urban scene . . . [and were] reinforced by their contacts with the Chicago School of Sociology, which offered them a sophisticated theory of urbanization."[14]

The most recent and extensive contribution to this sparse debate has been by Werner Sollors, who examines the representation of "modernity" through some of its most obvious symbols—the clock and the gramophone—in Richard Wright's "Long Black Song" and Zora Neale Hurston's "The Gilded Six-Bits."[15] Sollors relates these, on the one hand, to the modernization theories developed by Chicago sociologists and, on the other, to the universalist theories developed by Boasian anthropologists. While important ideological differences separated them, Sollors proposes, Wright and Hurston confronted analogous materials and conflicts—nature time vs. clock time, the South vs. the North, rural folk culture vs. modern urban civilization, modernity vs. tradition.[16] The sometimes antithetical resolution of these conflicts in their fictional work, Sollors suggests, might have had to do less with their views of African-American culture than with the divergent orientation of the disciplines of anthropology—especially at Columbia University in the 1920s—and sociology—especially at the University of Chicago in the 1920s and 1930s—disciplines that so deeply inspired the work of Hurston and Wright respectively:

> Anthropologists were more concerned with "culture," "folk," "tradition" and "adaptation," whereas sociologists looked into "civilization," "an urbanized population," "modernization" and "conflict." . . . The Boasian anthropologists in the period leaned toward an "internalist approach to the study of human groups—they focused primarily on the group considered in itself, its norms, institutions, and the patterns that gave it coherence." The Parkian sociologists, on the other hand, "highlighted the processes of interaction *between* groups" that were "being thrown into contact with each other, were reacting to each other, and mutually influencing each other in all sorts of ways." Thus "folk culture" often suggested the internalist perspective, whereas "urban civilization" summoned the interactionist approach.[17]

186 One might add, following Sollors's discussion, that while we must study these two important authors within the intellectual contexts of anthropology and sociology, we must also be wary of reproducing their half-a-century-old conceptual infrastructures by espousing ei-

ther Hurston and Boasian internalism or Wright and Parkian interactionism.[18] Unfortunately, it is in the vicinity of such ahistorical approaches, and of the first one in particular, that a number of recent critical reassessments of significance and consequence are to be found.

To take on Richard Wright at present is to confront two related critical trends within African-American literary criticism. Their challenge to the author can be summarized in the questions thrown at him. First, how can Wright continue to be the symbolic ancestor of African-American literature given his remarks on the absence of a "Black tradition?" Second, how can a literature so generously represented by women enshrine one who depicts them as "passive" and "inferior?" Finally, how is that African-American literary tradition to be rewritten in the poststructuralist 1990s were Wright to be moved from the center to the margins of that tradition?

Statements Wright made in *Black Boy* that concern the African-American tradition and, more generally, his politically qualified nationalism, his purported uncritical embrace of rationalism, the Enlightenment, and Western literature, and, finally, his purported Eurocentrism toward the Third World have become serious stumbling blocks to his status as the "symbolic ancestor" of African-American literature. Some critics have tried to redeem Wright by turning those statements on their head and making of Wright a more palatable proponent of cultural nationalism. Others have openly questioned his cultural and racial allegiance on the basis of his statements concerning African-American religion, family, community, and literary tradition.

Representative of these two strategies are Gunter Lenz and John McCluskey. Lenz presents Wright and Hurston as important precursors for the current self-consciousness toward and interest in the African-American folk tradition.[19] He claims that "Richard Wright's 'picture' of culture and community in the ghetto . . . should be complemented by . . . Zora Neale Hurston's work . . . [as] an alternative way of responding to the urban experience and of reconstructing black folk culture and community," and explains *Black Boy* specifically as an attempt to "[communicate] the meaning of the Southern folk heritage," bound by the need "to reject his immediate environment" and resulting in "rejection of the way of life of his own people."[20] This 187 he contrasts with "Blueprint for Negro Writing," where he finds evidence of Wright's "*reassessment of black folklore* as 'living and powerful.'" "Blueprint," Lenz finds, is "a far cry from his lament (in *Black Boy*) about the 'cultural barrenness of black life' and its traditions."[21] Lenz, however, makes no mention of the fact that "Blueprint" had been published some eight years before the autobiography and thus can hardly be used as evidence of Wright's newly achieved consciousness. If anything, the process took place in the reverse order. If Lenz's effort to minimize the disparity between Wright's and Hurston's views of the African-American folk tradition is admirable, he seems at times to do so by simplifying the complexities and ambiguities that made Wright's relationship—and that of many of his contemporaries—with his ethnic, national, and political cultures so conflictual and his relationship with Hurston rather contentious.

John McCluskey[22] takes the opposite route by raising the thorny issue of whether Wright can be at the "center of a modern Afro-American tradition," given his "uneasy relationship with [the] Afro-American vernacular," his dismissal of the church as an "ineffective and uncreative force," and, finally, his unwillingness "to use positive elements from his own culture."[23] Rather than minimizing these tensions, McCluskey points to a deep contradiction running through Wright's work: on the one hand are the author's pronouncements in favor of folklore and folk idioms, and on the other hand is his writing praxis, which creates heroes who have "weak, if non-existent" relationships with the Black community and in which heroes are "isolated men at odds with the world, fragmented victims and outsiders."[24] McCluskey's otherwise perceptive discussion closes with a puzzled and inconclusive reflection over the paradox of an artist, at once so conscious of "folk forms" yet so adamantly opposed to "tradition," "community," and "continuity."

With hindsight we can see how McCluskey anticipated, in the early eighties, what has become in the early nineties an openly polemical view of Wright. Written before the current rediscovery of Zora Neale Hurston, his essay reveals one reason for Hurston's new critical good fortune. Hurston, like Wright, theorized about the importance of the folk tradition and, unlike Wright, she practiced that theory through the representation of an ostensibly organic relationship between individual and group, intellectual and community, heroine and people. As a result, Hurston is now regarded as a positive alternative to Wright: an artist who succeeded precisely where Wright failed.[25]

While antithetical in their conclusions, Lenz and McCluskey typify the questions that have periodically surfaced within critical debates that did not question the centrality of Richard Wright overall. More hostile is the direction the debate has taken in the recent past. The questions raised by Lenz and the doubts voiced by McCluskey have turned into blunt attacks on Wright by prominent representatives of African-American literary criticism.

Robert Stepto has recently confronted the dilemma of Wright's position toward and within the African-American tradition.[26] Examining an episode from *American Hunger* in which Wright is ostracized by some Communist Party Black members for being an "intellectual," Stepto discerns not the familiar tension between "intellectuals" and "workers," which runs through the history of the Communist Party, but the unfaithfulness to a group of Blacks by a Black man who "refuses to *partake* of the essential intra-racial rituals."[27] Paradoxically, Wright is found guilty of exactly the same sin by the fictionalized Communist Party members—in *American Hunger*—and by Stepto. The religious connotations of Stepto's language—"to partake," "rituals"—are ultimately more revealing than his reading, showing this critic to be part of the very picture Wright, rightly or wrongly, created. Through a conscious and skilled use of religious language in his autobiography Wright links the family, the church, the school, the South, and the Communist Party—all of them bent upon enforcing allegiance on the recalcitrant modern individual—and finally rejects not so much each of them but the "partaking of rituals," which, in Wright's and in the Chicago sociologists' view of society, all these institutions demand.[28] More troubling than the misreading of an episode are Stepto's broader conclusions. Stepto castigates Wright for failing to stand by the "dimension of heroism" that is the essence of the tradition, for failing to create a "hero" or a "transcendent voice." To deny, as Stepto does, that heroism and transcendence are at the center of both *Native Son* and *Black Boy-American Hunger* is to ignore the process whereby Bigger Thomas and the autobiographical persona reach the "personal heroic voice." Bigger does so precisely when his fragmented sentences and painful insights—"'what I killed for must've been good'"—take over from Max's eloquent but ultimately ineffective summation. As Laura Tanner has argued, "Bigger has adopted Max's conclusions but changed their reference, adopted his language but changed the language game."[29] In the supreme heroism of reappropriating that language Bigger Thomas comes to "tell the story 'like he wanted it' . . . [finally] becom[ing] author and narrator of his own text, driving from the novel the voices that would overwhelm his own"—of the narrator, the lawyer, and perhaps even the literary critic. Going after the critics, especially of the sixties, who have "en-shrine[d]" Wright, Stepto concludes, very much in harmony with the larger tenets of American literary criticism, that "the black art-as-sociology and black aesthetic theories of the 1960s are outmoded . . . because . . . neither approach is fully in tune with the heartbeat of the artist and his art."[30]

Stepto's claims have been taken one step further by Henry Louis Gates. A critic who, in the recent past, has done much both archeologically—by recovering in print some of the lost milestones of the African-American literary tradition—and theoretically—by bringing African-American literary criticism up to date with the most recent developments in poststructuralist literary theory and by forc-ing literary theory to reflect over the issues raised by the African-American literary tradition—Gates has been a most vocal and promi-nent participant in the scholarly trend to decenter Richard Wright. Contrasting the "full voice," the "transcendent self," and the "lyrical shape of *Their Eyes Were Watching God*" with the "naturalism" of *Native Son*, and claiming that "this fiction of obliteration"—Wright's purported obliteration of the African-American heritage—is "the great divide in Black literature," Gates has done for African-American literature what has long since been done for American literature, where the natural-ist/realist tradition has been negatively defined as nonmodernist and excised, so to speak, to allow the transcendentalists to become the precursors of modernism.[31]

To deny, as Gates does, the lyricism of *Native Son*—in Bigger's per-ception of sailboats, airplanes, and even of the inimical snow and vio-lent water hose, for example—is to submit to precisely the dehuman-ized view of Bigger that caused *Native Son* to be written to begin with. Bigger's lyricism is perhaps more constrained, given the specific so-ciological, emotional, and existential subject Wright chose to write about. It is certainly no less powerful than that of many protagonists in American literature. More remarkable than the degree, pitch, or intensity of Wright's lyricism is that it never subsides, even in the grimmest moments. Gates's—and Stepto's—use of such loaded terms in a critical context where lyricism is routinely associated with art, and naturalism with non-art or bad art amounts to nothing less than a covert invitation addressed to literature to avoid those who cannot lyricize with "a full voice" or articulate a "transcendent self"—i.e., the people that the 1990 census takers failed to count and that the literary critics, apparently in agreement with the current administra-

190

tion, decided "do not count." Finally, and most important, to deny that Bigger's is a heroic and powerful voice is to define that voice so narrowly that the most powerful voices of American and African-American literature will be left out as well.

Gates also attacks Wright for presenting African-American culture as inferior to Western culture, for disclaiming his African-American literary "antecedents," and, conversely, for espousing the "Western" literary tradition as his source."[32] The terms Wright uses to characterize African-American culture and to dramatize his conflicts within it—"formless," lacking in "individuality," "elemental," "impulsive"— and that are so jarring to Gates and to our postsixties sensibilities define a point of view Wright shared with sociologists and modernist artists of the first half of this century. Very similar pronouncements, for example, inform Danny O'Neill's views of the Irish American community both in the *Studs Lonigan* trilogy and in the O'Neill pentalogy. Critics have found these views not just palatable but admirable and comparable to those expressed in the work of James Joyce, which is generally not labeled anti-Irish in spirit. We are entitled to critically assess the "modernist" and "modernizing" ideologies that underly Wright's views, but to dismiss his work because of concepts we have come to be skeptical of is to throw out the baby with the bathwater. Should we dismiss all of Zora Neale Hurston's and Langston Hughes's work because they received money from wealthy white patrons or, in the case of Hurston, for relying on forms of anthropological research that are now considered exploitative?

Gates faults Wright for reacting "stridently" against the Harlem Renaissance of the twenties and thus against the most important antecedent in African-American literary history. However, in the thirties Wright was not alone when he criticized the social relations and self-conscious alienation of art production of the twenties. Charles Johnson recently wrote that "Negritude—all kitsch—is a retreat from ambiguity, the complexity of Being occasioned by the conflict of interpretations, and a flight by the black artist from the agony of facing a universe silent as to its sense."[33] If we follow Johnson's sensitive remarks, we might see that Wright and many other intellectuals of the thirties were turning down—and contemporary critics are reviving— existential flight for political fight at a time when the universe stopped being silent, and interpretation ceased breeding despair. Both in the United States and in Europe writers came to attack the predominant aesthetic, ideological, and social relations of art and the artists of the previous decade, which suddenly came to appear complicitous with the totalitarianism of fascism and Nazism in Europe and with the tyranny of the Depression in the United States. These attacks notwithstanding, the African-American modernist literature of the 1930s is the most immediate heir to the Harlem Renaissance and to the literary modernism of the twenties, especially to that literature's heroic battles against the genteel tradition.

Wright is finally taken to task for encouraging young writers to appropriate what Gates terms, less than admiringly, the "great tradition of Western writing," and for stating that Black Americans had "no fictional works dealing with such problems."[34] However, the authors favorably mentioned by Wright—Eliot, Stein, Joyce, Proust, Hemingway, Anderson, Gorky, Barbousse, London, Dreiser, Balzac, etc.— were not simply "Western." Some were European and vernacular American modern authors. Some of these authors, even in the 1930s, were still considered so avant-garde that they had to be published through alternative presses and small magazines in the United States, were often sued for obscenity, and would most certainly not be found on the shelves of the public libraries; in large parts of Europe they were considered decadent, antisocial, or worse, revolutionary, and therefore openly banned, available only through underground illegal networks. They were most certainly not *the* canon that they became after the Second World War. Wright's literary referents also included some of the classics of European realism and naturalism and a few American realist and naturalist novels; in other words, the literature where an author like Wright, faced with the challenge of representing the modern city, migration, and urban poverty was most likely to find inspiration. As the many references scattered throughout his prose attest, Wright knew his "heritage" exceptionally well—minus, of course, the many texts that the painstaking labors of scholars like Gates are once again making available to us—but he knew of few literary predecessors, in the United States, who had dealt extensively with the urban, working-class, and lumpenproletarian world of cities like Chicago. He thus was not disavowing race as much as recommending certain authors unified by the aesthetics of realism and modernism and by a preoccupation with urban migration and social change. Wright preached the need to appropriate the work of white authors, much as many colonial writers did when confronted with the heritages of their native or ethnic culture, of the colonizer, and of their own intellectual upbringing. Like other colonial intellectuals formed

192

at once by the European intellectual heritage, the colonial context, and the vernacular cultures of their countries, he attempted to define a tradition that owed to both the international *and* the indigenous, to modern art *and* folk culture.

A different strategy from that of Stepto and Gates, one more useful to the project of recentering American literary history, is exemplified by Hazel Carby, who presents Nella Larsen's *Quicksand* (1928) "as a precursor not only to Richard Wright and Ralph Ellison but to a neglected strand of Afro-American women's fiction" that has been centrally concerned with the urban and social changes concurrent with migration.[35] She thus asks that we rethink the outlines of modern American and African-American literature. "In the search for a tradition of black women writers of fiction," she notes, "a pattern has been established from Alice Walker back through Zora Neale Hurston which represents the rural folk as bearers of Afro-American history and preservers of Afro-American culture." While easier to accomodate within mainstream American literary history, this rural-pastoral tradition "has effectively marginalized the fictional urban confrontation of race, class, and sexuality."[36] In a more recent essay Carby has added:

> Contemporary Afro-American cultural history and criticism is recreating a romantic discourse of a rural black folk in which to situate the source of an Afro-American culture. Indeed, much current critical work that is concerned with the construction, reconstruction, and revision of an Afro-American literary canon has expanded the discursive category of the folk to mythic proportions, and romantic readings of Hurston's *Their Eyes Were Watching God* are an integral part of that mythology.[37]

The disparaging of Wright is part of that mythology as well.

Gates has suggested that Hurston, Wright, and Ellison's texts all ask, "[I]n what voice would the Negro speak for her or himself in the language of fiction?" For Gates the voice should be the one that speaks in Hurston's and Ellison's texts, voices of "a common blackness" and "a unique black self." Hazel Carby, on the other hand, suggests that the question is more precisely, Who shall speak for the masses, and which masses will represent "the people" in the changed context of American advanced capitalism? For Hurston, one can answer, it was the citified, Westernized intellectuals of the North and the rural folks of the South, which some of those intellectuals had left behind and many had never known. For Wright it was the proletarian intellectuals and the urban proletariat of the northern Black Belts from which such intellectuals ideally came.

Parallel to and sometimes inscribed within the cultural nationalist argument that presents Richard Wright as a false supporter of African-American culture runs a feminist argument that presents him as misogynist and sexist.[38] Calvin Hernton's claim that "*Native Son* is an astounding Patriarchal achievement" with an "overriding phallic perspective"[39] has escalated into Alan W. France's claim that beneath Bigger Thomas's story of struggle against racism is another of struggle to "appropriate (and thus dehumanize) women," one that "takes the form of. . . the rape-slaying."[40] Bigger turns out to be a struggling patriarch, the rat scene a "struggle for phallic dominance with overtones of castration anxiety," the subtext a "system of sexual terrorism" carried out by Bigger against his mother, his sister, the daughter of his employer, and even his gang friends. Bigger discovers, according to France, not the existentially liberating power of murder but the mysogynistic power "of killing women." Ultimately siding with the prosecutor, this critic triumphantly reverses the verdict of not guilty that the lawyer, the narrator, and the reader for half-a-century have returned.[41]

Other extreme claims have been made by Nagueyalti Warren, who finds that Wright's Black female characters are "unwholesome," "stereotypical," "degrading," in short "bitches and "whores," and that this is due to the fact that "female sexuality [was] problematic for Wright."[42] It is not easy to dispute such a claim when sexuality has come to be problematic for many people and female sexuality specifically has come to preoccupy some of the most sophisticated minds of our time. It is more useful to observe Warren's work on a specific story, "Long Black Song." Warren rejects Sarah, the protagonist, as "stupid" and "hysterical" and as "the paragon of amoral sexuality and mindless stupidity." Her fault appears to be that "[s]he is not raped and is hardly seduced by the white salesman." Warren would apparently forgive her had Wright depicted the sexual encounter as unambiguously a rape. Instead, "she appears to lead the young man to her bed." My mother could have made herself no clearer in drawing the moral of similar real-life stories for the benefit of her young daughters. Finally, Warren explains Wright's "pathological" view of women with the theory that he hated himself and for that reason his characters—like Wright himself—whenever possible choose white over Black.[43] This is a choice that has become less and less acceptable in our times, and that is perhaps the context in which such reassessments must be understood. The inscription on the portals of our age might turn out to be "Woe to those who leave the safe enclosure of their class, race, and ethnic group."

Joyce Joyce has come to Wright's defense, but with less than successful results.[44] Joyce counters the accusations of sexism by also focusing on "Long Black Song." Her claim is that far from being a "stereotypical," "inferior," "instinctual," "primitive" character, Sarah is actually the center of consciousness of the story.[45] Surprisingly, however, Joyce reads the story as the seduction and rape of Sarah, a reading that indeed reduces the female protagonist to passive object and elevates the salesman to active agent. Emphasizing Sarah's passive role in her "sexual stimulation" and "arousal"—perhaps to protect her from the stigma of making improper advances to a man? or of weak resistance to a white man—Joyce seriously undermines her otherwise original and insightful thesis that Sarah is the center of consciousness in the story. By reading the story as a seduction activated by the salesman and Sarah's adultery as a sin activated by the husband's failure to "satisfy his wife sexually"[46] Joyce fails to recognize this as a rare literary representation of seduction and sex recorded through the consciousness of the female, Black, and poorer protagonist rather than the male, white, and richer one. More serious, by depicting her life as being in "harmony" with "the rhythmic pattern . . . of nature"[47]—natural harmony? for Black peasants in the South? in the 1930s?—Joyce reduces Sarah, precisely as others accuse Wright of doing, to "instinctual, primitive, and childlike nature."

The more moderate feminist critics have provided starting points for what could and should be an enlightening debate, not a witch hunt, about the representation of female characters by radical authors in the era preceding modern feminism. Jane Davis notes that "Wright depicts women of all types, whether Black or white . . . [as] threatening to men" and a threat to "their independence."[48] Maria Mootry adds that "we must accept [Wright's] treatment of the relations between men and women . . . [as] a metaphor for the struggle of an oppressed people to deal with history with dignity and meaning, a vision that for all its rigid compartmentalization into bitches, whores and woman-haters offers a painful and powerful truth of our history which should never be 'blotted out.'"[49] Finally, Kathleen Ochshorn notes that, in *Native Son*, more tragic than Bessie's lack of a protagonist role, or even the brutality of her murder, a brutality commensurate with the brutality of Bigger Thomas's life, is "[t]he minor role that Bessie's murder plays at Bigger's trial."[50] This "is the most poignant racism of the book." Following Mootry and Ochshorn, we must ask if we respond with horror to Bessie's murder because she is a woman or because it reproduces and indeed amplifies the brutality of life for people who are female, Black, and poor in a society that is sexist, racist, and classist.

The fact is that Wright presents all characters, Black and white, women and men, southern and northern, as passive in the face of different forms of coercion. Such representation cannot be understood apart from its underlying sociological premises. As the ensuing discussion demonstrates, Wright's representation of Black women and of the Black community rests on the conflict between group and individual, community and society, tradition and modernity, nature time and clock time. This conflict structures the autobiography as well as early sociological theory and literary modernism both in Europe and the United States. To read Richard Wright apart from these developments is to blind oneself to the tensions of his time. It is precisely in responding so deeply to those tensions that Wright produced great works of literature and ideas.

The same applies to the folk tradition-bearer Zora Neale Hurston, and to many artists and intellectuals of so-called modernism. In the case of Hurston in particular, we blind ourselves to the tensions between group and individual, folk culture and modern culture, tradition and modernity that underlie Janie's relationship with the porch people, with the community on the Muck, with the Black audience at her trial, and to the conflictual relationship between Hurston's autobiographical persona and the superstitious townspeople upon her mother's death. "No two authors in the tradition are more dissimilar than Hurston and Wright," Gates concludes from a comparison of the two mothers' death scenes in Hurston's and Wright's respective autobiographies. Hurston, it is argued, receives encouragement and inspiration to speak for and of the Black folk from her dying mother, taken to represent Black folk culture, while Wright receives not voice but somberness from his culture. Upon closer reading, however, one finds that the will of the dying mother, in Hurston's autobiography, is squarely and unambiguously set *against* the will, in this case the beliefs and superstitions, of the group. The injunction to speak that Gates hails is more precisely the ur-modernist injunction to speak as an in-

196

dividual *against* the community and its conformities, in other words the same that motivated Wright. Many other modern authors responded to that same injunction. Choosing to read Hurston's work as harmonic solution and integrated synthesis of conflicts that are apparently still with us puts us in the paradoxical position of hailing Hurston as the modernist ancestor we lost in Wright, while turning her more truly, and unfairly, into a rear-guard and belated representative of romanticism.

The following discussion in chapter 9 explores one important referent—sociological theory—for the disjunction between tradition and modernity that we find offensive in Wright and invisible in Hurston. Wright's so-called ambivalence toward Black culture should be recognized as part of broad historical tensions that span the political spectrum. The southern agrarians bypassed that tension by creating a religion of tradition; the Left went the opposite way. Neither found a conceptual solution beyond or above that basic dichotomy. Hopefully, Zora Neale Hurston, current "bearer and ancestor" of Black folk culture, will yet again be rediscovered and allowed to articulate this same disjunction when she presents the quest for voice—female, individual, and modern—as antithetical to the voice of the community—male, collective, and tradition-bound.

9

Sociology of an Existence: Black Boy-American Hunger by Richard Wright

While an overall assessment of the role played by sociology in the contexts of Richard Wright's larger work and of African-American literature—and, more generally, of Chicago literature and the literature of the 1930s—is a desirable but still premature task, enough has been said by Wright himself, by his biographers, and by literary critics to make the following analysis of *Black Boy-American Hunger*, as literary autobiography and sociological case history, both a step in that direction and a partial answer to the confusion that Wright's "unreliable" autobiography and "unsentimental" views about African-American culture have occasioned. Wright's two-volume autobiography is an emblematic product of a sociological grafting onto literature that is the acknowledged mark of the literature of the 1930s. More specifically, it is a remarkable expression of the tendencies that made the confluence of sociology and literature possible at that particular time of modern American history: on the one hand the tendency toward a more subjective sociology, a sociology that rediscovered the subjectivity of the individual as a social and cultural being; on the other the tendency toward a more objective literature, a literature that rediscovered the individual's unbreachable ties with the larger cultural and social spheres. Richard Wright's methodological and theoretical borrowings from the Chicago school of urban sociology and the content of that exchange will provide the two main axes for the present discussion.

The autobiography recounts the story of Wright's life between his setting fire to his parents' house, at age four, and his break with the Communist Party, at age thirty. The first volume is set in the South where, from an early age, the narrator is unable to comply with the rules that regulate social relations within the family and the primary community and, more broadly, between social groups and classes in a rural culture and in a racist society. Two intersecting narrative threads run through this story. One is the portrait-of-the-artist narrative, a story of violent clashes, both physical and psychological, with a world that hates books and knowledge—Blacks because of religious faith, whites because of racism. The other is the ex-slave narrative of escape to the North, the story of a modern quest for intellectual freedom that climaxes in the closing scene of *Black Boy*, with the narrator "aboard a northward bound train."

American Hunger continues with Wright's experiences in Chicago between 1927 and 1936, before his move to New York and the staggering success of *Native Son*. The confrontational pattern established in *Black Boy* is further developed in *American Hunger* through Wright's encounter with both the modern and urban North and the Communist Party. The racial and intellectual intolerance of the South, Wright soon learns, are oppressive presences in the North as well, even though they come dressed in different clothes. The North is not free of racism nor is the party more tolerant of dissent.

The first thing one notices in the autobiography are the many pages of documentary material that play no apparent role in the narrative economy of the story and are tangible signs that Wright's intent 199 was not simply the autobiography of an artist nor simply that of a modern-day southern slave who finds freedom in the North. These passages exemplify the methodology of participant observation in the tradition of the Chicago school of sociology.[1] As a participant-observer Wright captured, in many remarkable passages, the social worlds in which he found himself immersed:

> I would stumble upon one or more of the gang loitering at a standing in a field, or sitting upon the steps of somebody's house.
> "Hey." Timidly.
> "You eat yet?" Uneasily trying to make a conversation.
> "Yeah, man. I done really fed my face." Casually.
> "I had cabbage and potatoes." Confidently.
> "I had buttermilk and black-eyed peas." Meekly informational.

> And the talk would weave, roll, surge, veer, swell. . . . The culture of one household was thus transmitted to another black household, and folk tradition was handed from group to group. (BB 88–92)

In this and similar conversations Wright depicts what Frederic Thrasher and Louis Wirth called the "cultural milieu" of the street gang, its "moral and social codes."[2] It is Richard the gang-boy who, through his special gift for words, captures the fluid quality of the conversation; at the same time, it is Wright the sociologist who interprets it and distances himself in order to represent it.

Wright also described the white waitresses with whom he worked in Chicago: "I learned about their tawdry dreams, their simple hopes, their home lives, their fear of feeling anything deeply, their sex problems, their husbands" (AH 12). While sharing with the sociologists a dislike for the uniformity of the rural world, Wright was less sanguine in viewing the urban environment as a "new way of life." For him the "urbanism" that the waitresses represent—and that Bigger Thomas is also part of—is a despicable world filled with "radios, cars, and a thousand other trinkets . . . the trash of life . . . the words of their souls were the syllables of popular songs" (AH 14). It is the world of mass consumerism, which, for most presixties radicals and cultural critics, numbs the consciousness of people, especially the poor, with false images.

The same methodology allows Wright to capture another pole of "urbanism" that those who are excluded even from the "trash of life" represent: the world of the juvenile delinquent. Chicago sociologists focused on this social world for its supposed correlation with mass migration and cultural transition.[3] This is how Wright, who in the early thirties had worked at the Chicago South Side Boy's Club, recreates the world of juvenile delinquents:

> Each day black boys between the age of eight and twenty-five came to swim, draw, and read. They were a wild and homeless lot, cultur-ally lost, spiritually disinherited, candidates for the clinics, morgues, prisons, reformatories, and the electric chair of the state's death house. For hours I listened to their talk of planes, women, guns, politics, and crime. Their figures of speech were as forceful and colorful as any ever used by English-speaking people. (*AH* 88)

In the role of participant observer Wright thus capitalized on his first-hand experiences in a number of milieus that had been traditionally of interest to Chicago sociology and, while foreign to the sociologists, were thoroughly familiar to him. The ability to encompass many so-cial and cultural experiences had once been the prerogative of the picaro, the literary archetype who symbolized the individual's free-dom from social and cultural ties. This prerogative here becomes em-bodied in a sociological archetype—the migrant. Having moved away, the migrant can look back from a distance while still being part of the group. As a participant-observer Wright became that archetype: the migrant-picaro whose story confirms the achieved freedom from cultural and social strings.

If a sociological methodology tells us how Wright decided to tell his story, one still must understand what kind of story he actually chose to tell. Some of the pictures he draws of his relationship with his family, with his fellow comrades, with the worlds, first, of the South and, lat-er, of the North have been questioned as distorted or even false. It is not our task to challenge the claims of those who detect inconsisten-cies between Wright's life and the text. The truthfulness of Wright's account, however, should be sought less in the empirical record of a "real" life, to which no account, not even the municipal records, are ever fully faithful, than in his broader views of modern society and the modern world, views to which the theories and studies of the Chi-cago sociologists generously contributed and that Wright has repeat-edly acknowledged.

"Personal evolution," Chicago sociologists W. I. Thomas and Flo-rian Znaniecki theorized, "is always a struggle between the individual and society—a struggle for self-expression on the part of the individ-ual, for his subjection, on the part of society—and it is in the total

201

course of this struggle that the personality—not as a static 'essence' but as a dynamic, continuing evolving set of activity—manifests and constructs itself."[4] With this theory Thomas and Znaniecki postulated a dichotomy that is crucial to the narrative of *Black Boy-American Hunger*. This postulated struggle between individual and group provided the underlying structure for Wright's autobiography.

The use of personal documents and life histories in sociology owes its greatest debt to Thomas and Znaniecki as well. Determined to avoid the abstractions then in vogue among social scientists, Thomas had discovered in the letters and life histories of Polish immigrants a way to bring subjective reality within the purview of sociology. The result of his pathbreaking work has been described by a historian as "a synthesis of the anthropologist's or ethnographer's participant observations, the case study method of the social worker, and the content analysis procedures of the traditional humanistic disciplines."[5] In *The Polish Peasant* Thomas and Znaniecki examined first the primary group of the immigrant, the family, then the immediate community, the immigrant neighborhood, and finally the larger society, schools, churches, organizations, and associations.[6] *Black Boy-American Hunger* is organized precisely around that same conceptual progression. This was a model that the Chicago sociologists extensively used and increasingly refined as they dealt with immigrants' and migrants' transition from a peasant and traditional society to a modern and urban one.

The struggle between individual and society informs the two main concepts used in Wright's autobiography—"personality" and "environment." "Environment" is an inclusive term that indicates the group, the community, the culture, tradition, authority. Against the threat of these institutions the individual "personality" must strive for self-realization. These institutions become tangible living bodies, more real than the single individuals who form them. They are the challenges against which Richard, the autobiographical narrator, must contend.

Three types of institutions successively confront Richard: the family to which he belongs by blood, the South, epitomized by religion, school, and the racist white world, to which he belongs by culture, and the Communist Party to which he belongs by choice. As a ritual reenactment of the pyromaniacal action of the first scene in which he sets fire to his parents' home, the hero sets symbolic fire to these insti-

202

tutions. This seems to be the only way to keep his personality intact, until isolation emerges as his other alternative.

The hero's relationship with his family develops from passive to resentful submission to finally successful rebellion. Attempts at self-expression often spark the confrontations. Young Richard is punished for printing "four letter words describing physiological and sex-functions" that he had just learned in school (BB 32–33). He is punished for listening to the "Devil's stuff," the story of "Bluebeard and His Seven Wives" (BB 47). He is punished for speaking words "whose meaning I did not fully know" (BB 49). Many other times he is "slapped across the mouth" for saying something wrong.

Far from being a simple catalogue of punishments, the narrative illustrates the child's growing ability to rebel; each time he emerges from a confrontation with a family member, he keeps his personality intact through a progressive denial of kinship and a growing sense of isolation. In the first confrontation with his father, the narrator recalls the old man as a "stranger," as "always somehow alien and remote." (BB 17) By lynching the kitten that is disturbing his father's sleep he subverts his father's authority and ignites a process of estrangement for which the actual writing of the autobiography comes to appear as the culmination.

> A quarter of a century was to elapse . . . when I was to see him again. . . . I realized that, though ties of blood made us kin, though I could see a shadow of my face in his face, though there was an echo of my voice in his voice, we were forever *strangers*, speaking in a different language, living on vastly distant planes of reality. (BB 42, my emphasis)

Only through a denial of kinship ties, and thus at the cost of isolation, can the individual escape the familial institution and its violence against the individual personality.

Similar confrontations take place with Aunt Addie, who embodies those institutions—school, family, and church—that conspire to annihilate the individual. As Aunt Addie prepares to give Richard another lashing, and as he is considering whether or not to defend himself, reflections over the value of blood ties once more come to the fore:

> I was trying to stifle the impulse to go to the drawer of the kitchen table and get a knife and defend myself. But this woman who stood

before me was my aunt, my mother's sister, Granny's daughter; in her veins my own blood flowed; in many of her actions I could see some elusive part of my own self; and in her speech I could catch echoes of my own speech. (BB 119)

In spite of blood and, if need be, by spilling blood, Richard decides to defend himself. The result is a violent struggle of "kicking, scratching, hitting, fighting as though we were *strangers*, deadly enemies, fighting for our lives" (BB 120, my emphasis). Unlike the pupils in Aunt Addie's school whose personalities are "devoid of anger, hope, laughter, enthusiasm, passion or despair," and who are "claimed wholly by their environment and could imagine no other," Richard's personality defies submission to these institutions (BB 115–16).

The family, it turns out, represents the first but not the only environment that threatens Richard and against which his personality must struggle to preserve and affirm itself. Outside the family he must face the larger South, whose culture of racism cannot be fought with knives and razors and which he carries within himself at all times, even as he attempts to escape from it. The South pervades and comprises the outside world of religion, school, and work where young Richard must first begin to live as an adult.

External to the family and yet hardly distinguishable from it, religion comes uninvited to Richard, first in the guise of his grandmother's Seventh-Day Adventist Church and then of his mother's Black Methodist Church. A budding strength enables him at first to resist the potent machinery of family and friends and their attempts to save his soul: "The hymns and sermons of God came into my heart only long after my personality had been shaped and formed by uncharted conditions of life . . . and in the end I remained basically unaffected" (BB 124). Later, however, the social environment of the Methodist Church successfully seduces him: "I entered a new world: prim, brown, puritanical girls . . . black college students . . . black boys and girls. . . . I was so starved for association with people that I allowed myself to be seduced by it all" (BB 166–67). When a revival begins Richard is urged to attend and join the church: "'We don't want to push you,' they said delicately, implying that if I wanted to associate with them I would have to join" (BB 167). Much like the family, the church confronts the individual by asking him either to be a part of it or to remain alone. "It was hard to refuse," the narrator recalls, when refusal meant return to isolation. Besieged by the preacher, the congregation, and his mother, Richard and a few other lost sheep succumb to the group: "We young men had been trapped by the community, the tribe in which we lived and of which we were a part. The tribe, for its own safety, was asking us to be at one with it" (BB 169–70). Walking home "limp as a rag," feeling "sullen anger and a crushing sense of shame," the newly baptized Richard has experienced the nightmare that underlies the entire narrative: the domination of the group over the individual through the power of social consensus. This is a vision that becomes increasingly pronounced in the course of the narrative. The congregation, acting and constituted as a premodern tribe, emerges as a powerful abstract living body that, while formed by individuals, exists in and of itself, almost independently of the individuals who compose it. This reified perception becomes more acute in the portrayal of two other institutions in the South, school and racism, and culminates in the North with the Communist Party.

Outside the family and still in the South, while the soul finds nourishment in the church the intellect must find it in school. Central to the narrator's experiences is a confrontation over the speech that he is to deliver as class valedictorian. In another variation of the theme "group versus individual," three groups—family, school friends, and whites—ally themselves together against the protagonist. Chosen to deliver the graduation speech, Richard discovers that his principal has already written one. No other student has ever refused to comply, and if he will not submit, he will give up the chance to teach in the school system. For Richard, however, complying with the principal meant complying with the racist South: "He was tempting me, baiting me; this was the technique that snared black young minds into supporting the southern way of life" (BB 194). It also meant complying with his more submissive friends and with his family, all fervently opposed to his determination. Shortly before giving his own speech, recalls the narrator, "I was hating my environment more each day" (BB 196).

A larger and more threatening environment opens the moment Richard steps outside the school to find a job: the southern white world with its institutions of racism, segregation, and violence. At first this world allows Richard to distance himself from the previous ones and their values. "The truth was that I had—even though I had fought against it—grown to accept the value of myself that my old environment had created in me, and I had thought that no other kind of environment was possible" (BB 240).

205

Richard's experiences among whites illustrate various degrees of submission or adaptation to the "culture of terror" from which he will soon flee. Wright selects two individuals to illustrate how a personality can become identical with and therefore annihilated by its social environment. In Jackson Grigg wants Richard to learn how to act "like a black." Grigg says he hates whites, yet he submits completely to their racist assumptions and conventions. When he makes fun of them and begins to laugh Grigg covered "his mouth with his hand and bent at the knees, a gesture which was unconsciously meant to conceal his excessive joy in the presence of whites" (BB 204). Similarly, in Memphis Richard meets Shorty, "the most amazing specimen of Southern Negro" (BB 248). Shorty is willing to do anything for a quarter and even lets himself be kicked by a white man after having clowned around for him in the most shameless way.

Painfully aware of the destruction of individual personalities carried out within the institution of racism and as a result of submission to it, Wright presents Richard as the antithesis of that passive submission. Beaten for not saying "sir," fired for his looks, driven out of a job, forced to fight with another Black youth for the amusement of whites, Richard eventually begins to discover in the "civilized" culture seeping through to him from books and magazines the sustenance that he feels his own culture does not provide.

> From where in this southern darkness had I caught a sense of freedom? . . . The external world of whites and blacks, which was the only world that I had ever known, surely had not evoked in me any belief in myself. The people I had met had advised and demanded submission. . . . Whenever my environment had failed to support or nourish me, I had clutched at books. (BB 282)

Finding in books first a way to survive and later to escape, Richard gives himself new cultural birth and eventually reads his way out of the "darkness in daytime" postulated in the epigraph.

Finally heading north, reflecting over his experiences in the South, the narrator of Black Boy provides a summary of his life up to this point, a summary that reveals beneath the apparent formlessness of a life history some solid principles of selection: "I had been what my *surroundings* had demanded, what my *family*—conforming to the dictates of the whites above them—had exacted of me, and what the *whites* had said that I must be. Never being fully able to be myself, I had slowly learned that the *South* could recognize but a part of a man, could accept but a fragment of his *personality*" (BB 284, my emphasis). More than simply a record of Wright's experiences, *Black Boy* is a selection of episodes organized, like the sociologists' monographs, around the categories of family, culture, environment, and personality.

The contradictions between individual and group reach the starkest point in *American Hunger*, the second volume of Wright's autobiography, in the protagonist's relationship with the Communist Party. Unlike the family and the South, the party represents an institution that Richard chooses to join. Like the family and the South, the party provides a system of kinship, rituals, and allegiance against which the individual finds himself struggling only to discover, yet again, isolation as the only alternative.

In *The Polish Peasant* Thomas and Znaniecki theorized that social and political reorganization follows the disintegration of primary groups, such as family and community, caused by migration. They contrasted the rationality of "common ends and means" underlying new forms of cooperation, such as political and social organizations, with the "unreflective social cohesion brought about by tradition" that permeates social relations within the family and the ethnic community.[7] For the Chicago sociologists the city represents the destruction of "community," conservative and tradition-bound, but also its reconstitution, at a higher level, as modern and self-conscious cooperation.

As an immigrant to the "flat black stretches . . . black coal . . . grey smoke . . . dank prairie" of Chicago, Richard experiences precisely this transition. The Communist Party feeds his hunger for a sustained relationship without racism and for an intellectual light that will dissolve the epigraphic "groping at noonday as in the night." However, and once again, the party develops as an abstract power opposed to his personality, transcending yet subsuming all the institutions from which the narrator fled—the family, the church, and even the racist South.

The party, much like the family, is constructed as a kinship system. Both contain a degree of "oneness," which is fearfully portrayed in the purge trial of Ross. "Ross was one with all the members there, regardless of race or color: his heart was theirs and their hearts were his; and when a man reaches that state of *kinship* with others, that degree of *oneness*, or when a trial has made him *kin* after he has been sundered from them by wrongdoing, then he must rise and say . . . 'I'm guilty. Forgive me.'" (*AH* 124–25, my emphasis). Like a religion, the party hinges on a "common vision" and on notions of guilt. However, un-

207

like religion, it relies not on "mysticism" or the "invoking of God" but rather on a "moral code that could control the conduct of men, yet it was a code that stemmed from practical living, and not from the injunctions of the supernatural" (*AH* 121). Control is thus once more in the foreground, control by the group, the environment, the society. The party no less than the family and the church exacts a toll in exchange for "community."

The similarities between the party and the South are also noteworthy. At Ross's trial, the protagonist has a vision of his fellow comrades as people who are free of prejudice, but quickly realizes that the South has followed him in another guise: "I had fled men who did not like the color of my skin, and now I was among men who did not like the tone of my thoughts" (*AH* 119). The South has also followed him as the agent of distrust between Richard and other Blacks. In Memphis, the South had instilled fear between two Black youths who became unable to trust one another, so that whites could have the pleasure of seeing them fight. As in a déjà-vu experience, the Communist Party breaks up the friendship between Richard and Ross by once again spreading suspicion. "We two black men sat in the same room looking at each other in fear. Both of us were hungry. Both of us depended upon public charity. . . . Yet we had more doubt in our hearts of each other than of the men who had cast the mould of our lives" (*AH* 84). Wright constructs the party, as the family and the South before, as a tangible body; the party is more real than almost any other character, excepting the protagonist himself. Rather than being the accumulated consciousness or lack of consciousness of the individuals who form it, the party is envisioned as the personification of institutionalized control, with its own discipline, beliefs, and truths. Totally missing is an image of the party, or the family, or the church as embodiments of social relations, and of dynamics between and among people fighting historical battles. Instead, when the object becomes animated—Frankenstein-like—it turns against its creator.

The purge trial of Ross climaxes and epitomizes Wright's—and the Chicago sociologists'—view of social reality. Here is dramatized the view that the two contending litigants are the individual and the group. Ross is crushed and represents all those who were crushed previously in the autobiographical universe by the various institutions looming over it. "His hands shook. He held onto the edge of the table to keep on his feet. His personality, his sense of himself, had been obliterated. Yet he could not have been so humbled unless he

208

had shared and accepted the vision that had crushed him, the common vision that bound us all together" (*AH* 124).

The trial also contains the outline of what would become an American nightmare in the age of McCarthyism: the nightmare of the individual's loss of individuality and annihilation by "the party." The Communist Party offered a convenient target for working out deep social tensions over the relationship between individual and society. The tensions dramatized in Ross's trial and some of those acted out in the McCarthy trials as well must be seen as the tip of an iceberg. Beneath them are the South, the family, and many other social institutions, all on trial by proxy. A desirable and increasingly unattainable goal, one's identity as a social and not just an individual being—as part of a community, a culture, a group—was turned into an undesirable one. The self as a social being became the enemy to be fought against for the survival of the individual being. Through a collective process of projection the Communist Party became a symbol for the individual's loss of identity and for the fear of losing oneself in a changed social reality. As in a modern version of the passion plays, the Communist Party was made to bear the cross for a society plunging headlong into postwar affluence and alienation. The party was the lamb sacrificed on the altar of modernity.

In such a context, the concept of "personality" that Wright uses with stubborn insistence emerges as an attempt to build a bulwark against the rising tide of conformity, a bulwark designed by the Chicago sociologists a decade earlier. It is in this regard that Wright's debt to the Chicago school is most tangible. The two categories of "personality" and "environment" explicitly connect the cyclical and ever larger clashes between individual and group. The concepts allowed Wright to confront the rural racist environment in the South and the urban massified environment in the North. Through the use of these categories Wright became the sociologist of his own life. "I hungered for a grasp of the framework of contemporary living, for a knowledge of the forms of life about me, for eyes to see the bony structures of personality, for theories to light up the shadows of conduct" (*AH* 26). If in Marxist sociology Wright found the general ideas about capitalism and class relations, in Chicago sociology he found the more specific ideas about migration and social change that allowed him to 209 transpose his own story into a story of his times.

Black Boy-American Hunger is an exemplary product of the sociological imagination of the 1930s. Whether consciously or unconsciously,

Richard Wright wrote himself into a case study and thus became the informant of himself as a Black youth who grows up in the South and migrates to Chicago. In so doing he was able to make that story representative both of the specific experiences of Black migrants and of the more general facts of "social life" and "human nature" in modern society. It is in this light, as both participant observation record and representative case history, that Wright's autobiography, written at such an early age and interrupted before his move to New York and concurrent fame, becomes clearer. By the time he was living in New York his life had become far from representative: it had became exceptional.

At the conceptual level Wright's debt toward Chicago sociology is even more apparent. In *Black Boy-American Hunger* Wright appropriated from Chicago sociology a model of modern social reality as the site of relentless conflicts between the individual and the group. It is this model that is ultimately responsible for the problems that Wright's pronouncements on African-American culture have occasioned. Utilizing the strong points of such a model, Wright infused a classical form, the ex-slave narrative, with a most modern perception: like Park's marginal man, Wright's autobiographical persona is condemned to travel from bondage to bondage forever—never to find a "home." Utilizing the model's weak points, Wright committed the sociological fallacy of separating the individual from institutions, culture, environment, and, in the process, the subjective and the collective possibilities for change became lost. After having made the protagonist a representative of the community, the party, the group, Wright's autobiography closes by promoting not just rebellion but alienation from those very institutions.

Richard's last words are uttered in the emptiness of his total isolation, one from which he hoped to cause change and achieve self-expression. "My problem was here, here with me, here in this room, and I would solve it here or not at all. . . . I would hurl words into this darkness and wait for an echo, and if an echo sounded, no matter how faintly, I would send other words to tell, to march, to fight, to create" (*AH* 134–35). Unfortunately, these entombed words turned out to be not the call "to fight" that Wright had envisaged but the testament to a dying 1930s radical movement.

Notes

Introduction

1. Richard Wright, "Introduction," in *Black Metropolis*, pp. xvii–xviii.
2. James T. Farrell, *Studs Lonigan: A Trilogy*.
3. Nelson Algren, *Never Come Morning*.
4. Richard Wright, *Black Boy: A Record of Childhood and Youth* and *American Hunger*.
5. Fragments of the intellectual history that forms the background for these biases can be found in Terry Eagleton, "The Idealism of American Criticism"; Evan Watkins, "Conflict and Consensus"; Paul Lauter, "Race and Gender in the Shaping of the American Literary Canon"; Barbara Foley, "From New Criticism to Deconstruction"; Jonathan Arac, "F. O. Matthiessen"; Russell J. Reisling, *The Unusable Past*, pp. 30–36, 71–74, 96–99ff.; Paul Lauter, "Caste, Class, and Canon"; Michael Wood, "Literary Criticism"; Vincent B. Leitch, *American Literary Criticism*, pp. 102ff.; Gerald Graff and Michael Warner, eds., *The Origins of Literary Study in America*, pp. 1–14; William Ellis, *The Theory of the American Romance*, pp. 1–12.

6. Robert Lee, "Richard Wright's Inside Narratives," pp. 200–21.

7. Similar conclusions have been reached by an otherwise hetero-geneous array of scholars. A critic who in general has not automatically followed the prevalent antirealist ideologies, Houston A. Baker, Jr., claims, in *Long Black Song: Essays in Black American Literature and Culture*, that Wright's "use of naturalism was not the ideologically and literary self-conscious choice made by such men as Dos Passos, Mike Gold, and John Steinbeck"; Baker implies that Wright's must have been no more than a spontaneous, unreflective allegiance. Baker adopts a similar strategy when he minimizes Wright's involvement with the Communist Party by presenting it as a misguided and spontaneous attraction and by claiming that Black culture more than Marxist ideology shaped Richard Wright's views and works. Conscious that the naturalist reputation, just like the Communist reputation, is damaging to Wright, Baker pleads for a re-classification of this author outside the "Proletarian School" and suggests that "one cannot apply critical censures designed for American prole-tarian literature to Wright's work without just reflection" (pp. 126–28). Presenting *Native Son* as "tragedy" and Bigger Thomas as a "tragic hero," Joyce A. Joyce, in her *Richard Wright's Art of Tragedy*, rescues Wright from "so-ciological" and "thematic" studies, which she labels the "old critical ap-proach," and from "protest" and "naturalist" categorizations, which, she argues, blind us to the "intricacies," "complexities," "subtleties of tech-nique," in other words to the only aesthetic apparatus that New Criticism acknowledges. Reproducing the well-known view that "protest literature easily becomes dated while tragedy, striking at the core of what it means to be a human being, remains perpetually powerful," Joyce reproduces the assumptions that underly the most conservative versions of the Liter-ary Humanities curricula and the very rationale for the exclusion from those courses of all but a narrowly defined list of authors (pp. 5–23). Cf. also Joseph Bodziack's "Richard Wright and Afro-American Gothic." Bodziack claims that *Native Son* has "moments of gothic splendor"— "ghostly premonitions," "a curse," "Poe-sque" elements of "conscience and guilt," "mystery," and the "supernatural"—that are outside "the tenets of naturalism" and make it a legitimate member of the only legitimate novelistic traditon in American letters: the romance tradition.

8. Baker, p. 16.

9. See chapter 8.

10. To address these issues at present, one must do so through Rich-ard Wright. And to solve them for Richard Wright is to begin solving them for American literature as well. The motivation for one's need to engage this debate around Wright, rather than Farrell or Algren—in other words, where the debate is most active—becomes immediately apparent when one examines the 1981–91 MLA compact disk: 195 entries for Wright, 23 for Farrell, and 12 for Algren in the course of a whole decade. While it is accurate to say that all three authors are fairly low on the charts of Ameri-

can literary criticism—which presses and journals are publishing the criticism of these authors as well as the number of articles published attest to that—it would be a gross generalization to state that they are receiving equally neglectful attention. Wright is rarely the subject of a full-length article in the most prestigious literary journals, but one can hardly say that Wright is a neglected author. Irrespective of how prestigious the accomodations are, it is precisely around Wright that one can make out and engage the literary issues incumbent upon all three authors and the literary traditions under discussion. What has happened to Wright in the last two decades is both emblematic of what has happened to American literary naturalism and proletarian literature and significant of the way poststructuralist criticism has failed to alter the fundamental paradigms of American literature.

11. The number of new books and academic articles that focus on American literary realism and naturalism and the generally innovative approaches that many of them explore indicate that, the continuing disattention to the low critical status of these traditions notwithstanding, at least the long cycle of critical neglect toward them may be over. Cf. Mark Seltzer, "The Naturalist Machine"; Walter Benn Michaels, *The Gold Standard*; Daniel H. Borus, *Writing Realism*; Howard Horowitz, *By the Law of Nature*. See also Warner Berthoff, *The Ferment of Realism*; Eric J. Sundquist, *American Realism*; Donald Pizer, *Twentieth-Century American Literary Naturalism* and *Realism and Naturalism*; John J. Conder, *Naturalism in American Fiction*.

12. June Howard, *Form and History in American Literary Naturalism*, p. ix.

13. Lee Clark Mitchell, *Determined Fictions: American Literary Naturalism*, p. i.

14. Barbara Foley, "From New Criticism to Deconstruction," pp. 53ff., and *Telling the Truth: The Theory and Praxis of Documentary Fiction*, pp. 25, 68. More broadly, Foley argues that the marginalization of naturalism is tied to the denial within American literary criticism that an author "can observe, replicate, judge" or that the world has "independent ontological status." The estrangement from certain aspects of social reality experienced by specific authors and intellectuals of the modernist period at specific historical junctures, she also notes, became a generic and prescriptive estrangement: the mark of all good literature. Concerning the historical context within which realism develops, cf. also "Toward a Definition of Realism in the African Context," pp. 559–75, by Mineke Schipper, who, in the somewhat different context of the colonial and postcolonial novel, reminds us that "in different times and cultures, 'reality' is experienced and expressed . . . in different ways" and that an "author's belief that reality exists in itself as an object of knowledge" might procede from different assumptions and to different conclusions in the European context and in the African context during the nineteenth and twentieth centuries.

15. Amy Kaplan, *The Social Construction of American Realism*, p. 6ff. See also A. LaVonne Ruoff, Jr., and Jerry W. Ward, Jr., eds., *Redefining American Literary*

213

History; Gunter H. Lenz et al., eds., *Reconstructing American Literary History*; Sharon M. Harris, *Rebecca Harding Davis and American Realism*.

16. It might have been a courageous act, ten or twenty years ago, to call certain authors and texts that American literary criticism had relegated to the second-rate corner not just important authors and texts but a tradition. In the poststructuralist eighties it has become as daring to do so as it is in the postfeminist eighties for women to wear pants or smoke in public. Missing from many of these new literary traditions is a self-conscious effort to theorize how a particular literature, a new tradition, significantly alters the whole literature. Missing is the critical ambition that a new tradition should not be simply a tile in the mosaic and thus merely a belated version of the pluralist battles that historians fought and won fifty years ago. Under the pretense of separate-but-equal traditions, a pretense accepted by many if not all, these new traditions continue to be considered not quite as important as the Great American Authors and Texts of old. Certain literary traditions—modernism, the American Renaissance—continue to occupy the seats of honor and ultimately to dictate the priorities of the larger institution, the smaller traditions, and eventually what is written, published, taught, and read in the larger literary marketplace. Generally, these "major" authors and texts are not called a tradition, which, a traveler from literary Altruria would surmise, continues to refer to "minor," "neglected," or "neglectful" literatures.

17. Cf. Bernard Duffey, *The Chicago Renaissance in American Letters: A Critical History*; Hugh D. Duncan, *The Rise of Chicago as a Literary Center from 1885 to 1920*; Dale Kramer, *Chicago Renaissance: The Literary Life in the Midwest, 1900–1930*; Clarence A. Andrews, *Chicago in Story: A Literary History*; Carl S. Smith, *Chicago and the American Literary Imagination, 1880–1920*; Kenny Williams, *Prairie Voices: A Literary History of Chicago from the Frontier to 1893* and "'Creative Defiance': An Overview of Chicago Literature," pp. 7–24.

18. Judging by the number of studies and anthologies recently published, it appears that substantial and genuine interest in the literature of the 1930s is growing. Cf. Charlotte Nekola and Paula Rabinowitz, eds., *Writing Red*; Eric Homberger, *American Writers and Radical Politics*; Alan Wald, *The New York Intellectuals*; Carl Fleischauer and Beverly W. Brannan, *Documenting America*; Cary Nelson, *Repression and Recovery*; Hans Bak and Vincent Piket, eds., *Looking Inward, Looking Outward*; James F. Murphy, *The Proletarian Moment*; Walter B. Rideout, *The Radical Novel*.

19. If it may be difficult to sustain the view of three consecutive periods as a renaissance each and every one—the 1890s, the 1910s, and the 1930s—still there is no reason why such periodization should not be used and eventually more appropriate concepts than *renaissance* found to characterize the history of Chicago literature.

20. Cf. Kenny Williams, "Creative Defiance."

21. Raymond Williams, *Writing in Society*; see especially "Region and Class in the Novel," pp. 229–38; cf. also his *Marxism and Literature* and *The Sociology of Culture*.

22. Eric J. Sundquist, "Realism and Regionalism," p. 503.

23. Hazel Carby, *Reconstructing Womanhood: The Emergence of the Afro-American Woman Novelist*, pp. 163ff.

24. Ibid., p. 164.

25. As a result the old pivots of an embattled American literature—the American Renaissance, the Harlem Renaissance, the Lost Generation—continue to structure the periodization and the conceptualization of American and African-American literature, regardless of the plethora of new authors and texts that anticanonical scholarship has brought forth and notwithstanding the widely accepted claim that the old American literature was restricted by allegiances we spurn.

26. As Kenny Williams notes, "[T]roughout its history, [Chicago] has been blessed or cursed with being a city of superlatives. Everything is measured in terms of 'the most' this or 'the greatest' that . . . in terms of the number of firsts it has had . . . first in transportation . . . the first skyscraper . . . the largest stockyards" ("Creative Defiance," p. 9).

27. Richard K. Vedder and Lowell Gallaway, "Economic Growth and Decline in the Old Northwest," p. 301.

28. David C. Klingaman, "The Nature of Midwest Manufacturing in 1890," p. 291.

29. Quoted in Robert Conrow, *Field Days*, p. 152.

30. Cf. Bruce Nelson, *Beyond the Martyrs*; James Sloan Allen, *The Romance of Commerce and Culture*; Hartmut Keil and John Jentz, *German Workers in Chicago*; Arnold R. Hirsch, *Making the Second Ghetto*; Joanne J. Meyerowitz, *Women Adrift*; James Grossman, *Land of Hope*; Lizabeth Cohen, *Making a New Deal*; Ellen Fitzpatrick, *Endless Crusade*; Mary Jo Deegan, *Jane Addams and the Men of the Chicago School*; Eric Hirsch, *Urban Revolt*; William Cronon, *Nature's Metropolis*.

31. Cf. Amy Kaplan, *The Social Construction of American Realism*.

32. Margaret Walker, *Richard Wright: Daemonic Genius*, p. 319. This distinction, between the American Communist Party of the 1930s and modern Marxism, should be but is rarely observed in evaluating Wright's politics and epistemology. A thorough evaluation of Walker's memoir from a scholarly perspective can be found in Michel Fabre, "Margaret Walker's *Richard Wright*: A Wrong Righted or Wright Wronged?" pp. 429–50. Although Fabre has seriously undermined the credibility of Walker's biography of Wright, especially in areas concerning Wright's relationship with Walker and with women in general, I am not inclined to dismiss it altogether provided one approaches it with the same caution and caveats one would use with any memoir. For a discussion of the larger feminist reevaluation of Wright within which Walker can be situated, see chapter 8. In particular, Walker's evaluations and recollections of Wright's political 215 orientation vis-à-vis American Communism and, generally, Marxism seem more reliable and less biased than many of the personal or scholarly accounts available. Concerning Wright's relationship with the Communist Party and Marxism, see James Baldwin, *Nobody Knows My Name*;

Richard Crossman, ed., *The God That Failed*; Harold Cruse, *The Crisis of the Negro Intellectual*; Dan McCall, *The Example of Richard Wright*; Wilson Record, "The Negro Writer and the Communist Party," pp. 224–28; James R. Hooker, *Black Revolutionary*; Daniel Aaron, "Richard Wright and the Communist Party"; Michel Fabre, *The Unfinished Quest*; Raman K. Sing, "Marxism in Richard Wright's Fiction"; Cedric J. Robinson, "The Emergent Marxism of Richard Wright's Ideology" and *Black Marxism: The Making of the Black Radical Tradition*; Donald B. Gibson, *The Politics of Literary Expression*; John M. Reilly, "The Self-Creation of the Intellectual."

33. My claim that a fully vernacular American intellectual source, the Chicago school of urban sociology, played a central role in shaping the form and content of three Chicago novels that have generally been typed as "proletarian literature" should not be used to claim that this literature did not respond at the same time or deeply to intellectual and aesthetic currents outside the United States. It may be worthwhile to remember that while Lukács, Benjamin, Adorno, Brecht, and Bakhtin have become academic household items, the debates that provide the intellectual context for their formulations, in both Europe and the United States, and of which the literature under discussion is not just a relevant but an intrinsic part, are simply ignored as irrelevant, in the case of the European debate over the modern novel, or dismissed as uninteresting factional disputes, in the case of the American debate over the proletarian novel.

34. I do not agree with the terms I am using, especially the distinction between realism and modernism, but these are the terms in which this literary history is written and are useful here to make the point clear.

35. Robert Bone, "Richard Wright and the Chicago Renaissance," pp. 446–68.

36. Frederick Engels, *The Origin of the Family*; Walter Benjamin, "The Work of Art in the Age of Mechanical Reproduction."

37. Fred H. Matthews, "The Revolt Against Americanism: Cultural Pluralism and Cultural Relativism as an Ideology of Liberation," pp. 4–31.

38. Alain Calmes, *Le roman colonial en Algérie avant 1914*, p. 34–35.

39. George E. Marcus and Michael M. J. Fischer, eds., *Anthropology as Cultural Critique: An Experimental Moment in the Human Sciences*, see especially "The Repatriation of Anthropology as Cultural Critique," pp. 111–36.

40. Cf. Thomas Bender, *Community and Social Change in America*, pp. 17–21ff.

41. Robert Park, "The City: Suggestions for the Investigation of Human Behavior in the Urban Environment," in *The City*, pp. 1–46.

42. Ernest Burgess, "The Growth of the City: An Introduction to a Research Project," in *The City*, pp. 47–62.

43. Frederic Thrasher, *The Gang: A Study of 1,313 Gangs in Chicago*.

44. As Bender argues, these concepts laid the foundation in the United States for theories of modernization that came to enjoy great popularity in studies of ethnic and urban communities during the succeeding

decades and, outside academic discourse, still inform the representation of migration and social change.

45. Robert Park, "Human Migration and the Marginal Man," pp. 345–56.

46. Robert Redfield, *Tepoztlán: A Mexican Village. A Study of Folk Life*.

47. Louis Wirth, "Urbanism as a Way of Life," pp. 60–83.

48. Robert Redfield, *The Folk Culture of Yucatan*.

49. William Isaac Thomas and Florian Znaniecki, *The Polish Peasant in Europe and America*.

50. W. I. Thomas, *The Unadjusted Girl: With Cases and Standpoint for Behavior Analysis*.

51. James T. Farrell, *Studs Lonigan*.

52. Nelson Algren, *Never Come Morning*.

53. Richard Wright, *Black Boy and American Hunger*.

1. Between Literature and Science: Chicago Sociology and the Urban Literary Tradition

I am indebted for the title of the chapter to Wolf Lepenis's Between Literature and Science: The Rise of Sociology. *This insightful and original study traces the development of sociology in nineteenth-century Europe, and frames it within a dynamic and conflictual interaction between "literary" and "scientific intellectuals." While primarily concerned with intellectual history, Lepenis casts new light on the history of the novel and of modern literature by bringing the likes of Balzac, Flaubert, Dickens, Zola, and James into the midst of heated debates over the forms, genres, and discourses that were best equipped and therefore most authorized to represent modern society. "[F]rom the moment of its inception"—Lepenis writes—"sociology became both a competitor and a counterpart of literature. . . . When sociology desired to be sociography it came into conflict above all with the realistic novel over the claim to offer adequate reproduction of the 'prose of everyday circumstances'; when, on the other, it claimed to be social theory it incurred the suspicion of degenerating into a 'closet science,'" pp. 12–13.*

1. The interrelations of sociology and aesthetics are most insightfully discussed by Robert Nisbet, *Sociology as an Art Form* and Richard H. Brown, *A Poetics for Sociology*. For a recent and most original study of the historical relationship between literature and sociology see Wolf Lepenis, *Between Literature and Science*. Concerning different aspects of the relationship between literature and art, and sociology, see also Morroe Berger, *Real and Imagined Worlds*; Audrey Borenstein, *Redeeming the Sin*; John Kramer, "Images of Sociology and Sociologists in Fiction"; Donald C. Irving, "The Real World and the Made World"; Susan Krieger, "Fiction and Social Science"; Ellen A. Knodt, "Understanding *Main Street*." Most recent studies in this field have focused on other branches—anthropology and history—of the social sciences. Cf. Clifford Geertz, *The Interpretation of Cultures*; Hayden White, *Metahistory*; Vincent Crapanzano, "On the Writing of Ethnography"; Lawrence Stone, "The Revival of Narrative"; George E. Marcus and

217

Dick Cushman, "Ethnographies as Texts"; Paul Veyne, *Writing History*; George E. Marcus and Michael M. J. Fischer, *Anthropology as Cultural Critique*; James Clifford, *The Predicament of Culture*; Marc Manganaro, ed., *Modernist Anthropology*. Historians of the natural sciences have also been receptive to this new field of study. Cfr. Misia Landau, "Human Evolution as Narrative"; J. Edward Chamberlain and Sander L. Gilman, eds., *Degeneration*; Nancy L Stepan, "Race and Gender"; Donna Haraway, *Primate Visions*; L. J. Jordanova, ed., *Languages of Nature*.

2. Recent important studies of the Chicago school of sociology include Martin Hammersley, *The Dilemma of Qualitative Methods: Herbert Blumer and the Chicago Tradition*; Mary Joe Deegan, *Jane Addams and the Men of the Chicago School, 1892–1918*; Lee Harvey, *Myths of the Chicago School of Sociology*; Martin Bulmer, *The Chicago School of Sociology: Institutionalization, Diversity, and the Rise of Sociological Research* ; Lester R. Kurtz, *Evaluating Chicago Sociology*; J. David Lewis and Richard L. Smith, *American Sociology and Pragmatism: Mead, Chicago Sociology, and Symbolic Interaction*; Dennis Smith, *The Chicago School: A Liberal Critique of Capitalism*. Important recent contributions to specific aspects of this history can be found in Ellen Fitzpatrick, *Endless Crusade: Women Social Scientists and Progressive Reform*; John H. Ehrenreich, *The Altruistic Imagination: A History of Social Work and Social Policy in the United States*; Arthur J. Vidich and Stanford M. Lyman, *American Sociology: Wordly Rejections of Religion and Their Directions*; Rosalind Rosenberg, *Beyond Separate Spheres: The Intellectual Roots of Modern Feminism*; Steven J. Diner, *A City and Its Universities: Public Policy in Chicago, 1892–1919*; Ulf Hannerz, *Exploring the City: Inquiries Toward an Urban Anthropology*. Although no one has specifically treated the literary context of the Chicago school of sociology, a number of scholars have acknowledged such a conjunction; see especially James T. Carey, *Sociology and Public Affairs: The Chicago School*; Fred H. Matthews, *Quest for American Sociology: Robert Park and the Chicago School*; Martin Bulmer, *The Chicago School of Sociology*; Lee Harvey, *Myths of the Chicago School of Sociology*.

3. William Sharpe and Leonard Wallock, eds., *Visions of the Modern City*, pp. 9–10.

4. Alessandro Pizzorno, "Introduzione," p. xii, my translation. Pizzorno also identifies the beginning of a now dominant trend when he explains the progressive marginalization of the Chicago school in the years following the Second World War as a result of the idealist and internalist culturalist theories that originally grew as critiques of the Chicago school, specifically of the social ecological approach that had become the school's better known trademark. These theories, Pizzorno notes, eventually became the predominant antiempirical and antimaterialist forms of sociology altogether.

218

5. W. I. Thomas, "Life History," pp. 246–50.

6. Ibid.

7. Concerning the scarcity of primary and secondary material concerning W. I. Thomas see passim, chapter 4.

8. W. I. Thomas and Florian Znaniecki, *The Polish Peasant*, p. 294.

9. "Life Histories—Standpoint and Questionnaire, Americanization Study, Division of Immigrant Heritages," Robert Park Papers, Addenda 5:9.

10. Ibid.

11. William Isaac Thomas, "W. I. Thomas to Mrs. Donovan, Sep. 14, 1921," A-127.

12. Robert Park, "Notes on the Origins," p. 337.

13. See Matthews, *Quest*, and Winifred Raushenbush, *Robert Park: Biography of a Sociologist*.

14. Robert Park, "Life History," p. 253. At Park's memorial service Everett C. Hughes recalled Park as "a philosopher" who sought light "in the treatises of philosophers and in the arts—Greek tragedy, poetry, drama, novels, the stories of Ring Lardner, and the humblest human tragedy poured out on the pages of the daily newspapers." "Robert Ezra Park, 1864–1944. In Memoriam," (private printing), copy at University of Chicago, Regenstein Library, p. 9.

15. Park, "Notes on the Origins," pp. 238; Park, "Life History," pp. 253–54.

16. Quoted in Bulmer, *The Chicago School of Sociology*, p. 98.

17. Robert Park, *Race and Culture*, p. v.

18. Park, "Life History," p. 253.

19. Park, "Walt Whitman," University of Chicago, Regenstein Library, Special Collections (hereafter UCRL), Robert Park Papers, 5:13.

20. Ibid., pp. 2–3.

21. Quoted in Matthews, *Quest*, p. 108.

22. Warner J. Cahnman, "Robert E. Park at Fisk," p. 330. Cahnman also reports one of Park's sardonic comments on a study that heavily relied on numbers: "Of course, it would be interesting to know something about these people—wouldn't it?" ibid., p. 330.

23. Cited in Thomas and Znaniecki, *Methods in Social Science*, p. 12.

24. Matthews, *Quest*, p. 121.

25. Robert Redfield, "Addressed to Certain Writers of Verses," UCRL, Redfield Papers, Addenda 3:12.

26. Redfield, "Science as Humanity," UCRL, Redfield Papers, Addenda 6:7.

27. Ibid., p. 17.

28. Redfield writes: "There is more than a little in common between one of Freud's cases, as he wrote them down for us to read, and Lowes' study of Coleridge's creative mind." Ibid., p. 13.

29. Ibid., p. 19.

30. 'Department of Sociology Interviews" conducted by James Carey, UCRL.

31. "William Cater Interview, 3.17.1972," UCRL, 1:5, p. 13.

32. "Leonard Cottrell Interview, 3.28.1972, Part II," UCRL, pp. 11–12; "Robert Faris Interview, 5.24.1972, Part II," UCRL, p. 6; "Ruth Newcomb Interview, 5.22.1972, Part I," UCRL, 1:6, 1:8, 1:19, p. 12.

33. "Walter Reckless Interview, 6.28. 1972, Part II," UCRL, p. 9, ibid., 1:6. In the Robert Park Papers is also a long annotated bibliography of autobiographical and fictional writing, and prose "depicting the personal experiences of immigrants," produced by the Americanization Project, which includes among the titles Arthur Bullard, *Comrade Jetta* (1913), Willa S. Cather, *My Antonia* (1918), and *Song of the Lark* (1915), Rose Cohen, *Out of the Shadow* (1918), and Hamilton Holt, ed., *The Life Stories of Undistinguished Americans* (1906). "Immigrant Experiences, Bulletin No. 37, May 10, 1919," UCRL, Robert Park Papers, 3:1.

34. Ernest Burgess, "124, Urban Sociology—Study of the City through Literature and Art," July 26, 1929, UCRL, Ernest Burgess Papers, 27:1. The course description is subdivided in four sections, "Literature," "Poetry," "Art," and "Sculpture," and lists such authors as Charles Dickens, Victor Hugo, Theodore Dreiser, John Dos Passos, Sherwood Anderson, Edna Ferber as well as Jacob Riis, Jane Addams, and Lillian Wald.

35. Louis Wirth, "Index Cards," UCRL, Louis Wirth Papers, 39:8.

36. Ibid.

37. Ibid.

38. Louis Wirth, "Chapter 18 of Jules Romains, 'Men of Good Will'—Introducing Paris at Five C'Clock in the Evening," loose typed page, UCRL, Louis Wirth Papers.

39. Between 1918 and 1935 Robert Park reviewed many books of fiction, biography, and literary criticism for the *American Journal of Sociology*. Park regularly reviewed new works in African-American literature such as *The New Negro*, ed. Alain Locke, *The Book of American Negro Spirituals*, ed. J. W. Johnson, James Weldon Johnson, *God's Trombone*, ed. Countee Cullen, *Caroling Dusk*, *Plays of Negro Life*, ed. Alaine Locke and Montgomery Gregory, *Rainbow Round My Shoulder*, Howard W. Odum, *Longaree Sketches*, E. C. L. Adams. Park also reviewd immigrant literature such as M. E. Ravage, *An American in the Making*, Leah Morton, *I Am a Woman and a Jew*, Carl C. Jensen, *An American Saga*, and Michael Gold, *Jews Without Money*. In his obituary of Robert Park Horace R. Cayton quoted from the last letter he had received from Park: "Democracy is not something that some people in the country can have and others not have, not something to be shared and divided like a pie—some getting a small piece and some getting a large piece. Democracy is an integral thing. If any part of the country has it, they all have it. If any part of the country doesn't have it, the rest of the country doesn't have it. The Negro, therefore, in fighting for democracy for himself, is simply fighting the battle for our democracy. *The Pittsburgh Courier*, Feb. 26, 1944. Clipping in UCRL, Robert Park Papers, 1:15.

40. Robert Park, "The Negro in America," UCRL, Robert Park Papers, 1:15.

41. "Question XI. What is Negro Literature?" UCRL, Robert Park Papers, 1:12.

42. "Revised Program. Second Annual Institute for Social Research. University of Chicago, Aug. 18–27, 1924," UCRL, Ernest Burgess Papers,

21:8. The Summer Institute of the Society for Social Research was a yearly event, which for a number of years served as both a clearing house for new research projects and a means of contact with the profession by and for sociologists who had left Chicago for their teaching posts.

43. "The Use of Poetry," UCRL, Ernest Burgess Papers, 21:3. Judging by the extant proposal, this presentation focused on the "Songs," "Poetry," and "Folklore" of the "American Negro."

44. This is an interesting and broad discussion of the literary genre of exposure better known as muckraking literature and, in particular, of the nonfictional and fictional prose in the United States and Great Britain that constitutes the muckraking literary tradition.

45. "The Literature of Exposure," UCRL, Robert Park Papers, 2:10.

46. Nels Anderson, "The Poet and the Rebel Press," UCRL, Robert Park Papers, 3:5, pp. 1–2. Nels Anderson is best known for his study *The Hobo: Sociology of the Homeless Man* (1923).

47. Ibid., pp. 4, 9.

48. "VII. Write the History of Marginal Man," UCRL, Robert Park Papers, 2:2.

49. "Family Study II—Autobiographical and Biographical Material," UCRL, Ernest Burgess Papers, 27:11. This assignment sheet instructs students to select one book from a long list of autobiographical and biographical texts, to excerpt relevant passages and group the extracts under analytical headings provided in class or devised by the student, and finally to "make summaries, or state your own reaction to the material in the book" or "write according to directions for Plays and Novels."

50. Loose typed page, UCRL, Ernest Burgess Papers, 21:8.

51. Both Hugh D. Duncan's Ph.D. thesis, *The Rise of Chicago as a Literary Center from 1885 to 1920: A Sociological Essay in American Literature* (1948) and his Master thesis, "An Annotated Bibliography on the Sociology of Literature, with an Introductory Essay on Methodological Problems in the Field" (1947) were supervised by Louis Wirth. The first is a most insightful discussion of the literature of Chicago, of what contributed to that literature, and, in turn, of what that literature contributed to the literature of the United States, while the second remains a thorough reference work that still deserves to be consulted.

52. Louis Wirth, *The Ghetto* p. 287.

53. Pizzorno, "Introduzione," pp. xxi, xxiv, my translation. Louis Wirth expressed the same view of Park when he stated that "though he was the most empirical of sociologists, he was at the same time one of its greatest theorists and systematizers." "Robert Ezra Park, 1864–1944. In Memoriam," p. 22.

54. Fred Matthews, *Quest*, p. 127.

2. Maps, Models, and Metaphors: Theories of the City

1. Marcus, "Reading the Illegible," p. 263.

2. Robert Park, "The City: Suggestions for the Investigation of Human Behavior in the Urban Environment," p. 146; Ernest Burgess, "The Growth of the City: An Introduction to a Research Project," pp. 47–62; Frederic Thrasher, *The Gang: A Study of 1,313 Gangs in Chicago.*

3. Morris Janowitz, "Introduction," p. viii.

4. Park, "The City," p. 3.

5. Ibid., pp. 2, 4.

6. Ibid., pp. 4, 8.

7. Ibid., p. 1.

8. Ibid., p. 1.

9. Ibid., p. 3.

10. Ibid., p. 6.

11. Georg Lukács, *The Theory of the Novel,* pp. 29ff.

12. Ibid., p. 6.

13. James T. Farrell, *Reflections at Fifty and Other Essays.*

14. Park, "The City," p. 10, my emphasis.

15. Ibid., p. 40.

16. Ibid., p. 12.

17. Ibid., p. 41.

18. Ibid., p. 41, my emphases.

19. Ibid., pp. 40–41, my emphases.

20. Ibid., p. 41.

21. Ibid., p. 42.

22. Ibid., p. 42.

23. Ibid., p. 43.

24. Ibid., p. 43.

25. Ibid., p. 45.

26. Ibid., p. 45.

27. Burgess, "The Growth of the City," p. 50.

28. Ibid., p. 50.

29. Ibid., p. 53.

30. Ibid., p. 54.

31. Ibid., p. 54.

32. Ibid., p. 54.

33. Ibid., pp. 56–56.

34. Ibid., p. 54.

35. Ibid., p. 54.

36. Ibid., pp. 57–58.

37. Ibid., p. 57.

38. Cf. appendix 5 in Lee Harvey, *Myths of the Chicago School of Sociology,* for a bibliography of Ph.D. theses, pp. 284–93.

39. Frederic Thrasher, *The Gang;* James Short, "Introduction," p. xvi.

40. John Van Maanen, *Tales of the Field: On Writing Ethnography.*

41. Thrasher, *The Gang,* pp. ix–xi.

42. Ibid., p. 4, my emphasis.

43. Ibid., p. 3.
44. Ibid., p. 3.
45. Ibid., pp. xiii, 5.
46. Ibid., pp. 3, 6.
47. Ibid., p. 7.
48. Ibid., p. 7.
49. Ibid., p. 7.
50. Ibid., p. 8.
51. Ibid., p. 8.
52. Ibid., p. 9.
53. Ibid., pp. 8–15.
54. Ibid., pp. 15–18.
55. Ibid., p. 19.
56. Ibid., p. 20.
57. Ibid., pp. 3–9.
58. Ibid., p. ix, my emphases.
59. Ibid., pp. 3–6, my emphases.
60. Ibid., p. 19.
61. Ibid., pp. 22–23.
62. Ibid., pp. 14, 19.
63. Ibid., pp. 23, 20.
64. Ibid., pp. 3, 25.

3. "The Folk in a City World": Narratives of Transition, Theories of Modernization

1. Thomas Bender, Community and Social Change in America, pp. 17–21.
2. Ibid., see especially chapter 2.
3. Robert Park, "Human Migration and the Marginal Man," pp. 345–56. Robert Redfield, Tepoztlán: A Mexican Village. A Study of Folk Life; Robert Redfield, The Folk Culture of Yucatan; Louis Wirth, "Urbanism as a Way of Life," pp. 60–83.
4. Park, "Human Migration," pp. 345–46.
5. Ibid., p. 348.
6. Nancy Stepan, "Race and Gender: The Role of Analogy in Science"; see also Stepan, The Idea of Race in Science: Great Britain, 1800–1960.
7. Park, "Human Migration," pp. 352–55.
8. Ibid., p. 365.
9. Nancy Stepan, "Biology and Degeneration: Races and Proper Places," pp. 106–9.
10. J. M. Berthelot et al., "Les Sociologies et les Corps," pp. 47–48, my translation.
11. Redfield, Tepoztlán, pp. 12–14.
12. Ibid., pp. 93, 133, 193.
13. Ibid., p. 213.

14. Ibid., p. 213.

15. Ibid., p. 216.

16. Ibid., p. 216.

17. Two still useful discussions on the social changes resulting from the arrival of immigrants from peasant, rural, preurban, and preindustrial backgrounds are Herbert Gutman, *Work, Culture, and Society in Industrializing America*, especially chapter 1; and Rudolph Vecoli, "*Contadini in Chicago: A Critique of The Uprooted*".

18. Redfield, *Tepoztlán*, p. 219.

19. Wirth, "Urbanism as a Way of Life."

20. Bender, "Community and Social Change," p. 20.

21. Wirth, "Urbanism as a Way of Life," pp. 63–64.

22. Ibid., pp. 60–61.

23. Bender, "Community and Social Change," p. 40.

24. Ibid., pp. 61, 83.

25. Elizabeth Wirth Marvick, "Louis Wirth: A Biographical Memorandum," pp. 333–34.

26. Redfield, *The Folk Culture of Yucatan*.

27. Wright, *Black Boy*, p. 43.

28. Walter Benjamin, "Theses on the Philosophy of History," pp. 253–64.

4. Deviant Girls and Dissatisfied Women: A Sociologist's Tale

A version of this chapter has appeared in print under the same title in The Invention of Ethnicity, edited by Werner Sollors.

1. W. I. Thomas was born in rural Virginia in 1863 to Sarah Price and Thaddeus Peter Thomas, preacher by vocation and farmer by need. After completing a Ph.D. in classical and modern languages at the University of Tennessee, Thomas remained at that institution to teach Greek, Latin, French, German, and English for four years. He then decided to go to Germany to further his studies, a fairly popular intellectual trend at the time. In Berlin and Gottingen he continued to study philology while discovering the new disciplines of ethnology and folk psychology. Upon returning to the United States he obtained a position at Oberlin College, where his approach began to shift toward comparative literature. Here he read for the first time Herbert Spencer's *Principles of Sociology*. He remained at Oberlin until 1893 when, in a bold decision, he moved to Chicago and enrolled as one of the first graduate students in the newly organized department of sociology at the University of Chicago. After completing his doctorate, in 1896, Thomas became a professor there. His appointment was abruptly terminated in 1918 when, regardless of his prominence and seniority, a scandal over his "moral" conduct exiled him from the University of Chicago and relegated him to the margins of sociological research and teaching for the rest of his life. Since this is most of what is known

about Thomas's life, it would be a euphemism to say that it is scant. Fragments of information have to be gathered from a short autobiographical statement that Thomas wrote in 1927, upon Luther L. Bernard's request, as a contribution to a never published "History of Sociology in the United States" (see Thomas, "Life History"). Scarcely more will be found in Morris Janowitz's "Introduction" to W. I. Thomas, *On Social Organization and Social Personality*, pp. ix–xviii, and in "Biographical Note," ed. Edmund H. Volkart, *Social Behavior and Personality* pp. 323–24.

2. W. I. Thomas and Florian Znaniecki, *The Polish Peasant in Europe and America*.

3. Robert E. Faris, *Chicago Sociology, 1920–1932*, p. 17.

4. William Isaac Thomas, *The Unadjusted Girl: With Cases and Standpoint for Behavior Analysis*. All page references are to the 1923 edition and, hereafter, noted in parenthesis. The publication circumstances of *The Unadjusted Girl* go back to a time when social reform, academic research, and private philanthropy often overlapped. Thomas's study was commissioned and funded by Mrs. Ethel Dummer, the wife, daughter, and granddaughter of three Chicago bankers. A close associate of Hull House and many other associations of urban reformers, she was a model of early twentieth-century liberal philanthropy. Janowitz, "Introduction," p. xvi. *New York Times*, February 27, 5:13.

5. On the origins and development of Thomas's theory of the wishes and of the situation see Kimball Young, "Contributions of William Isaac Thomas to Sociology," 4 installments; Volkart, *Social Behavior and Personality*; Janowitz, "Introduction"; see also Herbert Blumer, *An Appraisal of Thomas and Znaniecki's "The Polish Peasant in Europe and America"*.

6. Several human types are determined by this wish. They include not only "the craftsman, the artist, the scientist, the professional man and to some extent the business man" (11) but also the vagabond, the criminal, the thief, the prostitute, the vamp, the charity girl, and the bohemian: in all of these types the desire for new experience is preponderant. The "philistine" and the "miser" are exemplary types of the wish for security.

7. Parental love and sexual love—in the form of courtship, mating, marriage, jealousy, flirting—as well as the love of the woman who is promiscuous but is nevertheless not a prostitute, all originate in the wish for response.

8. In fictional form, the episode in Richard Wright's autobiography where he is forced to join the church against his own will reproduces this very same model. See chapter 9.

9. See Sollors, *Beyond Ethnicity*, especially "Some Tales of Consent and Descent," pp. 149–73, for a discussion of symbolic kinship and of how romantic love can mediate or polarize ethnic and American identities. 225

10. Overall, Thomas's representation of the old world is markedly antipastoral. Thomas's old world, in fact, finds its closest complement in the work of three skillful critics of small-town America: Edgar Lee Masters,

Sherwood Anderson, and Sinclair Lewis, the writers who most contributed to demythologizing the image of an idyllic preurban America.

11. See Warren Susman's "Culture and Civilization: The Nineteen-Twenties," in his *Culture as History*, pp. 105–21, an essay that provides a useful historical framework for many of the themes discussed here.

12. A version of this same story appears in *The Rise of David Levinsky*, whose author, Abraham Cahan, was the editor of *Bintel Brief*—the letter column of the New York Jewish Daily *Forward* from which Thomas drew many of his documents. In a few of Cahan's short stories one can find some of the same concerns that occupy W. I. Thomas. The conflict between tradition and modernity also finds a remarkable expression in Cahan's short story "Yekl" (1896).

13. Written by the short story writer Hutchins Hapgood and quoted as "At Christine's (Manuscript)."

14. Written at a time when Thomas's work was a typical mixture of biologism, evolutionism, suffragism, and radicalism, "The Mind of Woman" was actually an article published in 1908 in the widely circulated *American Magazine*. That essay, together with "The Psychology of Woman's Dress," "The Older and Newer Ideals of Marriage," "Votes for Women," and "Women and the Occupations," represent Thomas's early attempts to uncover some of the social and cultural components of women's oppression. *Chicago Daily Tribune*, April 12, 1918.

15. Deegan and Burger, "William Isaac Thomas and Social Reform," p. 115.

16. Janowitz, "Introduction," p. xv.

17. Deegan and Burger, "William Isaac Thomas and Social Reform," p. 115; Janowitz, "Introduction," pp. x and xviii.

18. *New York Times*, April 22, 1918.

19. Janowitz, "Introduction," p. xiv.

20. Deegan, p. 118.

21. Janowitz, "Introduction," p. ix. In his foreword to Volkart's volume Donald Young has appropriately noted that "the man who established the personal document and the life history as basic sources in social sciences has left no such materials about himself."

22. *New York Times*, April 13, 1918.

23. See J. Edward Chamberlin and Sander L. Gilman, eds., *Degeneration: The Dark Side of Progress*, especially Robert Nye, "Sociology and Degeneration: The Irony of Progress," pp. 49–71, and Nancy Stepan, "Biology and Degeneration: Races and Proper Places," pp. 97–120.

24. See Stuart Ewen, *Captains of Consciousness: Advertising and the Social Roots of Consumer Culture;* also Stuart and Elizabeth Ewen, *Channels of Desire: Mass Images and the Shaping of American Consciousness.*

25. W. I. Thomas, "Life History."

26. The German philosopher and literary critic Walter Benjamin was, in a different context but in much the same years, also confronting urban

modernity. Both were flâneurs of the city. Walter Benjamin strolled the arcades of Paris, the harbor of Marseilles, the courtyards of Naples; W. I.Thomas strolled the backalleys of Chicago.

27. Ernest W. Burgess, "William I. Thomas as a Teacher," pp. 760–67.

28. *Bookman*, October 1923, p. 214.

29. Michel Foucault, "The Life of Infamous Men," p. 76.

30. I am referring on the one hand to Julia and Herman Schwendinger, "Sociology's Founding Fathers: Sexist to a Man" and to Carol Smart, *Women, Crime and Criminology: A Feminist Critique*, pp. 37–46; on the other to Mary Jo Deegan and John Burger, "William Isaac Thomas and Social Reform: His Work and Writings," pp. 114–25, and to Rosalind Rosenberg, *Beyond Separate Spheres: Intellectual Roots of Modern Feminism*. In these four discussions of W. I. Thomas are contained two antithetical positions, both within the framework of a feminist analysis. It may be that if read chronologically the four assessments reflect how feminist theory and analysis has evolved since the early seventies.

5. Ethnographers at Home: The Trilogy of Studs Lonigan

1. James T. Farrell, *Studs Lonigan: A Trilogy*. Originally published in three separate volumes as *Young Lonigan* (1932), *The Young Manhood of Studs Lonigan* (1934), *Judgment Day* (1935). All parenthetical references to the text are to the 1935 edition of the trilogy, and will be preceded by the respective abbreviations YL, YM, and JD.

2. Harold M. Meyer and Richard C. Wade, *Chicago: Growth of a Metropolis*, pp. 160–61. Edgar M. Branch, *James T. Farrell*, pp. 18–19.

3. James T. Farrell, *Young Lonigan: A Boyhood in Chicago Streets*.

4. Frederic Thrasher, *The Gang: A Study of 1,313 Gangs in Chicago*, see also passim, chapter 2.

5. Frederic Thrasher, "Introduction," p. vii.

6. Ibid., p. viii.

7. For a useful overview of the reviewers who brought up literary naturalism or sociology see Barry Wallenstein, "James T. Farrell: Critic of Naturalism," pp. 154–75.

8. *Review of Reviews*, January 1936, p. 7.

9. Horace Gregory, "Unspectacular Realism," p. 61.

10. Eunice Clark, "Chicago Boy," p. 40.

11. Critics followed a discourse whose origins were in the social chaos of late nineteenth-century American cities, in the large numbers of foreigners and poor packed in the urban slums, in the grim reality of children living in the streets, as well as in the trauma of a middle class besieged by foreigners whose childrearing practices, as a result of different cultural backgrounds and economics, directly threatened those of the middle class. Anthony Platt's study *The Child Savers* remains a classic analysis of the mid-ninteenth–century origins and development of the move-

ment to save the children of the urban poor through reform and correctional programs aimed at reasserting "parental authority, home education, domesticity, and rural values." See especially pp. 176ff.

12. James T. Farrell, "How *Studs Lonigan* Was Written," pp. 82–89.

13. Ibid., pp. 86–87.

14. James T. Farrell, "Author Defends Character Studs Lonigan," Schapiro Collection, Columbia University Libraries, New York City.

15. Cf. Richard Mitchell, "*Studs Lonigan*: A Scientific Novel"; Edgar Branch, "Freedom and Determinism in James T. Farrell's Fiction"; Alan M. Wald, *James T. Farrell: The Revolutionary Socialist Years*; William J. Lynch, "James T. Farrell and the Irish-American Urban Experience"; Donald Pizer, "James T. Farrell and the 1930s," pp. 19–21; Robert J. Butler, "Parks, Parties, and Pragmatism"; Bette Howland, "James T. Farrell's Studs Lonigan"; Lewis Fried, *Makers of the City*; Arnold L. Goldsmith, *The Modern American Urban Novel*.

16. Edgar M. Branch, "American Writer in the Twenties: James T. Farrell and the University of Chicago."

17. Ibid., p. 26.

18. James T. Farrell, "The Dance Marathons," Ernest Burgess Papers, Special Collections, Regenstein Library. My thanks to Lizabeth Cohen for directing my attention to this important document.

19. Ibid., pp. 3, 4, 8.

20. James T. Farrell, "How *Studs Lonigan* Was Written," pp. 84–85.

21. James T. Farrell to Meyer Schapiro, June 20, 1945.

22. James T. Farrell to Meyer Schapiro, June 2, 1942.

23. James T. Farrell, *Reflections at Fifty and Other Essays*, p. 184.

24. Eunice Clark, "Chicago Boy," p. 40.

25. Frank O'Malley, "James T. Farrell: Two Twilight Images," p. 255.

26. James T. Farrell to Morton D. Zabel, Dec. 5, 1934, Morton D. Zabel Papers, Modern Poetry, Special Collections, Regenstein Library.

27. Richard Mitchell, "*Studs Lonigan*: A Scientific Novel," p. 43.

28. Blanche H. Gelfant, *The American City Novel*.

29. Ann Douglas, "*Studs Lonigan* and the Failure of History in Mass Society: A Study in Claustrophobia," p. 493.

30. Jane Addams, "The Spirit of Youth Today," quoted in Thrasher, *The Gang*, pp. 128–30.

31. Thrasher, *The Gang*.

32. A useful discussion of the possible forms of visualization of the urban space can be found in Richard R. Wohl and Anselm L. Strauss, "Symbolic Representation and the Urban Milieu."

33. Douglas, "*Studs Lonigan* and the Failure of History," p. 492.

34. James T. Farrell, *Reflections at Fifty*, pp. 164–65.

35. Robert Park, "The City," pp. 10, 40.

36. For a more detailed discussion see passim chapter 2.

37. Thrasher, *The Gang*, pp. 5, 131.

38. Ibid., p. 74.

39. Ibid., p. 80.

40. Ibid., p. 251.

41. Ibid., p. 82.

42. Quoted by Philip A. Friedman in his "Afterword" to *Studs Lonigan*, p. 829.

43. Thrasher, *The Gang*, p. 131.

44. Farrell depicts the gangs's participation in the riots in one of the short but powerful italicized interchapters he experimented with in the second volume of the trilogy. Relying on a technique analogous to film montage, these interchapters bring into the novel and weave into the main narrative historical events, material drawn from the private lives of noncentral characters, sketches, and dialogues of parents and other people from the community. These interchapters comment on or contrast with the words and action of the main characters and create their meaning by way of juxtaposition.

45. Ernest Burgess, "The Growth of the City: An Introduction to a Research Project," pp. 47–62.

46. Burgess, "The Growth of the City," p. 57.

47. See passim chapter 2.

48. James T. Farrell, *Reflections at Fifty*, p. 193.

49. *Anthropology as Cultural Critique: An Experimental Moment in the Human Sciences*, ed. George E. Marcus and Michael M. Fisher, pp. 125–27.

6. Footnote Fellows: Cold Wars of American Letters

1. Simone de Beauvoir, *Force of Circumstance*, p. 327.

2. Nelson Algren, "I Ain't Abelard," p. 59.

3. Beauvoir, *Force of Circumstance*; see also Deirdre Blair's new biography *Simone de Beauvoir: A Biography* (New York: Summit Books, 1990).

4. Nelson Algren, "The Question of Simone de Beauvoir," p. 135.

5. Ibid.

6. Beauvoir, *Force of Circumstance*, pp. 166, 251.

7. Quoted in Duncan, *The Rise of Chicago as a Literary Center*, pp. viii–ix. Being of German stock in an intellectual world overwhelmingly dominated by Anglo-Saxon and New England descendents, Mencken naturally looked with sympathy toward Chicago, a city where people of Anglo-Saxon stock were rapidly becoming a minority as a new class of second-generation and, increasingly, native migrants—of Teutonic, Scandinavian, and Germanic origin—were rapidly moving upward in the spheres of cultural and industrial production of the city.

8. Alston Anderson and Terry Southern, "An Interview with Nelson Algren," p. 296.

9. Nelson Algren, *Chicago, City on the Make*, pp. 56, 85, 94.

10. "The Writer in Chicago: A Roundtable," *TriQuarterly* (Spring-Summer 1984), 60:336–37.

11. Jack Conroy to Will and Walt [nickname for Nelson Algren], Outgoing 1930s folder, Jack Conroy Collection, Newberry Library.

12. Ibid.

13. Nelson Algren, "Preface," p. xiv.

14. Fred Marsh, "Poles in Chicago"; Adam Margoshes, "Chicago." Critics thus confused their distaste for the subject matter with their evaluation of the novel. The *Partisan Review* drastically reversed Philip Rahv's earlier verdict on Algren. In 1935 Rahv hailed Algren's first novel *Somebody in Boots* in that magazine as "the first complete portrait of the lumpenproletariat in American revolutionary literature" and the author as "a young writer . . . inside the revolutionary movement." In 1942 Gertrude Buckman reviewed Algren's new novel for the same magazine. She complained that "Algren proposes no remedies" to what she described as the "easy brutality and [the] casual viciousness . . . [of] a social group whose moral tone is completely diseased." She also accused Algren of "[sparing] us any leavening glimpses into a life more wholesome and gentle," and after indicating some similarity between Algren and Faulkner, Brecht, and Celine, she proclaims the superiority of these authors for their ability to touch the "ultimate causes" and the "unmistakable implication of universal guilt." Gertrude Buckman's review of *Never Come Morning*—by far a more accomplished novel than the earlier *Somebody in Boots*—is emblematic of a shift, completed by the early forties, within the *Partisan Review* and large sectors of the American left as well. The shift away from historical and sociological specificity toward psychological universality that informs this last remark also informs Philip Rahv's reassessment of Algren. Reviewing *Never Come Morning* for the *Nation*, Rahv praised Algren for avoiding "sensationalism" and "left-wing propaganda," yet he found that this was a novel "about depressed people written by a depressed man" and that the author had a "compulsive feeling for low-life phenomena" to be found by "[scraping] the bottom of the social barrel." Finally, Rahv dismissed Richard Wright's sociological introduction as being "beside the point," since "truth" and "sincerity" have no particular sociological content. Philip Rahv, "The Lower Depths"; Gertrude Buckman, "A Slum on the Way to the End of the Night"; Philip Rahv, "No Parole."

15. Milton Hindus, "New Novels and Stories."

16. Malcolm Cowley, "Chicago Poem."

17. Benjamin Appel, "People of Crime."

18. Richard Wright, "Introduction," *Never Come Morning*, p. ix.

19. Ibid., p. x; Clifton Fadiman, *New Yorker*, 18:75; Wright, "Introduction," *Never Come Morning*, p. x.

20. Wright, "Introduction," *Never Come Morning*, p. x.

21. A useful overview and analysis of these critical shifts can be found

in Barbara Foley, "From New Criticism to Deconstruction"; Russell J. Reising, *The Unusable Past*; Kermit Vanderbilt, *American Literature and the Academy*; Richard Ohmann, *Politics of Letters*.

22. William Bittner, "The Literary Underground."

23. Norman Podhoretz, "The Man with a Golden Beef," 32:132.

24. Leslie Fiedler, "The Novel in the Post-Political World" and "The Noble Savages of Skid Row."

25. "Rough Stuff."

26. Lawrence Lipton, "A Voyeur's View of the Wild Side," 10:4–6.

27. Ibid.

28. Charles Walcutt, *American Literary Naturalism*; Alfred Kazin, *Contemporaries*; Chester E. Eisinger, *Fiction of the Forties*. See also Walter Allen, *The Modern Novel*; Kingsley Widmer, *The Literary Rebel*.

29. Edmund Fuller, *Man in Modern Fiction*, pp. 43–44.

30. Nelson Algren, "Author Bites Critic," 187:57–58; a copy of the original manuscript, which I have also used in the quotation, is located in the Alice Watkins Manuscript Collection—Watkins was Algren's agent at the time—and dated May-July 1958, Rare Book and Manuscript Library, Columbia University Libraries.

31. Nelson Algren to Malcom Cowley, July 25, 1952, Malcom Cowley Collection, Newberry Library.

32. Ibid., September 15, 1952.

33. Nelson Algren, "Introduction," pp. 10–11.

34. Respectively, James Robinson, "Nelson Algren's Spiritual Victims"; John Rymer, "A Changing Sense of Chicago," 4:378; David T. Boxer, "Social Allegory in the Novels of Nelson Algren," pp. 18, 22; Martha H. Cox and Wayne Chatterton, *Nelson Algren*, p. 94.

35. Elliot Podwill, "A 'Third-Person Society,' " p. 67.

36. Ibid., p. 118.

37. Cox and Chatterton, *Nelson Algren*, p. 93.

38. Podwill, "A 'Third-Person Society,'" p. 68.

39. Ibid., p. 114.

40. George Bluestone, "Nelson Algren," 22:40.

41. Boxer, "Social Allegory in the Novels of Nelson Algren," p. 15. Similar remarks can be found in Tom Carson, "The Man with a Golden Ear"; H. E. F. Donohue, "Algren's Innocence," p. 2; John Seelye, "The Night Watchman," 37:69.

42. R. W. Lid, "A World Imagined," p. 181.

43. Thus, instead of the "exhibition of vice among a particular ethnic group" Lid finds in Algren's novels "the culpability of the police"; instead of the criminal as a "casualty" of the slum, he sees the "righteous man," the "complacent man" as "[t]he source of the criminal act." Ibid.

44. For Lid Bruno is a "ghetto youth" who dreams of "sudden riches and overnight success . . . by the traditional routes open to the newly arrived and the poor and the ill-educated: the fight ring and the ball park."

In Bruno's mind, Lid notes, is "a cluster of tawdry hopes and aspirations pulled from the rag bag of American culture" that makes Bruno a representative, not a degenerate American. If occasionally Lid exceeds in detaching the symbolic from the empirical—he entitles his essay "A World Imagined" and writes that "the city Algren writes about isn't a real city, or even a segment of a real city"—he is perhaps overstating his case after finding himself surrounded by critics who either fail to see or actively deny the symbolic and empirical interpenetration of Algren's slum, and do so, in general, because they cannot conceive that the slum and its inhabitants can ever represent anything larger than themselves. Ibid., pp. 179–83.

45. The list is not very long: George Bluestone, "Nelson Algren"; Sheldon N. Grebstein, "Nelson Algren and the Whole Truth," pp. 299–309; R. W. Lid, "A World Imagined: The Art of Nelson Algren," pp. 177–96; Martha H. Cox and Wayne Chatterton, *Nelson Algren*; Bruce Bassoff, "Algren's Poetics in *The Man with the Golden Arm*"; Mary Ellen Pitts, "Algren's El: Internalized Machine and Displaced Nature"; James R. Giles, *Confronting the Horror: The Novels of Nelson Algren*; Bettina Drew, *Nelson Algren: A Life on the Wild Side*. Four dissertations have been written on Nelson Algren: Robert E. Omick, "Compassion in the Novels of Nelson Algren"; William E. Laukaitis, "Nelson Algren: A Critical Study"; David T. Boxer, "Social Allegory in the Novels of Nelson Algren"; Elliot Podwill, "A 'Third-Person Society': Flawed Human Relationships in the Work of Nelson Algren."

46. Kurt Vonnegut, "Introduction," p. xviii.

7. *A Walk on the Other Side:* Never Come Morning *by Nelson Algren*

"Why do you choose to live in Chicago?

If I lived in another city, even if life there were richer, I would lose my job. In Mexico City, I could not write about Chicago, because my way of writing about this city is not just that of recollection but rather of daylight reportage; as if I waited for a nightmare that returns at the same time each night and followed it until dawn. At times I wake up still sleepy and pursue my nightmare being careful not to disturb it; it's a sort of horror poetry. I'm sure that the lines of Baudelaire . . . have influenced my passion for that city" (my translation). Anne Pourtois, "Conversation avec Nelson Algren," *Europe* (October 1964), 52:76.

1. Nelson Algren, "The Mafia of the Heart,"p. 15.

2. Barbara Foley, *Telling the Truth: The Theory and Praxis of Documentary Fiction*, p. 16.

3. See William Stott's important study *Documentary Expression and Thirties America*.

4. Recent studies that have started to address this issue in relation to American literature are Mas'nd Zavarzadeh, *The Mythopoeic Reality: The Postwar American Nonfiction Novel*; John Hollowell, *Fact and Fiction: The New Journal-*

ism and the Nonfiction Novel; Sheely F. Fishkin, From Fact to Fiction: Journalism and Imaginative Writing in America; Robert Smart, The Nonfiction Novel; Barbara Foley, Telling the Truth.

5. Algren is referring to Donald Taft, at the time professor of criminology and human migration at the University of Illinois.

6. H. E. F. Donohue, Conversations with Nelson Algren, pp. 25, 30.

7. Ibid., pp. 89–90.

8. Cox and Chatterton, Nelson Algren, p. 41.

9. Nels Anderson, The Hobo; Harvey Zorbaugh, The Gold Coast and the Slum; Clifford Shaw, The Jack-Roller; Paul Cressey, The Taxi-Dance Hall.

10. It is remarkable to see how many novels and immigrant biographies were regularly reviewed in the pages of the American Journal of Sociology during the 1920s and the 1930s.

11. Donohue, Conversations with Nelson Algren, p. 154.

12. Respectively quoted in Martin Bulmer, The Chicago School of Sociology, p. 98, and in Werner J. Chanman, "Robert Park at Fisk," Journal of the History of the Behavioral Sciences (1978), 14:330.

13. Margaret Walker's new biography Richard Wright: Daemonic Genius contains a number of interesting references to the cultural life of Chicago during the 1930s.

14. All references to Never Come Morning will hereafter be in parenthesis and within the text; they are to the 1987 edition. I am following here Barbara Foley's discussion of documentary fiction and authentication, Telling the Truth, pp. 234ff.

15. Robert A. Perlongo, "Interview with Nelson Algren," p. 95.

16. Donohue, Conversations with Nelson Algren, p. 94.

17. Nelson Algren, "Preface," p. xv.

18. Frederick Thrasher, The Gang; W. I. Thomas, The Unadjusted Girl.

19. Thrasher, The Gang, pp. 63–67.

20. See passim chapter 2.

21. Nelson Algren, "When You Live Like I Done."

22. Ibid.

23. Jack Conroy Collection, Newberry Library.

24. Quoted by Ann Banks in First Person America, ed. Ann Banks (N.Y.: Knopf, 1980), p. xvii.

25. Ralph Ellison, "Harlem—Ahm In New York," May 10, 1939, Federal Writers Project Collection, Manuscript Division, Library of Congress.

26. Ralph Ellison, "Harlem," June 14, 1938, Federal Writers Project Collection, Manuscript Division, Library of Congress.

27. Jack Conroy, "Memories of Arna Bontemps," n.d. Jack Conroy Collection, Newberry Library.

28. B. A. Botkin, "WPA and Folklore Research: 'Bread and Song,'" p. 7; Botkin, "Living Lore of the New York City Writers' Project," p. 258.

29. These are mimeographed materials. I was able to see many of these manuals at the Historical Society Library of the University of Wisconsin-Madison. Jerre Mangione, The Dream and the Deal: The Federal

Writers' Project, 1935–1943; William F. McDonald, *Federal Relief Administration and the Arts*.

30. Nelson Algren to Millen Brand, May 21, 1940, Rare Book and Manuscript Collection Library, Columbia University Libraries.

31. McDonald, *Federal Relief Administration*, pp. 690, 714; M. Colby, ed., *Final Report on the WPA Program, 1935–1943*, pp. 63–65.

32. Foley, *Telling the Truth*, pp. 234, 260–67. See also a most interesting discussion of the elements of voice and subjectivity by Loy D. Martin, *Browning's Dramatic Monologues and the Post-Romantic Subject*.

8. Decentering and Recentering: Richard Wright, African-American, and American Literature

1. An earlier draft of chapters 8 and 9 has appeared in MELUS (Summer 1985), 12:25–43. All references are to *Black Boy: A Record of Childhood and Youth* and to *American Hunger*, hereafter cited in the text as BB and AH. *Black Boy* and *American Hunger* were originally composed as part of a single manuscript, to be called "American Hunger," which Wright completed in 1943. Following the suggestion of his publisher, Wright agreed to publish the first part as a separate text under the title *Black Boy*. The section dealing with his experience in the Communist Party came out separately in two installments in the *Atlantic Monthly* a few months later—the well-known "I Tried to Be a Communist." If one excludes Constance Webbs's limited edition of 1946, it was not until 1977 that the second part was published integrally. Diverging opinions on the reasons for the split publication can be found in Fabre, *The Unfinished Quest of Richard Wright*, pp. 254–56; John M. Reilly, "The Self-Creation of the Intellectual," pp. 213–14; Robert Kirsch, *Los Angeles Times*, May 29, 1977, pp. 1, 71; Darryl Pinckney, *Village Voice*, July 4, 1977, pp. 80–82; Bruno Cartosio, "Due scrittori afroamericani: Richard Wright e Ralph Ellison," pp. 395–431. For an overview and a critical assessment of this publication record see the newly published two-volume *Works: Richard Wright* by the Library of America edited by Arnold Rampersad. Richard Wright composed the two parts as one text and it is this unified single text that the present discussion examines. Since the structure and the narrative movement of the autobiography are central to the present discussion, it is not only justified but methodologically essential that the two parts be considered in their aesthetic and dialectical unity or "disunity." As Cartosio notes, by reintegrating the text one also notices the remarkable parallelism between the autobiography and *Native Son*. It is, he argues, in the last part of both texts that the equilibrium between narration and commentary gives way to a "didactical-moralistic anxiety" beneath which lay poorly hidden the unresolved contradictions of a whole political era.

2. Recent studies of Richard Wright include: Yoshinobu Hakutani, *Critical Essays on Richard Wright*; Joyce A. Joyce, *Richard Wright's Art of Tragedy*;

Harold Bloom, *Richard Wright*; James C. Trotman, *Richard Wright: Myths and Realities*; Harold Bloom, *Richard Wright's Native Son*; Eugene Miller, *Voice of a Native Son*; Kenneth Kinnamon, *New Essays on Native Son*. For recent discussions of *Black Boy-American Hunger* cf. Janice Thaddeus, "The Metamorphosis of Richard Wright's Black Boy"; Donald B. Gibson, "Richard Wright's Black Boy and the Trauma of Autobiographical Rebirth"; Jacob Howland, "Black Boy"; Yvonne Ochillo, "Black Boy: Structure as Meaning"; Abdul R. JanMohamed, "Negating the Negation." Earlier and still useful discussions of Wright's autobiography include Charles T. Davis, "From Experience to Eloquence"; Joseph T. Skerrett, Jr., "Richard Wright, Writing and Identity"; Robert J. Butler, "The Quest for Pure Motion"; Thymothy D. Adams, "I Do Believe Him Though I Know He Lies."

3. For a more detailed discussion of the concept of marginal man and of "peasant in the city" see passim, chapter 3.

4. This and similar passages have been read as evidence of Wright's negative views of the Black community and Black culture. Yet if one understands "Negro" in the passage to be synonymous with "recent southern migrant," "peasant in the city," and "poor, recently urbanized American," the figure of the Black migrant becomes representative of the experiences of other immigrants and migrants from peasant societies and the passage becomes both clearer and more resonant.

5. Houston Baker's reading of Wright's autobiography two decades ago and, specifically, of Wright's representation of the Black community contained suggestions that critics have failed to follow. The apparently unsympathetic remarks about Black culture made by Wright in *Black Boy-American Hunger*, according to Baker, are contingent upon the portrait-of-the-artist genre that informs the autobiography. This genre, in turn, informs the representation of the community and its cultural forms as enemies of the "young, gifted, black artist." Wright's pronouncements about the "essential bleakness of black life," Baker suggests, are tactical premises and aesthetic consequences of the "*struggling* artist" story. Baker also examines the apparent conflict between Wright's programmatic statements about and his fictional representation of Black culture, highlighting the positive and active role that Black culture plays in *Native Son* and in Wright's short story "Fire and Cloud." In the case of this short story Baker sustains his claim by arguing that the hero of the story is not communism but the reverend and the people "fused" through their religion. One might add that "Fire and Cloud" was at once a statement on the importance of the Black church and, more generally, of Black folk culture and a critique of the role of the party and the intellectual as the vanguard of the people predominant within the Left in the 1930s. Houston Baker, *Long Black Song: Essays in Black American Literature and Culture*, pp. 126–28, 138. For a recent essay that also deals with Wright's political and ethnic culture see Thomas Larson, "A Political Vision of Afro-American Culture: Richard Wright's 'Bright and Morning Star,'" pp. 147–59.

235

6. The most complete account of such relationship remains Michel Fabre's *The Unfinished Quest of Richard Wright*. References can also be found in Edward Margolies, *The Art of Richard Wright*, p. 11; Dan McCall, *The Example of Richard Wright*, p. 194; John A. Williams, *The Most Native of Sons*, p. 82; Kenneth Kinnamon, *The Emergence of Richard Wright*, pp. 196–97; Robert Felgar, *Richard Wright*, pp. 39–40, 138; Addison Gayle, *Richard Wright: Ordeal of a Native Son*, pp. 148ff.

7. St. Clair Drake and Horace Cayton, *Black Metropolis*, pp. xviii–xix.

8. Ibid., pp. xvii–xviii.

9. Fabre, *The Unfinished Quest of Richard Wright*, especially pp. 201, 232–34, 249, 267, 293–402.

10. Cf. Richard Wright's prefaces to Drake and Cayton's *Black Metropolis* and to his own *12 Million Black Voices*.

11. John M. Reilly, "Richard Wright Preaches the Nation: *12 Million Black Voices*," pp. 116–19; see also Reilly's very insightful "The Self-Creation of the Intellectual: *American Hunger* and *Black Power*," pp. 213–27.

12. Reilly's claim that Wright found sociology not by accident but in the epistemological process of actively looking for something proceeds from premises that the present discussion both shares and follows. It is hard, on the other hand, to believe that Wright was not influenced by the theories on nationalism of the Communist Party when he repeatedly and protractedly referred to Stalin's theories and policies on ethnic minorities. More interesting than such exclusionary hypotheses would be to explore the contradictions and confluences between the Communist Party and the Chicago sociologists' theories of nationalism and ethnicity and to pursue that examination aesthetically and thematically in Wright's work. One need not exclude the role of the Communist Party or, more generally, of Marxist theory in order to acknowledge the importance of Chicago sociology.

13. Robert Bone, "Richard Wright and the Chicago Renaissance," pp. 446–68.

14. Bone also explains that the figure who most prominently functioned as a link between the sociologists and the writers was the Chicago sociologist and Wright's close friend Horace Cayton, who "opened his research files [to Richard Wright], shared his notes for *Black Metropolis*, and provided Wright with a theoretical approach to the phenomenon of urbanization." Ibid.

15. Werner Sollors, "Modernization as Adultery: Richard Wright, Zora Neale Hurston, and American Culture of the 1930's and 1940's," pp. 22–75.

16. See chapter 3, passim.

17. Sollors, "Modernization as Adultery," p. 135. Cf. also Fred H. Matthews, "The Revolt Against Americanism: Cultural Pluralism and Cultural Relativism as an Ideology of Liberation" and Philip Gleason, "Americans

All: Ethnicity, Ideology, and American Identity in the Era of World War II," pp. 235–64.

18. Boas and Park cannot do for literary critics in the 1990s what they have long since ceased to do for anthropologists and sociologists. They are part of the intellectual history of the United States, and an important part, but the epistemological developments of the last decades have made many of those theories, concepts, and methods not only obsolete but politically fraught with problems.

19. Gunter Lenz, "Southern Exposures: The Urban Experience and the Reconstruction of Black Folk Culture and Community in the Works of Richard Wright and Zora Neale Hurston," pp. 3–39.

20. Ibid., p. 11.

21. Ibid., pp. 12, 21.

22. John McCluskey, Jr., "Two Steppin': Richard Wright's Encounter with Blue-Jazz.".

23. Ibid., pp. 333–36.

24. Ibid., pp. 338–43.

25. That the name and the literary criticism of Zora Neale Hurston should occupy such prominent space in a discussion devoted to Richard Wright is due to the nature of literary criticism in general and to this debate in particular. In the same way that the critical debate relevant to Farrell and Algren must in part be found and engaged in the vicinity of Richard Wright, the analysis of Zora Neale Hurston's work in the last few years has carried the heaviest load in the recentering of African-American literature. There one must engage critical issues that are most significant not only to Richard Wright but to American literature as well.

26. Robert Stepto, "I Thought I Knew These People: Wright and the Afro-American Literary Tradition," pp. 57–74.

27. Ibid., pp. 58–60, my emphasis.

28. See chapter 9, passim.

29. Laura Tanner, "Uncovering the Magical Disguise of Language: The Narrative Presence in Richard Wright's *Native Son*," pp. 412–31.

30. Stepto, "I Thought I Knew These People," p. 69.

31. Cf. Henry Louis Gates, *The Signifying Monkey: A Theory of African-American Literary Criticism*, pp. 118–20, 181–83, and Gates, "What's in a Name?"

32. Gates, "What's in a Name?" p. 491.

33. Johnson goes on, "But Negritude . . . as one answer to the problem of controlling meaning, still exerts in the 1980's a strong influence on contemporary black literary production," and by the 1990s, one should add, on literary criticism as well. Charles Johnson, *Being and Race*, p. 20.

34. Paradoxically, by juxtaposing the modernists T. S. Eliot, Stein, and 237 Joyce on the one hand and Black folk culture on the other, Gates is reproducing the same dichotomies that inspired the Chicago sociologists, Boa-

sian anthropologists, and the modernist artists themselves, which we are just beginning to recognize as historically and ideologically determined distinctions.

35. Hazel Carby, *Reconstructing Womanhood*, see especially pp. 163–75, and Carby, "Reinventing History/Imagining the Future," pp. 381–87.

36. Carby, *Reconstructing Womanhood*, p. 175.

37. Carby, "Reinventing History/Imagining the Future," p. 384.

38. For a partial bibliography of feminist essays on the representation of women by Richard Wright and, more broadly, within African-American literature, see Nagueyalti Warren's "Black Girls and Native Sons: Female Images in Selected Works by Richard Wright," pp. 59–77.

39. Calvin C. Hernton, *The Sexual Mountain and Black Women Writers*, p. 64.

40. Alan W. France, "Misogyny and Appropriation in Wright's *Native Son*," pp. 413–23.

41. France, "Misogyny and Appropriation," pp. 414–15, 419.

42. Warren, "Black Girls and Native Sons," pp. 59–77.

43. Ibid., pp. 69–70.

44. Joyce Ann Joyce, "Richard Wright's 'Long Black Song': A Moral Dilemma."

45. Ibid., pp. 380–82.

46. Ibid., p. 385.

47. In an odd combination of southern agrarianism and Afrocentrism Joyce explains that through Sarah's consciousness we perceive the inversion whereby "man inverts or ignores the *natural order of things*" (my emphasis), which, for Joyce, is identical with the rural "natural" world represented by Sarah and is antithetical to the "mechanical, rational, sterile egotistical society" represented by the clock, the gramophone, and the salesman. Ibid., p. 382.

48. Jane Davis, "More Force than Human: Richard Wright's Female Characters."

49. Maria K. Mootry, "Bitches, Whores, and Woman Haters: Archetypes and Typologies in the Art of Richard Wright."

50. Kathleen Ochshorn, "The Community of *Native Son*."

9. Sociology of an Existence: Black Boy-American Hunger by Richard Wright

The title of this chapter is derived from a statement by Irving Howe who writes of Richard Wright: "The sociology of his existence formed a constant pressure on his literary work, and not merely in the way this might be true for any writer, but with a pain and ferocity that nothing could remove" (my emphasis). From Howe's "Black Boys and Native Sons," p. 40. I would also like to acknowledge a particular debt that I owe for this chapter to Werner Sollors, whose seminar on kinship and ethnicity at Columbia University inspired this essay and whose suggestion that I explore the topic of Chicago sociology in relation to Richard Wright in my seminar paper was the original impetus for this study.

1. See Robert Park, "Sociological Methods," pp. 163, 166; Morris Janowitz, "Introduction," p. xxxv; James Short, "Introduction," *The Social Fabric of the Metropolis: Contributions of the Chicago School of Urban Sociology* (Chicago: University of Chicago Press, 1971), pp. xi–xlvi.

2. Louis Wirth, *On Cities and Social Life*, pp. 234–37; Wirth, *The Ghetto*, p. 287; Frederic Thrasher, *The Gang*.

3. See passim, chapters 3 and 4.

4. Cited in Robert Park, "Sociological Methods," p. 166.

5. Janowitz, "Introduction," p. xxiii.

6. W. I. Thomas and Florian Znaniecki, *The Polish Peasant in Europe and America*.

7. Janowitz, "Introduction," p. xxxv; Park, "Sociological Methods," p. 163.

Bibliography

Aaron, Daniel. "Richard Wright and the Communist Party." *New Letters* (Winter 1971).

Adams, Thymothy D. "I Do Believe Him Though I Know He Lies: Lying as Genre and Metaphor in Richard Wright's *Black Boy*." *Prose Studies* (Sept. 1985), 8:172–87.

Algren, Nelson. "Author Bites Critic." *Nation*, Aug. 2, 1958, 187:57–58.

—— *Chicago, City on the Make*. [1951.] New York: McGraw-Hill, 1983.

—— "I Ain't Abelard." *Newsweek*, December 28, 1964, 64:58–59.

—— "Introduction." In Nelson Algren, *The Neon Wilderness*. New York: Hill and Wang, 1960.

—— Letter to Millen Brand. May 21, 1940. Rare Book and Manuscript Collection Library, Columbia University Libraries, New York.

—— "The Mafia of the Heart." *Contact* (October 1960), 2:9–15.

—— *Never Come Morning*. New York: Harper and Brothers, 1942.

—— "Preface." In Nelson Algren, *Never Come Morning*. New York: Four Walls Eight Windows, 1987, pp. xi–xvi.

Bibliography

—— "The Question of Simone de Beauvoir." *Harper's*, May 1965, 230:134–36.

—— "When You Live Like I Done." July 17, 1939. Federal Writers' Project Records, Manuscript Division, Library of Congress, Washington, D.C.

Allen, James Sloan. *The Romance of Commerce and Culture: Capitalism, Modernism, and the Chicago-Aspen Crusade for Cultural Reform*. Chicago: University of Chicago Press, 1983.

Allen, Walter. *The Modern Novel*. New York: Dutton, 1964.

Anderson, Alston and Terry Southern. "An Interview with Nelson Algren." *Paris Review* (Winter 1965), vol 11. Rpt. in Nelson Algren, *The Neon Wilderness*. New York: Writers and Readers, 1986, pp. 294–304.

Anderson, Nels. *The Hobo*. Chicago: University of Chicago Press, 1923.

Andrews, Clarence A. *Chicago in Story: A Literary History*. Iowa City: Midwest Heritage, 1982.

Appel, Benjamin. "People of Crime." *Saturday Review*, April 18, 1942, p. 7.

Arac, Jonathan. "F. O. Matthiessen: Authorizing an American Renaissance." In Walter Benn Michaels and Donald E. Pease, eds., *The American Renaissance Reconsidered*. Baltimore: Johns Hopkins University Press, 1985.

Bak, Hans and Vincent Piket, eds. *Looking Inward, Looking Outward: American Fiction in the 1930s and 1940s*. European University Press, 1990.

Baker, Houston A. *Long Black Song: Essays in Black American Literature and Culture*. [1990.] Charlottesville: University of Virginia Press, 1972.

Bald, Wambly. *On the Left Bank, 1929–1933*. Athens: Ohio University Press, 1987.

Baldwin, James. *Nobody Knows My Name*. New York: Dial Press, 1961.

Bassoff, Bruce. "Algren's Poetics in the Man with the Golden Arm." *Etudes Anglaises* 40 (Oct.-Dec., 1987): 413–20.

Beauvoir, Simone de. *Force of Circumstance*. New York: Putnam, 1965.

—— *The Mandarins*. New York: World, 1956.

Bender, Thomas. *Community and Social Change in America*. New Brunswick: Rutgers University Press, 1978.

Benjamin, Walter. "Theses on the Philosophy of History." In *Illuminations*. New York: Schocken, 1969.

—— "The Work of Art in the Age of Mechanical Reproduction." In *Illuminations*. New York: Schocken, 1969.

Berger, Morroe. *Real and Imagined Worlds: The Novel and Social Science and Literature*. Cambridge: Harvard University Press, 1977.

Berthelot, J. M. et al. "Les Sociologies et les Corps." *Current Sociology*, 33(2):38–55.

Berthoff, Warner. *The Ferment of Realism: American Literature, 1884–1919*. New York: Cambridge University Press, 1981.

Bittner, William. "The Literary Underground." *Nation*, September 22, 1956, 183:249.

Bloom, Harold, ed., *Richard Wright*. New York: Chelsea House, 1987.

—— *Richard Wright's Native Son*. New York: Chelsea House, 1988.

Bluestone, George. "Nelson Algren." *Western Review* (Autumn 1957), 22:27–44.

Blumer, Herbert. *An Appraisal of Thomas and Znaniecki's "The Polish Peasant in Europe and America"*. New York: Social Science Research Council, 1939.

Bodziack, Joseph. "Richard Wright and Afro-American Gothic." In C. James Trotman, ed., *Richard Wright: Myths and Realities*. New York: Garland, 1988.

Bone, Robert. "Richard Wright and the Chicago Renaissance." *Callaloo* (Summer 1986), 9:446–68.

Borenstein, Audrey. *Redeeming the Sin: Social Science and Literature*. New York: Columbia University Press, 1978.

Borus, Daniel H. *Writing Realism: Howells, James, and Norris in the Mass Market*. Chapel Hill: University of North Carolina, 1989.

Botkin, B. A. "Living Lore of the New York City Writers' Project." *New York Folklore Quarterly* (November 1946), 2:252–63.

—— "WPA and Folklore Research: 'Bread and Song,' " *Southern Folklore Quarterly* (March 1939), 3:7–14.

Boxer, David T. "Social Allegory in the Novels of Nelson Algren." Ph.D. diss., University of Washington, 1970.

Branch, Edgar M. "American Writer in the Twenties: James T. Farrell and the University of Chicago." *American Book Collector* (Summer 1961), pp. 25–32.

—— "Freedom and Determinism in James T. Farrell's Fiction." In Sydney J. Krause, ed., *Essays on Determinism in American Literature*. Ohio: Kent State University Press, 1964, pp. 80–104.

—— *James T. Farrell*. New York: Twayne, 1971.

Brown, Richard. *A Poetic for Sociology: Toward a Logic of Discovery for the Human Sciences*. Cambridge: Cambridge University Press, 1977.

Buckman, Gertrude. "A Slum on the Way to the End of Night." *Partisan Review* (Sept.-Oct. 1942), 9:426–28.

Bulmer, Martin. *The Chicago School of Sociology: Institutionalization, Diversity, and the Rise of Sociological Research*. Chicago: University of Chicago Press, 1984.

Burgess, Ernest W. Collected papers. University of Chicago, Regenstein Library, Special Collections.

—— "The Growth of the City: An Introduction to a Research Project." Publications of the American Sociological Society, 1924. Rpt. in Park and Ernest Burgess, eds., *The City*. Chicago: University of Chicago Press, 1974, pp. 47–62.

—— "William I. Thomas as a Teacher." *Sociology and Social Research* (1918), 33(2):760–67.

Butler, Robert J. "Parks, Parties, and Pragmatism: Time and Setting in James T. Farrell's Major Novels." *Essays in Literature* (1983), 10(2):241–54.

243

———— "The Quest for Pure Motion in Richard Wright's *Black Boy.*" *MELUS* (Fall 1983), 10:5–17.

Cahan, Abraham. *The Rise of David Levinsky.* [1917.] New York: Harper and Row, 1976.

Cahnman, Warner J. "Robert Park at Fisk." *Journal of the History of the Behavioral Sciences* (1978), 14:328–36.

Calmes, Alain. *Le roman colonial en Algérie avant 1914.* Paris: L'Harmattan, 1984.

Carby, Hazel. *Reconstructing Womanhood: The Emergence of the Afro-American Woman Novelist.* New York: Oxford University Press, 1987.

———— "Reinventing History/Imagining the Future." *Black American Literature Forum* (Summer 1989), 23:381–87.

Carey, James T. *Sociology and Public Affairs: The Chicago School.* Beverly Hills: Sage, 1985.

Carpenter, Humphrey. *Geniuses Together: American Writers in Paris in the 1920s.* Boston: Houghton Mifflin, 1988.

Carson, Tom. "The Man with a Golden Ear." *Voice Literary Supplement* (November 1983), 21:16.

Cartosio, Bruno. "Dues scrittori afroamericani: Richard Wright e Ralph Ellison." *Studi Americani* (1971), 15:395–431.

Cayton, Horace R. "The Known City." *New Republic,* May 12, 1947, pp. 30–31.

Chamberlain, J. Edward and Sander L. Gilman, eds. *Degeneration: The Dark Side of Progress.* New York: Columbia University Press, 1985.

Clark, Eunice. "Chicago Boy." *Saturday Review of Literature,* April 27, 1935, pp. 40.

Clifford, James and George E. Marcus, eds. *Writing Culture: The Poetics and the Politics of Ethnography.* Berkeley: University of California Press, 1986.

Cohen, Lizabeth. *Making a New Deal: Industrial Workers in Chicago, 1919–1939.* New York: Cambridge University Press, 1990.

Colby, M., ed. *Final Report on the WPA Program, 1935–1943.* Washington, D.C.: Mimeo, 1946.

Conder, John J. *Naturalism in American Fiction: The Classic Phase.* Lexington: University Press of Kentucky, 1984.

Conrow, Robert. *Field Days.* New York: Scribner's, 1974.

Conroy, Jack. Collected papers. Newberry Library, Chicago.

Cowley, Malcolm. "Chicago Poem." *New Republic,* May 4, 1942, 106:613–14.

Cox, Martha H. and Wayne Chatterton. *Nelson Algren.* Boston: Twayne, 1975.

Crapanzano, Vincent. *Tuhamy: Portrait of a Moroccan.* Chicago: University of Chicago Press, 1980.

Cressey, Paul. *The Taxi-Dance Hall.* Chicago: University of Chicago Press, 1932.

Cronon, William. *Nature's Metropolis: Chicago and the Great West, 1848–1893.* New York: Norton, 1991.

Crossman, Richard, ed. *The God That Failed*. New York: Harper, 1965.

Cruse, Harold. *The Crisis of the Negro Intellectual*. New York: William Morrow, 1967.

Davis, Charles T. "From Experience to Eloquence: Richard Wright's *Black Boy* as Art." In Michael Harper and Robert Stepto, eds., *Chants of Saints: A Gathering of Afro-American Literature, Art, and Scholarship*. Urbana: University of Illinois Press, pp. 425–39.

Davis, Jane. "More Force than Human: Richard Wright's Female Characters." *Obsidian II* (Winter 1986), 1:68—-83.

Deegan, Mary Jo. *Jane Addams and the Men of the Chicago School, 1892–1918*. New Brunswick: Transaction, 1988.

Deegan, Mary Jo and John Burger. "William Isaac Thomas and Social Reform: His Work and Writings." *Journal of the History of the Behavioral Sciences* (1981), 17:114-—25.

Diner, Steven J. *A City and Its Universities: Public Policy in Chicago, 1892–1919*. Chapel Hill: University of North Carolina Press, 1980.

Donohue, H. E. F. "Algren's Innocence." In Nelson Algren, *Never Come Morning*. New York: Four Walls Eight Windows, 1987, pp. 285–91.

——— *Conversations with Nelson Algren*. New York: Hill and Wang, 1964.

Douglas, Ann. "*Studs Lonigan* and the Failure of History in Mass Society: A Study in Claustrophobia." *American Quarterly* (1977), 29:487–505.

Drake, St. Clair and Horace Cayton, *Black Metropolis*. New York: Harcourt and Brace, 1945.

Drew, Bettina. *Nelson Algren: A Life on the Wild Side*. New York: Putnam, 1990.

Duffey, Bernard. *The Chicago Renaissance in American Letters: A Critical History*. East Lansing: Michigan State College Press, 1954.

Duncan, Hugh D. *The Rise of Chicago as a Literary Center from 1885 to 1920*. Totowa, N.J.: Bedminster, 1964.

Eagleton, Terry. "The Idealism of American Criticism." *New Left Review* (May-June 1981), 127:53–66.

Ehrenreich, John H. *The Altruistic Imagination: A History of Social Work and Social Policy in the United States*. Ithaca: Cornell University Press, 1985.

Eisinger, Chester E. *Fiction of the Forties*. Chicago: University of Chicago Press, 1963.

Elliott, Emory, ed. *Columbia Literary History of the United States*. New York: Columbia University Press, 1988.

Ellis, William. *The Theory of the American Romance*.

Ellison, Ralph. "Harlem—Ahm in New York." May 10, 1939. Federal Writers' Project Records, Manuscript Division, Library of Congress, Washington, D.C.

Engels, Frederick. *The Origin of the Family, Private Property, and the State*. New York: International Publishers, 1985.

Ewen, Stuart. *Captains of Consciousness: Advertising and the Social Roots of Consumer Culture*. New York: McGraw-Hill, 1976.

245

Ewen, Stuart and Elizabeth Stuart. *Channels of Desire: Mass Images and the Shaping of American Consciousness*. New York: McGraw-Hill, 1982.

Fabre, Michel. "Margaret Walker's Richard Wright: A Wrong Righted or Wright Wronged?" *Mississippi Quarterly* (1989), 42:429–50.

—— *The Unfinished Quest of Richard Wright*. New York: Morrow, 1973.

Fadiman, Clifton. *New Yorker*, April 18, 1942, 18:75.

Faris, Robert E. *Chicago Sociology, 1920–1932*. San Francisco: Chandler, 1967.

Farrell, James T. "Author Defends Character Studs Lonigan." *Louisville Times*, November 22, 1960, 3:8.

—— "How Studs Lonigan Was Written." *The League of Frightened Philistines*. [1938.] New York: Vanguard, 1945.

—— Correspondence with Meyer Schapiro, Schapiro Collection, Rare Book and Manuscript Collection Library, Columbia University Libraries, New York.

—— Correspondence with Morton D. Zabel, Morton D. Zabel Papers, Modern Poetry, Special Collections, Regenstein Library, University of Chicago.

—— *Reflections at Fifty and Other Essays*. New York: Vanguard, 1954.

—— *Studs Lonigan: A Trilogy*. New York: Vanguard, 1935.

—— *Young Lonigan: A Boyhood in Chicago Streets*. New York: Vanguard, 1932.

Felgar, Robert. *Richard Wright*. Boston: Twayne, 1980.

Fiedler, Leslie. "The Noble Savages of Skid Row." *Reporter*, July 12, 1956, 15:43–44.

—— "The Novel in the Post-Political World." *Partisan Review* (Summer 1956), 23:360–61.

Fishkin, Sheely F. *From Fact to Fiction: Journalism and Imaginative Writing in America*. New York: Oxford University Press, 1985.

Fitch, Noel Riley. *Sylvia Beach and the Lost Generation: A History of Literary Paris in the Twenties and Thirties*. New York: Norton, 1983.

Fitzpatrick, Ellen. *Endless Crusade: Women Social Scientists and Progressive Reform*. New York: Oxford University Press, 1990.

Fleischauer, Carl and Beverly W. Brannan, *Documenting America: 1935–1943*. Berkeley: University of California Press, 1988.

Fleming, Robert E. "The Chicago Naturalistic Novel, 1930-—1966." Ph.D. diss., University of Illinois, Urbana, 1967.

Foley, Barbara. "From New Criticism to Deconstruction." *American Quarterly* (Spring 1984), 36:43–64.

—— *Telling the Truth: The Theory and Praxis of Documentary Fiction*. Ithaca: Cornell University Press, 1986.

Foucault, Michel. "The Life of Infamous Men." In Meaghan Morris and Paul Patton, eds., *Michel Foucault: Power, Truth, Strategy*. Sydney: Feral Publications, 1979.

France, Alan W. "Misogyny and Appropriation in Wright's *Native Son*." *Modern Fiction Studies* (Autumn 1988), 34:413–23.

Fried, Lewis. *Makers of the City*. Amherst: University of Massachusetts Press, 1990.

Friedman, Philip A. "Afterword." In James T. Farrell, *Studs Lonigan*. New York: Signet, 1965, pp. 821–40.

Fuller, Edmund. *Man in Modern Fiction*. New York: Random House, 1958.

Gates, Henry Louis. *The Signifying Monkey: A Theory of African-American Literary Criticism*. New York: Oxford University Press, 1988.

——— "What's in a Name?' *Dissent* (Fall 1989), 36:487–95.

Gayle, Addison. *Richard Wright: Ordeal of a Native Son*. New York: Anchor, 1980.

Gelfant, Blanche H. *The American City Novel*. Norman: University of Oklahoma Press, 1954.

Gibson, Donald B. *The Politics of Literary Expression*. Westport, Conn.: Greenwood, 1981.

——— "Richard Wright's Black Boy and the Trauma of Autobiographical Rebirth." *Callaloo* (Summer 1986), 9:492–98.

Giles, James R. *Confronting the Horror: The Novels of Nelson Algren*. Kent, Ohio: Kent State University Press, 1989.

Gleason, Philip. "Americans All: Ethnicity, Ideology, and American Identity in the Era of World War II." In Rob Kroes, ed., *The American Identity: Fusion and Fragmentation*. European Contributions to American Studies 3. Amsterdam: Amerika-Instituut, 1980, pp. 235–64.

Goldsmith, Arnold L. *The Modern American Urban Novel: Nature as "Interior Structure."* Detroit: Wayne State University Press, 1991.

Graff, Gerald, and Michael Warner, eds. *The Origins of Literary Study in America*. New York: Routledge, 1989.

Grebstein, Sheldon N. "Nelson Algren and the Whole Truth." In Warren French, ed., *The Forties*. Deland, Fla.: Everett/Edwards, 1969.

Gregory, Horace. "Unspectacular Realism." *Nation*, July 20, 1932, p. 61.

Grossman, James. *Land of Hope: Chicago, Black Southerners, and the Great Migration*. Chicago: University of Chicago Press, 1989.

Gutman, Herbert. *Work, Culture, and Society in Industrializing America*. New York: Random House, 1977.

Hakutani, Yoshinobu, ed., *Critical Essays on Richard Wright*. Boston: G. K. Hall, 1982.

Hakutani, Yoshinobu and Lewis Fried, eds. *American Literary Naturalism: A Reassessment*. Heidelberg: Anglistiche Forschungen, 1975.

Hammersley, Martin. *The Dilemma of Qualitative Methods: Herbert Blumer and the Chicago Tradition*. New York: Routledge, 1989.

Hannerz, Ulf. *Exploring the City: Inquiries Toward an Urban Anthropology*. New York: Columbia University Press, 1980.

Haraway, Donna J. "In the Beginning Was the World: The Genesis of Biological Theory." *Signs* (1981), 6:469–-81.

Harris, Sharon M. *Rebecca Harding Davis and American Realism*. Philadelphia: University of Pennsylvania Press, 1991.

Harvey, Lee. *Myths of the Chicago School of Sociology.* Brookfield, Vt.: Gower, 1987.

Hernton, Calvin C. *The Sexual Mountain and Black Women Writers: Adventures in Sex, Literature, and Real Life.* New York: Anchor, 1987.

Hindus, Milton. "New Novels and Stories." *New York Herald Tribune,* April 26, 1942, book review section.

Hirsch, Arnold R. *Making the Second Ghetto: Race and Housing in Chicago, 1940–1960.* New York: Cambridge University Press, 1985.

Hirsch, Eric. *Urban Revolt: Ethnic Politics in the Nineteenth-Century Chicago Labor Movement.* Berkeley: University of California Press, 1990.

Hollowell, John. *Fact and Fiction: The New Journalism and the Nonfiction Novel.* Chapel Hill: University of North Carolina Press, 1977.

Homberger, Eric. *American Writers and Radical Politics, 1900–1939.* New York: St. Martin's, 1986.

Hooker, James R. *Black Revolutionary: George Padmore's Path from Communism to Pan-Africanism.* New York: Praeger, 1970.

Horowitz, Howard. *By the Law of Nature: Form and Value in Nineteenth-Century America.* New York: Oxford University Press, 1991.

Howard, June. *Form and History in American Literary Naturalism.* Chapel Hill: University of North Carolina Press, 1985.

Howe, Irving. "Black Boys and Native Sons." Rpt. in Yoshinobu Hakutani, ed., *Critical Essays on Richard Wright.* Boston: G. K. Hall, 1982.

Howland, Bette. "James T. Farrell's Studs Lonigan." *Literary Review* (Fall 1983), 27:22–25.

Howland, Jacob. "Black Boy: A Story of Soul-Making and a Quest for the Real." *Phylon* (June 1986), 47:117–27.

JanMohamed, Abdul R. "Negating the Negation as a Form of Affirmation in Minority Discourse: The Construction of Richard Wright as Subject." *Cultural Critique* (Fall 1987), 7:245-66.

Janowitz, Morris. "Introduction." In Morris Janowitz, ed., *W. I. Thomas, On Social Organization and Social Personality.* Chicago: University of Chicago Press, 1969, pp. vii–lviii.

Johnson, Charles. *Being and Race: Black Writing Since 1970.* Indiana University Press, 1988.

Joyce, Joyce A. *Richard Wright's Art of Tragedy.* Iowa City: University of Iowa Press, 1986.

—— "Richard Wright's 'Long Black Song': A Moral Dilemma." *Mississippi Quarterly* (Fall 1989), 42:379–85.

Kaplan, Amy. *The Social Construction of American Realism.* Chicago: University of Chicago Press, 1988.

Kazin, Alfred. *Contemporaries.* Boston: Little, Brown, 1962.

Keil, Hartmut and John Jentz. *German Workers in Chicago: A Documentary History of Working-Class Culture from 1850 to World War I.* Urbana: University of Illinois Press, 1983.

248

Kinnamon, Kenneth. *The Emergence of Richard Wright: A Study in Literature and Society.* Urbana: Illinois University Press, 1972.

—— *New Essays on Native Son.* New York: Cambridge University Press, 1990.

Kirsch, Robert. Untitled. *Los Angeles Times,* May 29, 1977, 1:71.

Klingaman, David C., ed. *Essays on the Economy of the Old Northwest.* Athens: Ohio University Press, 1987.

—— "The Nature of Midwest Manufacturing in 1890." In David C. Klingaman, ed., *Essays on the Economy of the Old Northwest.* Athens: Ohio University Press, 1987.

Kramer, Dale. *Chicago Renaissance: The Literary Life in the Midwest, 1900–1930.* New York: Appleton-Century, 1966.

Krieger, Susan. "Fiction and Social Science." *The Mirror Dance: Identity in a Women's Community.* Philadelphia: Temple University Press, 1983, pp. 173–97.

Kurtz, Lester R. *Evaluating Chicago Sociology: A Guide to the Literature, with an Annotated Bibliography.* Chicago: University of Chicago Press, 1984.

Landau, Misia. "Human Evolution as Narrative," *American Scientist* (May-June 1984), 72:262–68.

Larson, Thomas. "A Political Vision of Afro-American Culture: Richard Wright's 'Bright and Morning Star.'" In C. James Trotman, ed., *Richard Wright: Myths and Realities.* New York: Garland, 1988, pp. 147–59.

Laukaitis, William E. "Nelson Algren: A Critical Study." Ph.D. diss., University of Maryland, 1968.

Lauter, Paul. "Caste, Class, and Canon." In Marie Harris and Kathleen Aguero, eds., *A Gift of Tongues: Critical Challenges in Contemporary American Poetry.* Athens: University of Georgia Press, 1987, pp. 57–82.

—— "Race and Gender in the Shaping of the American Literary Canon: A Case Study from the Twenties." *Feminist Studies* (Fall 1983), 9:435–63.

Leclerc, Gerard. *L'observation de l'homme: une histoire des enquête sociales.* Paris: Editions du Seuil, 1982.

Lee, Robert. "Richard Wright's Inside Narratives." In Richard Gray, ed., *American Fiction: New Readings.* London: Vision, 1983.

Leitch, Vincent B. *American Literary Criticism from the Thirties to the Eighties.* New York: Columbia University Press, 1988.

Lennox, Bouton Grey. "Chicago and the Great American Novel: A Critical Approach to the American Epic." Ph.D. diss., University of Chicago, 1935.

Lenz, Gunter. "Southern Exposures: The Urban Experience and the Reconstruction of Black Folk Culture and Community in the Works of Richard Wright and Zora Neale Hurston," *New York Folklore* (1981), 7:3–39.

Lenz, Gunter H. et al., eds. *Reconstructing American Literary History and Historical Studies.* New York: St. Martin's, 1990.

Lepenis, Wolf. *Between Literature and Science: The Rise of Sociology.* Cambridge: Cambridge University Press, 1988.

Lewis, J. David and Richard L. Smith. *American Sociology and Pragmatism: Mead, Chicago Sociology, and Symbolic Interaction.* Chicago: University of Chicago Press, 1980.

Lid, R. W. "A World Imagined: The Art of Nelson Algren." In Yoshinobu Hakutani and Lewis Fried, eds., *American Literary Naturalism: A Reassessment.* Heidelberg: Anglistiche Forschungen, 1975.

Lipton, Lawrence. "A Voyeur's View of the Wild Side." *Chicago Review* (Winter 1957), 10:4–14.

Lukács, Georg. *The Theory of the Novel.* [1916.] Cambridge, MIT Press, 1982.

Lynch, William J. "James T. Farrell and the Irish-American Urban Experience." *Proceedings of the Comparative Literature Symposium. Ethnic Literatures Since 1776: The Many Voices of America.* Lubbock, Tex.: Texas Technical Press. 1978, pp. 243–54.

McCall, Dan. *The Example of Richard Wright.* New York. Harcourt and Brace, 1969.

McCluskey, John. "Two Steppin': Richard Wright's Encounter with Blue-Jazz." *American Literature* (1983), 55:332—-44.

McDonald, William F. *Federal Relief Administration and the Arts.* Columbus: Ohio State University Press, 1969.

Mangione, Jerre. *The Dream and the Deal: The Federal Writers' Project, 1935–1943.* Boston: Little, Brown, 1972.

Marcus, George E. and Michael M. Fischer, eds. *Anthropology as Cultural Critique: An Experimental Moment in the Human Sciences.* Chicago: University of Chicago Press, 1986.

Marcus, Steven. *Engels, Manchester, and the Working Class.* New York: Random House, 1974.

—— *Freud and the Culture of Psychoanalysis: Studies in the Transition from Victorian Humanism to Modernity.* Boston: G. Allen and Unwin, 1984.

—— *The Other Victorians; A Study of Sexuality and Pornography in Mid-Nineteenth-Century England.* New York: Basic Books, 1966.

—— "Reading the Illegible." In H. J. Dyos and Michael Wolff, eds., *The Victorian City: Images and Reality.* Boston: Routledge and Kegan, 1978, pp. 257–76.

Margolies, Edward. *The Art of Richard Wright.* Carbondale: Southern Illinois University Press, 1969.

Margoshes, Adam. "Chicago." *Current History* (1942), 12:467–68.

Marsh, Fred. "Poles in Chicago." *New York Times Book Review,* May 10, 1942, p. 6.

Martin, Loy D. *Browning's Dramatic Monologues and the Post-Romantic Subject.* Baltimore: Johns Hopkins University Press, 1985.

Marvick, Elizabeth Wirth. "Louis Wirth: A Biographical Memorandum." In A. Reiss, ed., *Louis Wirth, On Cities and Social Life.* Chicago: University of Chicago Press, 1964, pp. 333–34.

Matthews, Fred H. *Quest for American Sociology: Robert Park and the Chicago School.* Montreal: McGill-Queen's University Press, 1979.

———"The Revolt Against Americanism: Cultural Pluralism and Cultural Relativism as an Ideology of Liberation." *Canadian Review of American Studies* (Spring 1970), 1:4–31.

Meyer, Harold M. and Richard C. Wade. *Chicago: Growth of a Metropolis.* Chicago: University of Chicago Press, 1969.

Meyerowitz, Joanne J. *Women Adrift: Independent Wage Earners in Chicago, 1880–1930.* Chicago: University of Chicago Press, 1988.

Michaels, Walter Benn. *The Gold Standard and the Logic of Naturalism: American Literature at the Turn of the Century.* Berkeley: University of California Press, 1987.

Miller, Eugene. *Voice of a Native Son: The Poetics of Richard Wright.* Jackson, Miss.: University Press of Mississippi, 1990.

Mitchell, Lee Clark. *Determined Fictions: American Literary Naturalism.* New York: Columbia University Press, 1989.

Mitchell, Richard. "Studs Lonigan: A Scientific Novel." *Toth* (1959), 1(2):35–44.

Mootry, Maria K. "Bitches, Whores, and Woman Haters: Archetypes and Typologies in the Art of Richard Wright." In Richard MacKesey and Frank E. Moorer, eds., *Richard Wright: A Collection of Critical Essay.* Englewood Cliffs, N.J.: Prentice-Hall: 1984. 117–27.

Murphy, James F. *The Proletarian Moment: The Controversy Over Leftism in Literature.* Urbana: University of Illinois Press, 1991.

Nekola, Charlotte and Paula Rabinowitz, eds. *Writing Red: An Anthology of American Women Writers, 1930–1940.* New York: Feminist Press, 1986.

Nelson, Bruce. *Beyond the Martyrs: A Social History of Chicago Anarchists, 1870–1900.* New Brunswick, N.J.: Rutgers University Press, 1988.

Nelson, Cary. *Repression and Recovery: Modern American Poetry and the Politics of Cultural Memory, 1910–1945.* Madison: University of Wisconsin Press, 1989.

Nisbet, Robert. *Sociology as an Art Form.* New York: Oxford University Press, 1976.

Nye, Robert. "Sociology and Degeneration: The Irony of Progress." In J. Edward Chamberlain and Sander L. Gilman, eds., *Degeneration: The Dark Side of Progress.* New York: Columbia University Press, 1985, pp. 49–71.

Ochillo, Yvonne. "Black Boy: Structure as Meaning." *Griot* (Spring 1986), 6:49–54.

Ochshorn, Kathleen. "The Community of Native Son." *Mississippi Quarterly* (Fall 1989), 42:387–92.

Ohmann, Richard. *Politics of Letters.* Middletown, Ct.: Wesleyan University Press, 1987.

O'Malley, Frank. "James T. Farrell: Two Twilight Images." In Harold C. Gardiner, ed., *Fifty Years of the American Novel.* New York: Scribner, 1951, pp. 237–56.

Omick, Robert E. "Compassion in the Novels of Nelson Algren." Ph.D. diss., University of Iowa, 1967.

Park, Robert. "The City: Suggestions for the Investigation of Human Behavior in the Urban Environment." *American Journal of Sociology* (1915). Rpt. in Park and Ernest Burgess, eds., *The City*. Chicago: University of Chicago Press, 1974, pp. 1–46.

——— Collected papers. University of Chicago, Regenstein Library, Special Collections.

——— "Human Migration and the Marginal Man." *American Journal of Sociology* (1928). Rpt. in Everett C. Hughes, ed., *Race and Culture*. New York: Arno, 1974, pp. 345–56.

——— "Life History." *American Journal of Sociology*, 79(2):251–60.

——— "Notes on the Origins of the Society for Social Research." *Journal of the History of the Behavioral Sciences*, 18:332–40.

——— *Race and Culture*. New York: Arno, 1974.

——— "Sociological Methods of W. G. Sumner, and of W. I. Thomas and F. Znaniecki." In Stuart A. Rice, ed., *Methods in Social Science: A Case Book*. Chicago: University of Chicago Press, 1931, pp. 154–75.

Perlongo, Robert A. "Interview with Nelson Algren." *Chicago Review* (1957), 2:92–98.

Persons, Stow. *Ethnic Studies at Chicago, 1905–1945*. Chicago: University of Illinois Press, 1987.

Pinckney, Darryl. Untitled. *Village Voice*, July 4, 1977, pp. 80–82.

Pitts, Mary Ellen. "Algren's El: Internalized Machine and Displaced Nature." *South Atlantic Review* (November 1987), 52:61–74.

Pizer, Donald. "James T. Farrell and the 1930s." In Ralph F. Bogardus and Fred Hobson, eds., *Literature at the Barricades: The American Writer in the 1930s*. Tuscaloosa: University of Alabama Press, 1982.

——— *Realism and Naturalism in Nineteenth-Century American Literature*. Carbondale: Southern Illinois University Press, 1984.

——— *Twentieth-Century American Literary Naturalism: An Interpretation*. Carbondale: Southern Illinois University Press, 1982.

Pizzorno, Alessandro. "Introduzione." In *La Città*. Milano: Comunitá, 1987.

Platt, Anthony. *The Child Savers: The Invention of Delinquency*. Chicago: University of Chicago Press, 1969.

Podhoretz, Norman. "The Man with the Golden Beef." *New Yorker*, June 2, 1950, 32:132–39.

Podwill, Elliot. "A 'Third-Person Society': Flawed Human Relationships in the Work of Nelson Algren." Ph.D. diss., Kent State University, 1983.

Pourtois, Anne. "Conversation avec Nelson Algren." *Europe* (October 1964), 52:72–77.

"Proletarian." *Review of Reviews*, January 1936, p. 7.

Rahv, Philip. "The Lower Depths." *Partisan Review* (July-August 1935), 2:63–64.

———— "No Parole." *Nation*, April 18, 1942, 154:466—-67.

Rampersad, Arnold. "Notes to the Text." In *Works: Richard Wright*. New York: Library of America, 1991.

Raushenbush, Winifred. *Robert Park: Biography of a Sociologist*. Durham: Duke University Press, 1979.

Record, Wilson. "The Negro Writer and the Communist Party." In C. W. E. Bigsby, ed., *The Black American Writer*. Delend, Fla.: Everett/Edwards, 1969.

Redfield, Robert. Collected Papers, University of Chicago, Regenstein Library.

———— *The Folk Culture of Yucatan*. [1941.] Chicago: University of Chicago Press, 1961.

———— *Tepoztlán: A Mexican Village. A Study of Folk Life*. [1930.] Chicago: University of Chicago Press, 1973.

Reilly, John M. "Richard Wright Preaches the Nation: *12 Million Black Voices*." *Black American Literary Forum* (1982), 16:116–19.

———— "The Self-Creation of the Intellectual: *American Hunger* and *Black Power*." In Yoshinobu Hakutani, ed., *Critical Essays on Richard Wright*. Boston: G. K. Hall, 1982, pp. 213–27.

Reising, Russell J. *The Unusable Past: Theory and the Study of American Literature*. New York; Methuen, 1986.

Rideout, Walter B. *The Radical Novel in the United States, 1900–1954*. New York: Columbia University Press, 1956, 1992.

Robinson, Cedric J. *Black Marxism: The Making of the Black Radical Tradition*. Atlantic Highlands, N.J.: Zed Books, 1983.

———— "The Emergent Marxism of Richard Wright's Ideology," *Race and Class* (1978), 19: 221–37.

Robinson, James. "Nelson Algren's Spiritual Victims." *The Gypsy Scholar* (1976), 3:3–12.

Rosenberg, Rosalind. *Beyond Separate Spheres: The Intellectual Roots of Modern Feminism*. New Haven: Yale University Press, 1982.

"Rough Stuff." *Time*, May 28, 1956, 67:106.

Ruoff, A. LaVonne, Jr., and Jerry W. Ward, Jr., eds. *Redefining American Literary History*. New York: Modern Language Association, 1990.

Rymer, John. "A Changing Sense of Chicago in the Works of Saul Bellow and Nelson Algren." *The Old Northwest* (December 1978), 4:371–83.

Schipper, Mineke. "Toward a Definition of Realism in the African Context." *New Literary History* (1985), 16:559–75.

Schwendinger, Julia and Herman Schwendinger. "Sociology's Founding Fathers: Sexist to a Man." *Journal of Marriage and the Family* (1971), 33:783–99.

Seelye, John. "The Night Watchman." *Chicago* (February 1988), 37:69–72.

Seltzer, Mark. "The Naturalist Machine." In Ruth Bernard Yeazell, ed., *Sex, Politics, and Science in the Nineteenth-Century Novel*. Baltimore: Johns Hopkins University Press, 1986, pp. 116–47.

253

Sharpe, William and Leonard Wallock, eds. *Visions of the Modern City.* [1983.] Proceedings of the Heyman Center for the Humanities, Columbia University, New York. Baltimore: Johns Hopkins University Press, 1987.

Shaw, Clifford. *The Jack-Roller.* Chicago: University of Chicago Press, 1930.

Short, James. "Introduction." In Frederic Thrasher, *The Gang: A Study of 1,313 Gangs in Chicago.* Chicago: University of Chicago Press, 1927.

Sing, Raman K. "Marxism in Richard Wright's Fiction." *Indian Journal of American Studies* (1974), 4:31–47.

Skerrett, Joseph T., Jr. "Richard Wright, Writing and Identity." *Callaloo* (Oct. 1979), 2:84—94.

Smart, Carol. *Women, Crime and Criminology: A Feminist Critique.* London: Routledge and Kegan Paul, 1976.

Smart, Robert. *The Nonfiction Novel.* New York: University Press of America, 1985.

Smith, Alson J. *Chicago's Left Bank.* Chicago: Henry Reghery, 1953.

Smith, Carl S. *Chicago and the American Literary Imagination, 1880–1920.* Chicago: University of Chicago Press, 1984.

Smith, Dennis. *The Chicago School: A Liberal Critique of Capitalism.* Houndmills, Basingstoke: Macmillan, 1988.

Sollors, Werner. *Beyond Ethnicity: Consent and Descent in American Culture.* New York: Oxford University Press, 1986.

———— "Modernization as Adultery: Richard Wright, Zora Neale Hurston, and American Culture of the 1930's and 1940's." In Steve Icknigwill, ed., *Looking Inward/ Looking Outward.* European Contributions to American Studies 18. Amsterdam: Amerika-Instituut, 1990, pp. 22–75.

Sollors, Werner, ed. *The Invention of Ethnicity.* New York: Oxford University Press, 1989.

Stepan, Nancy. "Biology and Degeneration: Races and Proper Places." In J. Edward Chamberlain and Sander L. Gilman, eds., *Degeneration: The Dark Side of Progress.* New York: Columbia University Press, 1985, pp. 97–120.

———— *The Idea of Race in Science: Great Britain, 1800–1960.* London: MacMillan, 1982.

———— "Race and Gender: The Role of Analogy in Science." *ISIS* (June 1986), 77:261–77.

Stepto, Robert. "I Thought I Knew These People: Wright and the Afro-American Liteary Tradition." In Harold Bloom, ed., *Richard Wright.* New York: Chelsea House, 1987, pp. 55–74.

Stott, William. *Documentary Expression and Thirties America.* New York: Oxford University Press, 1973.

Sundquist, Eric J. *American Realism: New Essays.* Baltimore: Johns Hopkins University Press, 1982.

———— "Realism and Regionalism." In Emory Elliott, ed., *Columbia Literary History of the United States.* New York: Columbia University Press, 1988.

254

Susman, Warren. *Culture as History: The Transformation of American Society in the Twentieth Century.* New York: Pantheon, 1984.

Tanner, Laura. "Uncovering the Magical Disguise of Langauge: The Narrative Presence in Richard Wright's *Native Son.*" *Texas Studies in Literature and Language* (Winter 1987), 29:412–31.

Thaddeus, Janice. "The Metamorphosis of Richard Wright's *Black Boy.*" *American Literature* (May 1985), 57:199–214.

Thomas, William Isaac. "Life History." Ed. Paul Baker. *American Journal of Sociology* (September 1973), 79(2):246–50.

—— "The Mind of Woman." *American Magazine* (December 1908), 67:146–52.

—— *The Unadjusted Girl: With Cases and Standpoint for Behavior Analysis.* Boston: Little, Brown, 1923.

—— Ethel S. Dummer Papers. Radcliffe College, Schlesinger Library, Cambridge, Mass.

Thomas, William Isaac and Florian Znaniecki. *Methods in Social Science: A Case Book.* Ed. S. Rice. Chicago: University of Chicago Press, 1931.

—— *The Polish Peasant in Europe and America.* 5 vols. Chicago: University of Chicago Press, 1918–20.

Thrasher, Frederic. *The Gang: A Study of 1,313 Gangs in Chicago.* Chicago: University of Chicago Press, 1927.

—— "Introduction." In James T. Farrell, *Young Lonigan.* New York: Vanguard, 1932.

Trotman, C. James, ed. *Richard Wright: Myths and Realities.* New York: Garland, 1988.

Vanderbilt, Kermit. *American Literature and the Academy.* Philadelphia: University of Pennsylvania Press, 1986.

Van Maanen, John. *Tales of the Field: On Writing Ethnography.* Chicago: University of Chicago Press, 1988.

Vecoli, Rudolph. "Contadini in Chicago: A Critique of *The Uprooted.*" *Journal of American History* (1964), 51:404–17.

Vedder, Richard K. and Lowell Gallaway. "Economic Growth and Decline in the Old Northwest." In David C. Klingaman, ed., *Essays on the Economy of the Old Northwest.* Athens: Ohio University Press, 1987.

Vidich, Arthur J. and Stanford M. Lyman. *American Sociology: Worldly Rejections of Religion and Their Directions.* New Haven: Yale University Press, 1985.

Volkart, Edmund H., ed. *Social Behavior and Personality: Contributions of W. I. Thomas to Theory and Social Research.* New York: Social Science Research Council, 1951.

Vonnegut, Kurt, "Introduction." In Nelson Algren, *Never Come Morning.* New York: Four Walls Eight Windows, 1987.

Walcutt, Charles. *American Literary Naturalism: A Divided Stream.* Minneapolis: University of Minnesota Press, 1956.

Wald, Alan M. *James T. Farrell: The Revolutionary Socialist Years.* New York: New York University Press, 1978.

—— The New York Intellectuals: The Rise and Decline of the Anti-Stalinist Left from the 1930s to the 1980s. Chapel Hill: University of North Carolina Press, 1987.

Walker, Margaret. Richard Wright: Daemonic Genius. New York: Warner, 1988.

Wallenstein, Barry. "James T. Farrell: Critic of Naturalism." In Yoshinobu Hakutani and Lewis Fried, eds., American Literary Naturalism: A Reassessment. Heidelberg: Anglistiche Forschungen, 1975, pp. 154–75.

Warren, Nagueyalti. "Black Girls and Native Sons: Female Images in Selected Works by Richard Wright." In C. James Trotman, ed., Richard Wright. New York: Garland, 1988, pp. 59–77.

Watkins, Evan. "Conflict and Consensus in the History of Recent Criticism." New Literary History (Winter 1981), 12:348–50.

Widmer, Kingsley. The Literary Rebel. Carbondale: Southern Illinois University Press, 1965.

Williams, John A. The Most Native of Sons. New York: Doubleday, 1970.

Williams, Kenny. "'Creative Defiance': An Overview of Chicago Literature." Midwestern Miscellany (1986), 14:7–24.

—— In the City of Men: Another Story of Chicago. Nashville: Townsend, 1974.

—— Prairie Voices: A Literary History of Chicago from the Frontier to 1893. Nashville: Townsend, 1980.

Williams, Raymond. Marxism and Literature. New York: Oxford University Press, 1978.

—— The Sociology of Culture. New York: Schocken, 1981.

—— Writing in Society. London: Verso, 1981.

Wirth, Louis. Collected papers. University of Chicago, Regenstein Library, Special Collections.

—— On Cities and Social Life. Ed. A. Reiss. Chicago: University of Chicago Press, 1964.

—— The Ghetto. [1928.] Chicago: University of Chicago Press, 1982.

—— "Urbanism as a Way of Life." American Journal of Sociology (1938). Rpt. in Albert J. Reiss, Jr., ed., On Cities and Social Life. Chicago: University of Chicago Press, 1981, pp. 60–83.

Wohl, Richard R. and Anselm L. Strauss. "Symbolic Representation and the Urban Milieu." American Journal of Sociology (1958), 63:523–32.

Wood, Michael. "Literary Criticism." In Emory Elliott, ed., Columbia Literary History of the United States. New York: Columbia University Press, 1988, pp. 993–1018

Wright, Richard. American Hunger. New York: Harper and Row, 1983.

—— Black Boy: A Record of Childhood and Youth. New York: Harper and Row, 1966.

—— Black Power. Westport: University of Connecticut Press, 1954.

—— "Blueprint for Negro Writing." New Challenge (Fall 1937), 2:53–66.

—— "Introduction." In St. Clair Drake and Horace Cayton, eds., Black Metropolis. New York: Harcourt and Brace, 1945, pp. xvii–xviii.

———— "Introduction." In Nelson Algren, *Never Come Morning*. New York: Harper and Brothers, 1942, pp. ix–x.

———— *Lawd Today*. [1937.] New York: Walker, 1963.

———— *Pagan Spain*. New York: Harper and Row, 1957.

———— *12 Million Black Voices*. New York: Arno, 1941.

———— *Works: Richard Wright*. New York: Library of America, 1991.

Young, Kimball. "Contributions of William Isaac Thomas to Sociology." *Sociology and Social Research* (October 1962), 47:3–24; (January 1963), 47:123–37; (April 1963) 47:251–72; (July 1963), 47:381–97.

Zavarzadeh, Mas'nd. *The Mythopoeic Reality: The Postwar American Nonfiction Novel*. Urbana: University of Illinois Press, 1972.

Zorbaugh, Harvey. *The Gold Coast and the Slum*. Chicago: University of Chicago Press, 1929.

Index

261

263

267

269

Designer: Teresa Bonner
Text: Joanna
Compositor: The Composing Room of Michigan, Inc.
Printer: Book Crafters
Binder: Book Crafers